*Texas Society of Certified Public Accountants*

# Texas Society of

# Certified Public Accountants

## A History, 1915–1981

### REVISED EDITION

BY

## JAMES A. TINSLEY

*Published for the*
*Texas Society of Certified Public Accountants by*
*Texas A&M University Press*
*College Station*

Library of Congress Cataloging in Publication Data

Tinsley, James A.
    Texas Society of Certified Public Accountants.

    Bibliography: p.
    Includes index.
    1. Texas Society of Certified Public Accountants—
History. I. Texas Society of Certified Public
Accountants. II. Title.
HF5616.U5T56 1983        657'.06'0764        82–45890
ISBN 0–89096–152–2

*Manufactured in the United States of America*
First published 1962. Revised edition 1983

# *Contents*

# *Foreword*

THE first history of the Texas Society of Certified Public Accountants (TSCPA) was published in 1962. As Heloise Brown Canter indicated in her foreword to that edition, we owe it to the pioneers of the accounting profession in Texas "to record their works" and to "form a record of their achievements." So much of lasting importance has occurred in our maturing organization since 1962 that the activities of that period must also be reported. Only then can we complete the record of achievements of all the outstanding leaders who brought our profession in Texas to its present effective and remarkable maturity. Accordingly, in January, 1979, President-elect Carl S. Chilton, Jr., asked me to serve as chairman of the TSCPA History Committee to accomplish the objective set out in his letter: "I would like you to organize a project to get our published history up to date." Our committee soon set out to plan a revision of the 1962 history.

The committee decided that a completely new manuscript, rather than a supplement, was needed because events after 1962 were so interwoven with the earlier events. A more cohesive history of the Society was the goal. Therefore, this new edition contains a history of early days of accountancy as well as annals of the Society from its origin in 1915 to the present time.

The files in the Society in the last twenty years are so substantial that an extraordinary and skillful effort was needed to record properly our activities. The scope of this effort, together with the need for extensive interviews with past presidents and other key people, as well as the wish to delineate the relationship of prior history with current events, caused the committee to turn to the author of the 1962 edition, Dr. James A. Tinsley, who was engaged to write the revision. He is now executive director of the Texas Gulf Coast Historical Association, and thus we have had the benefit of that relationship. The committee worked with Dr. Tinsley for nearly three years to complete the research and related activities necessary for him to produce the manuscript for the book.

Our committee's extensive study of the roots, development, and growth of the Texas Society convinces us that its efforts for almost seven decades, particularly during the explosive growth in membership in recent years, form a base for a powerful continuing service to the profession and the rapidly expanding economy and population we serve.

KENNETH W. HURST, CPA, Chairman
Society History Committee

---

### *In Memoriam and Dedication*

Shortly before the long-awaited arrival of this book, Kenneth W. Hurst died on March 19, 1983. Even though he didn't see the final product, he knew his project was almost in print. A member of the Texas Society of CPAs for forty-eight years, this dedicated Tyler CPA knew and respected the role of TSCPA in the world of accounting. Because he wanted others to understand the profession and the people who made it great, this TSCPA history is in existence.

Mr. Hurst served as president of the Society in 1963–64 and received its highest awards—Meritorious Service to the Public Accounting Profession in Texas, Distinguished Public Service, Honorary Fellow. He also played a dominant part in the ongoing success of TSCPA's Educational Foundation. Six CPAs have been accorded the honor of being named Kenneth W. Hurst Fellows for significant contributions to the Foundation. As a CPA, a volunteer, and a man, Ken Hurst will be missed, but his indomitable spirit will linger in the hearts of many.

CARROLL W. PHILLIPS, CPA
1982–83 TSCPA President

# *Preface*

TWENTY years ago, in 1962, the Texas Society of Certified Public Accountants published my history of the Society down to that time. I was pleased, therefore, when Kenneth Hurst and the Society History Committee invited me to revise and update the history in 1979. Not having followed developments in the profession closely, however, I was surprised at the changes that had occurred in the interim. What at first appeared to be a relatively simple exercise of picking up where I had left off turned into a job requiring considerable restudy of the accounting profession. It has been a stimulating intellectual experience, however, and I hope I have accurately described the workings of the Texas Society as well as correctly interpreted the major forces at work within the profession.

As was the case in writing the first history, my task was made immeasurably easier by the cooperation I received from Society officials and leaders in the profession. Each former president of the Society gave generously of his time to discuss matters relating to the Society and the profession. In addition, Lloyd Weaver and Don Lyda, former chairmen of the Texas State Board of Public Accountancy, granted lengthy interviews and read parts of the manuscript. Bob Bradley, Joe Holloman, and Fern Spaulding, also of the Texas State Board of Public Accountancy staff, responded to many specific requests for information. Ernest Wehner and Melvin Bergeron assisted at crucial points in my research. William Quimby, the Society's former executive director, took time to review select chapters.

My greatest debt of gratitude is owed to members of the Texas Society's History Committee. Under the guidance of Kenneth Hurst, committee members patiently read and wisely criticized several drafts of the manuscript, to the enlightenment of the author and the improvement of the book. Wayne Tidwell, Robert Hibbetts, Robert Knox, Walter Bielstein, William Giese, Ennis Hawkins, Daniel Kilgore, Carl Chilton, Stanley Scott, Johnnie Ray Seale, and Rowland Pattillo served on the committee. Kathleen Klein, director of communications for the Society, provided valuable and important liaison services and gently prodded the author to meet deadlines.

It goes without saying, the efforts of all those named prevented many mistakes and added greatly to the finished product. The flaws remaining are my own. In language every CPA understands, "the opinions expressed" in the book are those of the author.

JAMES A. TINSLEY

*Texas Society of Certified Public Accountants*

# 1

## *The Emergence of Professional Accounting in America*

THE history of the Texas Society of Certified Public Accountants (TSCPA) appropriately begins with some reference to the emergence of the accounting profession in Scotland and England in the middle of the nineteenth century and to the early years of professional growth in the United States. For while accountants in Texas organized their society in 1915 in response to local conditions that were sometimes unique, they did so against the backdrop and within the context of professional standards established a half-century earlier.

Public accounting is generally recognized to be one of the youngest professions, barely a century old by some standards. It is well to remember, however, that men "skilled in accounts" were vital to the commerical life of ancient Greece and Rome. Also, the revival of trade and commerce which marked the end of the Middle Ages was facilitated by the formation of colleges of accountants that demanded rigorous training of their members. The system of double-entry bookkeeping, in fact, evolved during the age of the Italian merchant prince.[1]

Accounts and accounting remained relatively uncomplicated, however, until the industrial revolution of the nineteenth century. The simple business forms of the agrarian age were then swept away and replaced with more intricate accounting systems. Equally important social and political changes followed in the wake of industrialism. By the twentieth century the public demanded the right to look more deeply into the operations of the great public service corporations. Businesses were required to disclose financial operations always before considered private matters. These conditions demanded a new class of experts to audit, analyze, and advise management, government, and the public.

1. Among the many descriptions of accountancy, one of the most concise is John Bauer, "Accounting," *Encyclopedia of Social Sciences*, 1: 404–12.

## The British Influence

The chartered accountants in Scotland and England responded first to the demands of the new industrial age. In Scotland it became common practice by the 1840s for "expert accountants" to act as agents of the court in bankruptcy cases. Guilds or "institutes of accountants" were organized in Edinburgh and Glasgow in 1853, and in Aberdeen in 1867. While these Scottish institutes worked together closely, they were not merged into one body until 1951. In England, the Companies Acts of 1845, 1862, and 1868 required public audits of certain firms, principally railroads, and thus provided the impetus for professional accounting. Institutes of accountants soon appeared in Liverpool and London (1870), Manchester (1873), and Sheffield (1877). In 1880 these institutes merged into a federated union, the Institute of Chartered Accountants in England and Wales.

The English and Scottish accountants styled their profession along lines similar to law. Because of conditions arising out of the late Middle Ages, England's legal profession was left very much to itself insofar as public regulation or control was concerned. When medieval canon law, taught by the universities, became obsolete and was ignored, common law took its place. Apprentices in common law received instruction from guilds of practicing lawyers at the Inns of Court rather than from the universities. Consequently, these guilds were soon recognized by the government as having the sole right to admit new members to the bar, a privilege which carried the responsibility of keeping their professional house in order. Accountants sought to establish this same type of control over their professional affairs. Thus the apprenticeship system predominated in the training of young accountants. However, in Scotland a certain number of university law courses were required of accountants, and in England, the five years of apprenticeship were reduced to three years for persons with a college degree. The institute schools provided all other formal education. Examinations leading to the licensing of chartered accountants were prepared, given, and graded by the institutes. A professional journal, the *Accountant*, was first published by the English profession in 1874.[2]

2. See Nicholas A. H. Stacey, *English Accountancy 1800–1954* (London: Gee and Company, 1954), pp. 19–27.

## Professional Accounting Crosses the Atlantic

The chartered accountant's dexterity in analyzing intricate business affairs, along with his independence and impartiality in performing audits and rendering decisions, won respect for the new profession at home and abroad. British investors soon dispatched chartered accountants to the United States to report on their investments. For instance, Quilter, Ball & Co. and Turquand, Young & Co. were engaged in 1870 to help untangle the affairs of the Erie Railroad. Price Waterhouse & Co. sent accountants to the United States several years before the firm established a resident agent in New York in 1890. The first English firm to open formal offices in the United States was Barrow, Wade, Guthrie & Co., organized in 1883 when two partners in the English firm of Thomas, Wade, Guthrie & Co. took into partnership an English-born New York accountant and actuary, John Wylie Barrow. Barrow lived only fifteen months after the arrangement was made, however, and James T. Anyon came over from England to take charge of the office.

Other English accountants migrated to the United States on their own initiative. William Henry Vesey, who, one writer says, "never foreswore allegiance to Queen Victoria," came in the 1850s and had a strong firm established by 1866. James Yalden and William J. Calhoun came in the 1870s. The Yalden firm, formed in 1876, was probably the strongest firm, foreign or domestic, in the United States by 1896. Louis M. Bergtheil, J. R. Robertson, Thomas C. Roberts, George Wilkinson, and others came in the 1880s.[3]

English accountants in the United States organized a professional society in 1886 when a group of ten or twelve of their number from the New York–Philadelphia area gathered in the Barrow, Wade, Guthrie & Co. offices for discussions with Edwin Guthrie. Guthrie was in this country on client matters but he was also a willing missionary for the profession. He advised his listeners to form a guild of the most reputable accountants along the same lines that had just proven so successful in England. He predicted that such an association, with high membership requirements, complete control over professional affairs, and a strict code of ethics, would soon become the accepted voice of the profession in America. Duly inspired, his audience organized the

3. *New York CPA* 26 (June, 1956): 364ff.

American Association of Public Accountants, the first national society purporting to speak for professional public accountants.

The American Association of Public Accountants retained a distinctive British flavor for many years. Of the original officers, including James Yalden as president, William H. Vesey as treasurer, and James T. Anyon as secretary, only John Heins of Philadelphia, the vice-president, was American-born and -educated. It is also noteworthy that seven of the eight association secretaries from 1887 to 1906 were British. The eighth, Frank Broaker, was trained by and was the partner of a Scottish accountant in New York. Until 1906, the time of its merger with the Federation of Societies of Public Accountants, 102 of the association's 266 members had come to the United States from England and Scotland.[4]

The association, of course, was not the only organized voice of accountancy at that time. Records of sixteen different bookkeeping and accounting societies in the 1870s and 1880s have been found. Many were fraternal societies existing primarily to find jobs and to provide sickness and burial benefits for the members, most of whom were in private employment. However, the New York Institute of Accountants, organized in 1882, and the Bookkeepers Beneficial Association of Philadelphia, formed in 1874, were dedicated to more professional pursuits as well. Some members of these two societies were in public practice, and in New York, English accountants took an active role in the institute's affairs. Frequent meetings were held at which papers on the theory and practice of accounting were read and discussed.[5]

The English guild system met only limited success in this country. While recognizing the excellence and high standards set by the American Association of Public Accountants, many good accountants remained outside the organization. Annual membership rarely exceeded thirty persons, 90 percent of whom lived in New York. American notions of democracy and amateurism, which tended to keep the doors of all professions open to anyone who wished to hold himself out as a practitioner, also ran counter to the aristocratic presumptions of the Association. Association efforts to establish a school of accounting also

4. Norman E. Webster, comp., *The American Association of Public Accountants: Its First Twenty Years* (New York: American Institute of Accountants, 1954), is the best source of information on this subject.
5. Ibid., pp. 9–17.

failed. In 1894, the New York School of Accounts, underwritten by the association and modeled after the institute schools in England and Scotland, opened under the jurisdiction of the Board of Regents of the University of New York. Two years later it closed for lack of students and funds. A different approach was clearly needed to build the profession in the United States.

## State Certification in New York, 1896

Professional accounting in America moved in new directions in 1896, the year New York's legislature adopted the nation's first public accountancy act. The New York law created a certification board with authority to set minimum professional standards and to designate those who met the standards "certified public accountants" (CPAs).[6] The law was permissive, the state merely reserving the title of certified public accountant for those who qualified by examination and experience. No attempt was made to register all accountants, nor was the practice of accountancy restricted to CPAs. The law was significant in two ways, however. Implying a partial rejection of the English guild system, it used the state licensing authority to provide the stamp of professional excellence which the guild had been unable to accomplish alone. At the same time, the assumption that practitioners would control the state licensing board meant control of professional matters would only be shared with rather than surrendered to the state. The effect of the law, therefore, added the certification power of the state to the persuasive power of the guild, thereby providing a mechanism for elevating the profession. Other states soon followed New York's example. By 1923 all forty-eight states and the District of Columbia had enacted permissive CPA legislation.[7]

State certification, beginning in 1896, solved some problems; it created others. Accountants opposed in principle to surrendering or even sharing the power to license with the state ignored the certification pro-

6. Ibid., pp. 207–40.

7. Three articles by James Don Edwards record some of the high points of the profession. See "Some Significant Developments of Public Accounting in the United States," *Business History Review* 30 (June, 1956): 211–25; "Public Accounting in the United States from 1913 to 1928," ibid. 32 (Spring, 1958): 74–101; "Public Accounting in the United States from 1928 to 1951," ibid. 30 (Dec., 1956): 444–71.

cedures. Personality clashes between state board members and applicants for certificates often prevented qualified persons from receiving certificates. For whatever reason, accountants who failed or refused to become certified soon lost many of the better clients. They were also relegated to a second-class professional citizenship when denied membership in the new state societies of CPAs. The lack of reciprocity between states created other difficulties, particularly handicapping firms engaged in national practice. State certification, furthermore, hindered the development of an organization that could speak for the profession in national affairs. But the principal weakness of state certification was the wide variance in standards that existed from state to state. Under Gresham's law, the cheap CPA certificates drove out the good and debased the certificate wherever it was found.

## Toward a National Profession

The search for ways to correct the defects and retain the strong points of state certification taxed the energies of the best minds in the profession after 1896. Supporters of the American Association of Public Accountants, who might be dubbed "nationalists," attempted to control the profession on the national level. They were lukewarm toward the state certificate and upheld the right of the association to be the sole judge of its own membership. Others, who might be called "federalists," believed strongly in states' rights for the profession. They saw recognition of the certificate as the highest order of the profession and advocated a federal union of the state societies to represent the profession on the national level.

The nationalists and federalists clashed soon after New York enacted the 1896 law. The American Association of Public Accountants, while essentially a local New York group, was nearer to being a national society than any other in existence in 1896. Many association members received New York certificates but some did not. The association was officially cool toward the idea that the state certificate should automatically qualify an accountant for membership. The first major threat to the association came in 1902 when George Wilkinson of Illinois and Charles W. Haskins of New York formed the Federation of Societies of Public Accountants in the United States. The federation was made up of state societies which had just won CPA legislation in their respective states or were working toward that end. Membership in the federation came only through joining one of the state societies for which the certificate was a prerequisite. For three years the federation threatened to eclipse the association, but Haskins died and the New York Society of CPAs withdrew from the federation. The defection of the New York society was a mortal blow. No accounting society could presume to speak for the profession unless this large and influential body of accountants was represented. The association absorbed the federation in 1905, but it granted major concessions to the federalists who, for the most part, represented the profession in the southern, middle, and far western sections of the country. Presidents of the state societies of CPAs were declared vice-presidents of the association, and all who held membership in the state societies were accepted into the association's membership without question.[8]

The state of affairs lasted barely a decade. In 1916 a committee of the association sharply criticized differences existing between states in educational and experience requirements for the certificate, which made reciprocity between states difficult and the quality of membership uneven. In short, the committee called for more uniform standards of admission to the profession.

In the light of this report, pronounced nationalists urged the association to take out a national charter. A reminder that this might open the way to regulation by the national government caused the idea to be dropped. The association, however, was renamed the American Institute of Accountants under a charter from the District of Columbia. The new institute then gained tighter control over admissions by requiring applicants to pass a uniform examination. These examinations were in turn made available to the state boards of accountancy for their use in testing applicants for state certificates. The nationalists also gained strength by the provision that officers of the institute be nominated and elected by the membership at large. This, in effect, turned the institute back into the hands of the eastern accountants. To complete their conquest, the nationalists secured the adoption of a professional code of ethics by the institute in 1917.[9]

8. Webster, *American Association*, pp. 308–17.
9. "A History of the American Institute of Accountants," in *The American Institute of Accountants Fiftieth Anniversary Celebration* (New York: American Institute of Accounts, 1938), pp. 14–17.

Accountants were concerned with more than organizational problems after 1896. Government regulation of business, the passage of federal income tax laws, and World War I all had profound impact on professional development. An editorial in the new *Journal of Accountancy* addressed itself directly to this point in 1908. Writing optimistically concerning the "Prospects for Young Accountants," the editor claimed that a "special reason for expecting a steady enlargement of the accounting field . . . may be found in the political situation." Fifteen years ago, he said, the American people "were greatly concerned over the money question; today they are aroused over the abuses of corporate franchises." The people "are demanding publicity with regard to the affairs of railroads, banks, insurance companies, gas companies, telephone companies, street railway companies, in fact, from all corporations which enjoy special or exclusive privileges. Whatever one's own opinion may be on this subject," he declared, "it is impossible . . . to escape the conviction that the day is near when none of our giant corporations will be permitted to operate in the dark." "Indeed," the article continued, "the transition from darkness to light is now under way, and the calls for public accountants are multiplying in consequence." "The public accountant," it was added, "never becomes the hired man of any corporation for whose balance sheet he vouches. His audit is an independent one, and before long, it will be the only audit which the people will accept with any confidence."[10] In 1913 the ratification of the Sixteenth Amendment opened up the field of income tax work for accountants. This reliance upon CPAs for tax expertise had the corollary effect of enhancing the businessmen's respect for other services the accountant could render. World War I brought new opportunities. An excess profits tax demanded professional interpretation and handling. Equally important, accounting firms were called upon to render expanded services to the purchasing agents for the English and French governments in the United States and to our own government in its business with contractors of war goods.

## Texas at the Turn of the Century

Public accounting in Texas grew out of circumstances at the turn of the century very similar to those that gave rise to the profession in

10. *Journal of Accountancy* 6 (Sept., 1908): 351–54.

other states. In the late nineteenth century the network of Texas railroads fell into place, stimulating commercial and industrial expansion. Cotton and cattle, the older forms of Texas wealth, were "money crops," the sale and management of which involved increasingly complex financial records. The lumber industry came of age in 1900, and the discovery of oil at Spindletop in 1901 along with the production of sulphur in 1912 gave dramatic evidence of the new direction the Texas economy would take in the twentieth century. The value of products manufactured in Texas increased 300 percent in the period 1899 to 1911. Dallas and Fort Worth in the north and Galveston, Houston, and San Antonio in the south became centers for the wholesale and retail distribution of goods and the accumulation of investment capital. In 1903 Texas chartered the first life insurance company organized with local money, and in 1905 the state resumed the issuance of bank charters after a lapse of almost thirty years. Population increased at the rate of approximately 25 percent each decade and gave promise of providing a stable demand for professional services of all kinds, including accounting.

Responding to that demand, Marion Douglas in Galveston and Daniel Kernaghan in Fort Worth opened accounting offices in 1896, making them probably the first practitioners of public accounting in the state. Little is known about Douglas's background and professional career aside from his being recognized as a man of character and integrity, the possessor of a ready wit and an engaging personality. In addition to his public practice, Douglas was from time to time city auditor of Galveston, agent for the American Surety Company of New York, and secretary of Dolson Incorporated of Galveston. Somewhat more is known about Kernaghan, who was born in 1851 in New Orleans, Louisiana. He was trained to follow his father's vocation of watchmaker, but instead he went to work for a firm of cotton merchants in 1872 in Jefferson, then a major trading center for northeast Texas. He was employed a few years later by the wholesale grocery firm of Bateman & Brothers, which moved its offices to Fort Worth in 1882. Kernaghan became head bookkeeper for the firm and, in 1891, was appointed trustee to liquidate the assets of the firm. For a while afterward he was a merchant broker before announcing his public accountancy practice in 1896.

Marion Douglas and Daniel Kernaghan were each destined for

leadership roles in the Texas Society of Certified Public Accountants, though two decades would elapse before the Texas certificate became a reality. During that time, approximately fifty more accountants began to practice in Texas and joined in advancing the cause of the profession.

# 2

## The Public Accountancy Act of 1915:
## Birth of the Texas Society

WILLIAM PRESTON PETER of Peter & Company in Dallas took the lead in organizing accountants and securing legal recognition for the profession in Texas. Born in 1866 in Springfield, Kentucky, Peter attended Browder Institute and afterward found employment as a store clerk, a newspaper reporter, and a mercantile adjustor. It is not known when he moved to Texas, but his duties as secretary of the Texas Wholesale Credit Association provided extensive auditing experience which he relied upon in 1907 to establish his firm and enter the public accounting field.[1] Peter also showed an early interest in professional organizations. Along with C. W. Roberts of Abilene, he was a member of the National Association of Accountants and Bookkeepers at the turn of the century.[2]

His later activities suggest that Peter was probably instrumental in 1909 in persuading Representative Claude M. McCallum of Dallas to introduce a bill in the state legislature calling for the recognition of "the profession of certified public accountants . . . and authorizing the Secretary of State to issue certificates granting . . . use of the title 'Certified Public Accountant.'" The bill was reported out of committee adversely, however, ending any hope of its adoption at that session.[3] Two years later, Peter wrote Representative George A. Harmon of Dallas that he and "several of the boys [again] were heartily in favor of the C.P.A. bill," but no record exists of the measure's being introduced in

1. Rita Perine Merritt, ed., *The Accountants' Directory and Who's Who, 1925* (New York: Prentice-Hall, 1925), p. 617; and Albert G. Moss to author, Dec. 24, 1958.
2. Norman E. Webster, comp., *The American Association of Public Accountants: Its First Twenty Years* (New York: American Institute of Accountants, 1954), p. 280.
3. *House Journal*, 31st Legislature, Regular Session (1909), p. 1316.

the legislative sessions of 1911 or 1913.[4] Here the matter rested until 1915.

## Prelude to Certification: The Texas State Society of Public Accountants, 1911–1915

Meanwhile, recognizing that legislation might be secured more easily if accountants were better organized, Peter set events in motion leading to the organization of the Texas State Society of Public Accountants. Early in March, 1911, he requested from chambers of commerce throughout Texas the names of public accountants in each city. Using the list he thus compiled, Peter then wrote to individual accountants that he and other Dallas accountants had "no doubt" an organization formed along "right lines" would be beneficial to practicing accountants throughout the state. Asking if they "could afford to spend a day" to take up this important matter, Peter proposed a meeting in Galveston as soon as the railroads had a "low rate" to the resort city.[5] The response to Peter's invitation was prompt and encouraging. At the end of the month, he wrote Marion Douglas to make arrangements for the meeting.

On May 22, 1911, seventeen public accountants and six junior staff accountants met at the Hotel Tremont in Galveston to form the Texas State Society of Public Accountants. In addition to Peter and Douglas, those attending included Milton Morris of Austin; Charles F. Bridewell of Beaumont; Charles H. Schoolar, Harry E. Gordon, Charles Byers, and J. W. Hurst of Dallas; Clarence Longnecker of El Paso; P. B. Potter, Charles E. Scales, and Vernon Davis Bierman of Fort Worth; B. F. Albertson, D. Maples, and George Kidd, Jr., of Houston; and B. L. Raborn and William M. Aikman of San Antonio. The junior accountants present were I. D. Roberts of Beaumont; Daniel A. McKeever of Dallas; J. A. Phinney and J. P. Longon of Fort Worth; and Lynn Walker and A. A. Van Alstyne of Galveston.

Peter called the meeting to order and Scales served as temporary secretary. For the committee on credentials, Gordon proposed and the

4. William P. Peter to George A. Harmon, Jan. 31, 1910, Peter MSS in Texas Society Archives (the Society records are referred to hereinafter as TSCPA).
5. William P. Peter to Hugo R. Burnaby, Beaumont, Mar. 14, 1911, Peter MSS, TSCPA.

group approved two classes of membership. Fellow membership was bestowed upon the seventeen accountants present, who were in turn described as Texas citizens of good moral character "practicing the profession of public accountancy on their own behalf, or on the behalf of another, or who were members in good standing of societies in other states having equal qualifications." Junior accountants regularly employed as assistants of fellow members were eligible for associate membership.

The membership established, Schoolar reported for the constitution committee. The society was organized, he stated, to elevate and improve the profession; to bring public accountants together; to promote a standard of ethics; to establish a code of honor between accountants, their clients, and the public; to demonstrate that public accountants were safeguards to the industrial and financial development of the state; and to encourage the development of guilds of accountants interested in the upbuilding of the profession. Future members, both fellow and associate, were to be admitted only by examination or reciprocity. Initiation fees of $35 and $15, respectively, were established, and annual dues were set at $10 and $5 for the two types of members. By-laws adopted at the same time provided for standing committees on membership, program, guilds, auditing examinations, and legislation.

Members of the new society next elected permanent officers. Gordon was elected president; Bridewell, vice-president; and Peter, secretary-treasurer. Four directors were also elected: Potter, Longnecker, Raborn, and Schoolar. President Gordon accepted the duties of president and challenged each of the officers to do "his whole duty or we cannot hope to attain marked success." The body then selected a corporate charter and seal, voted its thanks to the hosts, had its photograph taken, and selected Dallas as the site for the first annual meeting on October 21, 1911.[6]

In the interval between the organizational meeting and the first annual gathering in Dallas, the Board of Directors met again in Galveston on July 10. Four new fellow members were elected at that time: Thomas A. Thurston of El Paso, W. V. Lauraine of Houston, Joseph Elliot Hutchinson, Sr., of Dallas, and Horace Pickett of Waco. Stonewall Jackson Von Koenneritz of Austin was elected to associate mem-

6. "Minutes of Convention for Organization, May 22, 1911," Peter MSS, TSCPA.

bership. The board then selected Longnecker to represent the society at the September meeting of the American Association of Public Accountants in San Francisco and to petition for membership in the AAPA. The success of Longnecker's mission was evidenced later in an address by Edward L. Suffern, president of the AAPA, who welcomed the state societies of Texas and Alabama into membership. "Both of these societies," Suffern declared, "start under promising auspices and we hope will increase and develop in the near future."[7]

Fourteen members and eleven guests gathered in the parlors of the Oriental Hotel in Dallas for the first annual meeting of the Texas State Society of Public Accountants. At a Board of Directors meeting held just before the general session, Harry Vivian Robertson of Amarillo, C. A. Richardson and Stuart A. Giraud of Beaumont, Charles G. Morgan, Sr., of Waco, and Charles G. Morgan, Jr., of Dallas were elected fellow members. Five associate members were elected concurrently: Albert G. Moss, Arthur C. Upleger, and Joseph E. Hutchinson, Jr., of Dallas, and Frank J. McDonald and W. H. McDonald of San Antonio. The minutes of the board meeting also report that John B. Geijsbeek, CPA, of Denver, Colorado, and chairman of the Educational Committee of the American Association of Public Accountants, "favored the Board several times with valuable advice based upon his experience in these matters."[8]

Several items of business were brought up in the Society's general meeting. The qualifications for fellow membership were raised, to admit only senior accountants of two or more years' experience who passed examinations in three areas: theory and practice, accounting problems, and commercial law. The examination was waived for applicants who held CPA certificates from other states. Annual membership dues were then raised to $25 and $15 for fellow and associate members, respectively.

George Kidd was elected vice-president to fill the post vacated when Bridewell temporarily moved from Texas, and Schoolar was chosen to a full three-year term on the board of directors. Notice was also given at this meeting that the Society had been duly chartered by the State of Texas on October 12, 1911. At the conclusion of the business session, Geijsbeek formally addressed the members and their guests.

7. "The President's Address," *Journal of Accountancy* 12 (Nov., 1911): 505.
8. "Minutes . . . Board of Directors, October 21, 1911," Peter MSS, TSCPA.

The official minutes of subsequent meetings of the Texas State Society of Public Accountants are missing. However, a newspaper report of the third annual meeting, held in Fort Worth on October 24, 1913, indicates that the membership had expanded to include A. A. Hart of San Antonio; Edward J. Archinard, Kernaghan, and G. L. Rawlings of Fort Worth; O. F. Schubert, George H. Bird, Loyd B. Smith, Louis A. Williams, and A. C. Miller of Dallas; and Frank G. Masquelette of Houston. Kernaghan was elected president of the society on this occasion. Selected to serve with him were Douglas, vice-president; Bridewell, treasurer; and Scales, secretary. Judging from this report, legislation was uppermost in the minds of the membership. Bridewell, Giraud, and Hart reported as a legislative committee that good educational work had been done and that the chances of getting a CPA bill through the next legislature (1915) were very bright.[9]

Biographical information regarding the forty-eight known members of the Texas State Society of Public Accountants is difficult to find.[10] By 1915, Kernaghan was sixty-four years of age and perhaps the oldest member. Von Koenneritz and Hutchinson, Sr., were in their early fifties. Peter was forty-nine, Thurston was in his middle forties, Schoolar and Bridewell were forty-three and forty-one, respectively, and Masquelette was forty. Aikman was thirty-nine, Robertson and Upleger were thirty-two, and Moss and Hutchinson, Jr., were twenty-nine and twenty-six, respectively. At least three were CPAs from other states. Bierman held Ohio certificate number 114 dated 1910, Masquelette held Louisiana certificate number 123 dated 1908, and Bridewell held Oregon certificate number 25 dated 1913. Some had college training. Gordon, McKeever, and Upleger were fresh from the New York University School of Commerce; Bridewell had studied at Tulane; Hutchinson, Sr., went through the junior year at the University of Alabama and Southern University of Birmingham; Robertson took four years of engineering at the Agricultural and Mechanical College of Colorado; and Masquelette was a Northwestern University graduate.

The membership was made up exclusively of accountants in local firms. Two national firms opened offices in Texas in 1915; Peat, Mar-

9. *Dallas Morning News*, Oct. 25, 1914.
10. This information was gathered from several sources: Merritt, *The Accountants' Directory*; the author's interviews with past presidents of the Texas Society; and a folder marked "Biographies" compiled by the History and Archives Committee of the Texas Society.

wick, Mitchell & Co. and Ernst & Ernst. But neither of these firms was represented in the society membership. As previously noted, Douglas and Kernaghan probably had the oldest practices in the state, having opened offices in Galveston and Fort Worth, respectively, in 1896. In 1911, Kernaghan and Archinard formed a partnership that continued until 1916. Schoolar organized a firm in Dallas in 1906 and soon admitted Bird to partnership. Peter and Company, organized in 1907, had on its staff at various times Hutchinson, Sr., Upleger, Gordon, McKeever, and Moss. Moss became a partner in 1913, and the firm name changed to Peter and Moss. Also in Dallas, Hutchinson, Sr., organized his firm late in 1907, and by 1915 Smith was a partner in the firm Hutchinson and Smith. Upleger, Gordon, and McKeever left Peter to organize their own firm, but this arrangement lasted less than a year. Upleger then worked briefly for Hutchinson and Smith before opening the offices of Upleger & Falk, Inc., in Waco in 1913. The date Byers established himself in Dallas is not known, but by 1910 he had a thriving practice. Masquelette moved from New Orleans, Louisiana, in 1909 to open offices in Houston for Robinson and Masquelette. This partnership was dissolved in 1913, by which time F. G. Masquelette & Co. had offices in Houston and El Paso. In Amarillo, Robertson quit private employment as a bookkeeper for the Amarillo Power and Light Company to open his public practice in 1910. Aikman arrived in San Antonio in 1911 to continue the profession he had entered as an apprentice in Indiana in 1896. Richardson and Giraud were partners in a firm that had offices in Beaumont and Houston by 1913. Bridewell worked several years for Standard Oil Company and Armour Packing Company before going into public practice. Scales was more in private work than public. He was auditor for one of the Fort Worth meat-packing plants and operated his public practice on the side. Von Koenneritz was primarily a banker in Austin who engaged in public accounting "during his leisure time." At least two of these men, Robertson and Byers, were English-born, though Robertson was reared and educated in New Mexico and Colorado. In later years, at least twenty-six of the forty-eight members of the Texas State Society of Public Accountants secured certificates from the Texas State Board of Public Accountancy.[11]

11. A. A. Hart, referred to in a preceding paragraph, was probably Alexander Hart, who was elected secretary of the Certified Accountants of Louisana in 1906 two years before that state enacted a CPA law. Hart was admitted to membership in the

## The Public Accountancy Act of 1915

The Texas State Society of Public Accountants was looked upon as the first step toward state certification. The second step occurred in 1915 when State Senator J. C. McNealus of Dallas introduced and secured the adoption of Senate Bill 222 creating the Texas State Board of Public Accountancy. The bill was sponsored in the House of Representatives by George W. Dayton of Valley View. Thirty states had already passed CPA laws by 1915, and Texas was one of six states joining the ranks that year. The states adjoining Texas secured CPA laws in the following order: Louisiana, 1908; Arkansas, 1915; Oklahoma, 1917; and New Mexico, 1921.

The Texas CPA statute was a permissive law similar to those of most other states. It provided that the governor appoint a board composed of five practicing accountants, each of whom was to have had a minimum of three years' experience in public accounting. The first board members were permitted to grant themselves certificates if they met the requirements of the law. After January, 1917, all board members were required to be certificate holders. The board was authorized to hold periodic examinations to test applicants in theory of accounts, practical accounting, auditing, and commercial law. Candidates were required to be at least twenty-one years old, citizens of good moral character, and to have had three years' study and practice in accounting. A waiver clause excused from examination those who had practiced the last two of the preceding three years in Texas, provided the application for waiver was filed before January 1, 1916. Cancellation of the certificate was permissible under the law in the event the holder was convicted of a felony or fraud, was declared insane or incompetent, or was guilty of an act detrimental to the profession. Any CPA who knowingly and willfully misrepresented a report was subject to a fine of $100 to $1,000 and forfeiture of certificate. The practice of accountancy was not restricted to certificate holders, but noncertified accountants who posed as CPAs were liable to misdemeanor charges and a $200 fine.[12]

---

American Association of Public Accountants in 1907. *Journal of Accountancy* 4 (May, 1907): 66.

12. A copy of the bill may be found in the legislative journals and, more accessibly, in *Journal of Accountancy* 19 (May, 1915): 375–80.

On March 22, Governor James E. Ferguson signed the bill into law, and on June 11 he appointed Peter, Archinard, Morris, Robertson, and Edgar F. Hunter of San Antonio to the first Texas State Board of Public Accountancy. Meeting for the first time in Fort Worth's Westbrook Hotel on June 22, the board set about implementing the new act, the business at hand being to organize and accept applications for certificates by waiver, examination, or reciprocity. Initially awarding themselves waiver certificates numbered 1 through 5 in the order named above, the board members delayed granting other waivers for the moment. They then elected Archinard chairman and Robertson secretary-treasurer and adopted the Missouri state board's definition of "public accountant," the intention being to make it difficult for persons only marginally engaged in public practice to qualify for a certificate. Finally, the dates of July 26–29 were set for the first examinations in Galveston. As the AIA uniform examination was not available until 1916, and then not used by the Texas board until 1919, each board member except the chairman assumed responsibility for one part of the test.

Prior to the Galveston meeting, controversies arose between Peter and Archinard over Peter's failure to submit a formal application for his certificate and between Peter and Scales, whose application for a waiver was before the board. At a special meeting in Fort Worth on July 23, which Peter failed to attend, the board, over Hunter's objection, renumbered the first five certificates in new order: Morris (1), Robertson (2), Archinard (3), and Hunter (4). Certificate number 5, while reserved for Peter, was held up pending resolution of the disputes with Archinard and Scales. Meanwhile, the board began to act on other waiver applications and awarded certificate number 6 to Kernaghan and numbers 8 and 9 to Joseph Hutchinson, Sr., and Loyd Smith, respectively.

Three candidates appeared for the examination in Galveston, two of whom were successful: Jesse E. Buford and Ambrose G. MacMahon. The board awarded them certificates 25 and 26 and at the same time approved waiver certificate number 7 for Raborn and numbers 14–23 for Thurston, Aikman, Samuel Williams, Schoolar, Douglas, Charles Snyder, Bridewell, Anthony Grondona, Jesse Nelson, and Louis Williams.

Following the Galveston meeting, the board members reconvened on July 31 in Fort Worth, where, Peter having reconciled his problems with Archinard and Scales, the board awarded his certificate along with five others: numbers 10 through 13 to Moss, Frank McDonald, Scales, and Byers and number 24 to Grider.

The flurry of meetings in June and July completed the board's formal activity for 1915. While twenty-six certificates had been issued, that many more applications, some from persons prominent in professional society affairs, were still pending. And by January 1, 1916, the deadline for waiver applications, the board had a total of sixty-one unanswered applications on hand.

The board reduced the backlog of waiver applications at a three-day session in March, 1916, by awarding certificates 27–35 to Victor Buron, Joseph Hutchinson, Jr., von Koenneritz, Ira Harris, John K. Breeden, A. R. Washington, Henry Fisher, W. H. Rankin, and I. Schwartz. Then, following a two-day session in June, waiver certificates 36–48 went to Joseph Higgs, M. W. Mattison, Paul Williams, C. W. Roberts, Charles Morgan, Jr., A. E. Myles, Upleger, H. M. Heinzie, L. B. Peyton, Giraud, W. M. Ballard, Kidd, and O. C. Van Zandt. Finally, in August the board issued a waiver certificate to W. J. Loverien (number 49), and in October, to Charles L. Armstrong (number 57) and Victor Roos (number 58).

This was thought to have completed the waiver process, approximately two-thirds of the applications received having been approved. In 1917, however, certificate number 47 was revoked on grounds of personal character, and in 1918 the board belatedly issued certificate number 67 to Longnecker upon reconsideration of his waiver application. The last waiver certificate was issued in 1920 to John S. Oglesby (number 72) upon order of the district court of Tarrant County, which agreed with Oglesby that he was entitled to recognition by the board. Thus, the board issued a net total of fifty waiver certificates under the 1915 act.[13]

## Texas Society of Certified Public Accountants

Meanwhile, soon after the CPA law was enacted, changes were made in the professional society that reflected the new status of Texas

13. See Minute Books of the Texas State Board of Public Accountancy for the years 1915–1920.

accountancy. At a meeting held in the Fort Worth offices of Kernaghan & Archinard on October 27–28, 1915, the Texas State Society of Public Accountants gave way to a new organization, the Texas Society of Certified Public Accountants. Sixteen persons, each the holder of a waiver certificate, were present in person or represented by proxy at the first meeting of the new society. Fourteen were former members of the old association. Along with Kernaghan, Archinard, and Scales, who were the hosts, Byers, Louis Williams, Snyder, Joseph Hutchinson, Sr., and Jesse Nelson of Dallas; Thurston from El Paso; and Douglas and Bridewell of Galveston were there in person. Loyd Smith of Dallas, Robertson of Amarillo, Grider of El Paso, Morris of Austin, and Samuel Williams of Houston were there by proxy.

Peter was noticeably absent from this meeting and consequently from charter membership in the Texas Society of Certified Public Accountants. While no conclusive evidence has been found that explains his absence, it is likely that his quarrels with Archinard and Scales kept him away.

The first order of business was the election of officers for the new society. Kernaghan, having already served two terms as head of the parent organization, was again chosen president. Smith, though not present, was elected vice-president, and Scales was elected secretary-treasurer. Thurston and Byers were elected directors to complete the executive body of the new society. A motion was then approved which limited charter membership in the Texas Society of Certified Public Accountants to the sixteen present in Fort Worth or represented by proxy. It was further agreed that in the future members would be elected by ballots in which "three black balls" would defeat an applicant's petition. Initiation fees were set at $10 and annual dues at $15 for fellow members. Seven members constituted a quorum, and the second Monday in August was picked to be the date of the annual meetings. The Board of Directors was empowered to call a special meeting in March, 1916, however, for the purpose of ratifying the constitution and by-laws.[14]

The meeting to adopt the constitution was delayed until August 14, 1916. While no record of it has been found, there was either a second meeting of the Society or an election of members before Au-

14. "Minutes . . . October 27–28, 1915," TSCPA.

gust, for a list of fellow members dated July, 1916, included the names of Peter, Moss, Hutchinson, Jr., and Schoolar in addition to those who were at the October, 1915, meeting. The same document listed Bird, Gordon, Austin H. Cole, and Miller of Dallas; A. F. De Loach and P. L. Sanders of Galveston; and Harvie Kernaghan of Fort Worth as additional associate members.[15] Therefore, there were twenty-seven members of record when the Texas Society of Certified Public Accountants met again in Fort Worth to adopt a constitution.

The preamble to the constitution declared that the Society was incorporated "for the purpose of maintaining and elevating the standard of proficiency, integrity and character, and promoting the interests of certified public accountants, and cultivating professional cooperation and social intercourse amongst its members." Two types of membership were provided. Fellow membership was open to any white citizen holding the Texas certificate and practicing "the profession of public accountant on his own behalf or in the employ of another public accountant, as a senior accountant." Associate membership of distinctly inferior rank was open to "any white citizen of the United States, eighteen years of age or over, who is engaged in the practice of the profession of public accountancy." Only fellow members were eligible to vote and hold office in the Society. Honorary membership could be bestowed on accountants and nonaccountants by the Society. Neglected payment of dues, recall of certificate by the Texas State Board of Public Accountancy, or conviction of a felony act resulted in forfeiture of membership.[16]

Following adoption of the constitution and by-laws, fellow members of the Society voted on two applications for fellow membership and four applications for associate membership, their votes revealing personality disputes and a bias against national firms. The applicants for fellow membership were Hunter, who held certificate number 4 and was a member of the Texas State Board of Public Accountancy, and Victor E. Buron of Texarkana, who held certificate number 27. Fourteen Society members voted on the applications, but neither Hunter nor Buron received the twelve affirmative votes needed for admission.

Three of the four applications for associate membership, George

15. See pamphlet entitled "Texas Society of Certified Public Accountants: Constitution and By-Laws Adopted August 14, 1916," TSCPA.
    16. Ibid.

Marr Hofford, MacMahon, and Alexander Norman Young, were from the Dallas office of Peat, Marwick, Mitchell & Co., and they, along with C. V. Paulk of Dallas, were voted down also. Hofford, fifty years old at this time, was manager of the new Texas office and had held extensive auditing assignments in private industry before joining Peat, Marwick, Mitchell & Co. In October, 1916, two months after being denied membership, Hofford was awarded a Texas certificate. Mac-Mahon was born in Canada in 1885 and was educated at Guildhall School in London, England. He qualified for his Texas certificate in July, 1915. Young was born in Aberdeenshire, Scotland, in 1879 and was licensed a chartered accountant in 1908. As an apprentice to A. S. Mitchell in Aberdeen, Young had been with Peat, Marwick, Mitchell & Co. since the firm's inception.

Minutes of this meeting also indicate that Governor James E. Ferguson was elected an honorary member of the Texas Society of Certified Public Accountants; however, another list of members indicates that as early as July, 1916, Ferguson, Pickett, and J. S. Morris Goodloo of New York had been elected honorary members. The reasons for honoring the governor who signed the 1915 accountancy act are self-evident and understandable. The reasons for honoring Pickett, a charter member of the Texas State Society of Public Accountants who did not receive a certificate from the Texas State Board of Public Accountancy, and Goodloo, who was prominent in Ohio and New York accounting circles, are not so evident and are unrecorded in Society minutes.

Thus, amid some confusion as to exact dates of membership and sharp disagreements over personalities, the Texas Society of Certified Public Accountants was formally launched.

# 3

## The Texas Society's Early Years, 1916–1931

THE first years were difficult ones for the Society. Some accountants refused to attend professional meetings and discuss problems with fellow practitioners because of personality conflicts or fear of client encroachment. They also split over the issues that divided the national profession into two camps in 1921, one represented by the American Institute of Accountants and the other by the American Society of Certified Public Accountants. In spite of these problems, however, a new spirit surfaced by the middle 1920s. The Society enlisted new members, instituted a publications program, and achieved a degree of financial stability. A code of ethics, adopted with reasonable expectations of compliance, further reflected professional development. In 1928 the Texas Society won first prize in a contest sponsored by the American Society of Certified Public Accountants to determine which of several competing state societies had made the most progress that year. Also in 1928, Arthur C. Upleger became president of the American Society of Certified Public Accountants, and Loyd Smith and George Armistead went on the Council of the American Institute of Accountants. The Society's momentum faltered in 1931 when efforts to pass a regulatory bill in Texas failed and the debilitating effects of the national depression set in, but the presidents who presided over Society affairs from 1916 to 1931 had good reason to feel that their efforts had resulted in a foundation for solid growth in the future.

### A National Profession Divided

A major rift in the national profession occurred when many accountants became disgruntled with the actions of the American Institute of Accountants in 1916 that seemed to encroach upon the prerogatives of state boards and the importance of state certification. Under the leadership of Durand Springer of Michigan, critics of the institute formed the American Society of Certified Public Accountants in 1921 and thereby divided the profession again roughly along the lines that had existed from 1902 to 1905 between federalists and nationalists. The American Society grew rapidly and further enhanced the state certificate as the hallmark of the profession in America. The American Society made the certificate a prerequisite for membership, whereas the institute did not. The American Society endorsed two-class regulatory laws while the institute held back. The American Society also led the fight against the National Association of Certified Public Accountants, a private corporation, formed in 1921, that was flooding the nation with cheap imitations of state certificates. A court injunction eventually forced the mail-order firm out of business, thereby adding weight to the American Society's claim to leadership of the profession.

Divided leadership at the national level was reflected within the state. As noted above, the Texas Society furnished leaders to both the American Society of Certified Public Accountants and to the American Institute of Accountants, and the tension reflected in the different philosophies of the two organizations was often evident in the affairs of the Texas Society.

## Members, Meetings, and Finances

Personality problems and fears of client encroachment were more basic reasons for the poor membership and professionalism of the Texas Society in its early years. From 1915 to 1920, the Texas State Board of Public Accountancy issued seventy-five certificates, each holder being a potential member of the Texas Society. Membership remained static at twenty fellows, however, the same number represented at the 1916 meeting. Annual meetings of even this number were difficult to arrange. Nine fellow members were in Dallas for the 1917 meeting, but the next year the meeting failed for lack of a quorum, and no meeting was attempted in 1919.

In 1920 the Society snapped out of its lethargy. Four meetings were held that year, one in Galveston and three in Dallas. Thirteen new members, including two who had been denied membership in 1916, were added to the roster, the first additions since 1916. The number included Arthur C. Upleger of Waco; Ira Harris, George Hofford, Ambrose MacMahon, Austin H. Cole, and Charles Morgan, Jr., of Dallas; Thomas Elbert Allday and A. E. Myles of Wichita Falls; Charles S. Jones of El Paso; E. D. Newman of Fort Worth; Joe C. Harris of San Antonio; Robert T. Ronaldson of Beaumont; and Frank J. Huey of Houston.

Further evidence that the Society members had to large degree risen above personality differences was demonstrated in 1921, 1922, and 1923 when all fourteen persons who applied for membership were elected. Thomas J. Tapp of Houston and Bouldin S. Mothershead of Fort Worth, and later, Harlingen, joined in 1921. The next year George Armistead and Jay A. Phillips of Houston, Frank G. Rodgers of San Antonio, and W. D. Brunkern of Waco became members. In 1923 Percy W. Pogson of El Paso; Herbert Himes of Monterey, Mexico; Adrian V. Seay of Houston; Luke B. Garvin and J. C. McNamara of Dallas; Mac Killough of Palestine; and James Rudolph Isleib and Frank L. Wilcox of Waco joined the Society ranks.

The subject of membership enlistment was thoroughly discussed at the Society's annual meeting in 1924, the first held in Houston. Frank Rogers explained why some of the older San Antonio accountants had not joined. They "have a grievance against the old Society, that is to say, the Society of former years, and also probably against some members of the first Board of Accountancy," Rodgers said. "They ought to be members of the Society alright," he continued, but it must be shown "that this Society is not like it used to be . . . we have cut out a lot of that wrangling and differences and have a common ground now." Charles Scales seconded Rodgers's remarks. "Some difficulty occurred in the old Society," he admitted, but "the troubles of the old Society have been wiped out . . . and we have been working harmoniously for years."[1] Later that year Armistead remarked in his presidential report that the early trouble with memberships was "the prevalent distrust of accountants with each other." Texas accountants, he said, "need a dignified conception of our profession which will at once make us considerate in thought and temperate in speech."[2]

In line with this philosophy, the Society moved closer toward the

---

1. "Minutes . . . May 16, 1924," pp. 46–47, TSCPA.
2. "Minutes . . . November 15, 1924," p. 25, TSCPA.

position that membership was a professional matter open to all certificate holders. Some discriminations formerly practiced were abandoned. To this end the constitution was amended in 1928 to provide for balloting on prospective members by mail.[3] If no more than two votes were cast against a candidate's application for membership within thirty days after the name had been mailed out, the person was declared elected. Three negative notes forced a referral of the election to the board of directors, where four affirmative votes out of ten were sufficient to elect. Only in very rare cases thereafter was the election of members referred to the members in convention.

Other changes made during the 1920s put membership on a more professional plane. Associate membership, first looked upon a means of bringing apprentice and junior accountants into the Society on a nonvoting basis, was redefined in 1923 to declare that "any associate member who shall fail to obtain a certificate . . . within three years after the date of admission . . . shall be suspended."[4] In 1928 noncertified accountants were denied any form of membership, and the associate rank was retained only for certified accountants no longer in public practice. At this same time honorary membership in the Society, previously open to persons outside the profession, was restricted to certificate holders only who, by reason of foreign citizenship, could not qualify for fellow status.[5]

The new philosophy regarding membership brought an increase in the Texas Society's ranks. Records are not clear on the exact number of fellow members initiated in the middle 1920s. There were apparently eight additions in 1924 and three in 1925. No records exist for 1926, though membership certificates start with the number 100 in 1927. This figure undoubtedly represented associate and honorary memberships as well as fellow members, however. Twenty-three new members were added in 1927, twenty-seven in 1928, and twenty in 1929. Approximately 171 membership certificates were issued in the period 1916 to 1931.[6]

3. "Constitution . . . Adopted . . . November 30, 1928," TSCPA.
4. "Constitution . . . As . . . Revised October 27, 1923," TSCPA.
5. "Constitution . . . Adopted . . . November 30, 1928," TSCPA.
6. In 1924: J. J. Gannon, William H. Rankin, J. G. Bixler, Charles Edgar Miller, Otho G. Roquemore, Herman A. Barsun, E. V. Becker, and D. B. Griffin. In 1925: Clinton E. Smith, Thomas Franklin Kennedy, and Forrest Mathis. In 1927: Raymond I.

These figures did not always represent clear gain, however, for some let their memberships lapse and others moved away. Average paid-up membership in any given year in the late 1920s was slightly over one hundred. The largest group to attend an annual meeting during this interval was thirty-three, the number that gathered in San Antonio in 1928.

More attractive programs at annual meetings sparked new interest in the Society. President Marion Douglas in 1920 promised during his tenure of office "there would be a regular program provided including addresses and discussions on live topics by members or others from prepared papers."[7] Later that year Nathan Adams, a prominent Dallas banker, was the featured speaker at a banquet honoring applicants for examination by the Texas State Board of Public Accountancy. At the meeting of the Board of Directors in June, 1921, Upleger and Albert Moss were instructed to prepare technical papers for the annual meeting in August. Joseph Hutchinson, Sr., was charged with providing an after-dinner speaker. Thus the pattern was established that conventions of the Society have followed in an expanded manner down to the present. Among the members and guests who participated in programs during the decade were W. M. Hauhart of Southern Methodist University; F. M. Law of the First National Bank of Houston; Spurgeon Bell, George H. Newlove, Chester Lay, and H. C. Walling of the University of Texas;

---

Mehan, C. H. Cavness, John S. Oglesby, O. H. Maschek, Arthur H. Carter, George B. Simpson, Charles R. English, Victor E. Buron, J. R. Maceo, H. Tracy Nelson, Ben M. Davis, N. O. Richardson, C. F. Milledge, Rene J. LeGardeur, Thomas B. Cornell, Arthur C. Woods, C. R. Phelps, Edwin H. Wagner, Edward A. Stenzel, Carneal B. Sheffield, E. R. Burnett, Jacob Irl Weatherby, William M. Aikman, and Y. D. Harrison, Jr. In 1928 the Executive Committee meeting on March 17 declared Robert Emmett Seay, L. R. Carter, and Lawrence R. Chenault elected. At the annual meeting, Nov. 30, 1928, the chairman of the Membership Committee reported twenty additional persons elected but failed to include their names in the record. At the meeting, however, E. E. C. Smith, William D. Prince, Thomas C. McNeil, and Walter L. McBride were elected to membership by the convention and their names were thus recorded. In 1929 the Executive Council met on July 29 and declared the following elected subject to the expiration of the thirty-day period for filing protests: Howard H. Hull, Hatcher Andrew Pickens, John Tom Devanney, Theodore W. Mohle, Ross Charles Rodgers, Claude Thomas Lynn, Cloize A. King, Revely A. Moore, Darcy Robert Bonner, and Alex M. Cameron. Douglas B. Bagnell also applied for membership at this time but withdrew his application before it was approved. After 1929 the minutes and committee reports rarely contain the names of members elected during the year.

7. "Minutes . . . August 14, 1920," TSCPA.

Elkin Moses, CPA, of New Orleans; Durand Springer of the American Society of Certified Public Accountants; John Carey of the American Institute of Accountants; Paul Carrington of the American Arbitration Association; Frank Wilcox of Waco; John W. Ballard of Texas Christian University; Archie M. Smith of the Louisiana State Board of Public Accountancy; and Walter L. McBride of the U.S. Internal Revenue Service.

Membership had a direct bearing on the Society's financial condition. Dues were reduced in 1917 to $5 and $2.50 for fellow and associate members, respectively. Three years later it appeared that the millennium in money matters was reached when dues of the past two years were remitted! "This was done," the secretary recorded, "for the reason that the Treasurer reported that there were sufficient funds on hand to run the society up to that time."[8] It should be added quickly that this condition did not exist long and no remission of dues has occurred since. Instead, dues went back up to $10 for fellow members in 1923 and to $5 for associate members in 1928. The elevation of dues and an expanded membership provided the Society with an average annual income of slightly over $1,000 from 1926 to 1931. In the fiscal year ending November, 1929, receipts reached $1,740.53, highest of the decade. Expenditures were proportionate to income, however, so while an adequate surplus of about $500 was kept on hand each year, expenditures of the Society very nearly matched receipts. Characteristic expenditures were convention expenses, which in those days included payment for the annual banquet, printing costs, travel expenses for the officers, and legislative costs. Commencing in 1929 the Society paid the secretary-treasurer a token salary, first set at $300 annually.

## Enforcing the Law

At the same time the Society launched a positive program of professional development, it helped carry on a rearguard fight to defend the 1915 law and the designation "CPA" from fraudulent misuse. Individual members of the Society and the Texas State Board of Public Accountancy carried this burden more than the Society, though meetings of the latter were used to plan strategy. The prime target was the

8. "Minutes . . . January 31, 1920," TSCPA.

National Association of Certified Public Accountants, referred to earlier, which was actively selling diplomas in Texas.[9] El Paso accountants pressed charges in February, 1922, against a local man who was accredited by this agency and was using the designation "C.P.A.(N.A.)" behind his name. In due time the case reached the Texas Court of Criminal Appeals. There the conviction in the lower courts was affirmed and the constitutionality of the 1915 law was upheld.[10] A similar case arose in Wichita Falls about the same time and was handled successfully in the lower courts.

The cost of the El Paso case was borne initially by the Texas State Board. Armistead paid the expenses of the Wichita Falls case, about $100, in the name of the Law Enforcement Association of Accountants. At a Society meeting in Houston in 1924, Loyd Smith and Upleger proposed $250 be subscribed to reimburse the State Board for its expenses, as there was some question concerning the board's authority to spend money for such purpose.[11] Later that same year, in Fort Worth, Armistead spoke out strongly on this point. "I here venture to lay down the proposition," he said, "that we should not, as accredited practitioners, look to the State Board, or to any other agency to enforce the law. The remedy is in ourselves individually, if we but act and meet the violations as we find them. To fight the thing out on our own battleground, ours should be the spirit of Cromwell's pikemen who rejoiced greatly when they beheld the enemy."[12]

## A Code of Ethics

Fending off outsiders who were threatening the integrity of the certificate was less important and more easily accomplished than formulating a code of professional ethics that would oblige Society members to strengthen the profession from within. At issue, however, was the necessity that the Society, in the absence of the State Board's authority under the 1915 law to do so, formulate a clear statement of the profession's obligation to the public and regulate the professional conduct and competitive behavior of its members. In the context of the

9. See p. 26.
10. Henry v. State of Texas, 260 S.W. 190.
11. "Minutes . . . May 16, 1924," TSCPA.
12. "Minutes . . . November 15, 1924," TSCPA.

times, this meant imposing restraints on crass commercial advertising, open solicitation of accounts, and competitive bidding that many were convinced drove down the quality of service rendered by CPAs. Bouldin Mothershead voiced the matter in his presidential report to the membership in 1928. "The most significant advancement of the year," Mothershead told the thirty-three delegates gathered in San Antonio's St. Anthony Hotel, "lies in the tendency toward crystalization in the minds of Certified Public Accountants of the conception of professional obligations to the economic and business life of our state." Accountants in Texas were beginning to get a "clearer understanding" of what distinguishes a profession from a vocation and to realize that they must "render a distinct contribution to the society as a whole aside and apart from those functions that we as individuals perform for a consideration."[13] Consistent with this enlightened attitude, the Society adopted its first code of professional ethics the following year in Beaumont.

Mothershead, William Peter, and Armistead drafted the code, which addressed several of the broad issues troubling the profession. Willful mistatements or gross negligence in financial reporting became grounds for expulsion. Conditions under which Society members could use the initials "CPA" were carefully described and limited to professional engagements, care also being taken to require that CPAs practicing in the name of a Society member's firm be members of the Society and thereby subject to its ethical code. In spite of a strong feeling that contingent fees should be permitted in federal tax cases, the code declared improper these financial arrangements as well as the acceptance of commission and brokerage fees. Soliciting accounts was declared unethical behavior, and professional advertising was severely limited. The enticement of one member's staff accountant into the employ of another was deemed to be unprofessional. Any member proposing changes in the public accountancy act was required to give notice to the state Society. Finally, the code restrained members from associating with accounting schools and colleges that conducted their affairs in unprofessional ways.[14]

The adoption of a code of ethics did not necessarily mean compliance, and for many years it was weakly enforced. The first code also

13. "Minutes . . . December 1, 1928," TSCPA.
14. *Texas Accountant* 2 (Nov., 1929): 3–4.

remained silent on the whole issue of competitive bidding. However, by 1929 the Texas Society had at least raised a standard around which the profession in the state could rally.

## Advertising the Profession

While professions generally decry individual advertising or publicity, they nevertheless attempt to put themselves before the public in the most favorable light and to educate the public to a further understanding of the services their members perform. Public accounting, because it was a new profession, needed to undertake such a program, more so than older professions, like law, or professions further removed from the laity's comprehension, like medicine. The Texas Society therefore established a publicity committee in 1920 vested with "full power to act towards spreading propaganda favorable to holders of Certified Public Accountant certificates issued by the State of Texas."[15] Later that same year Loyd Smith, Scales, Upleger, and George Hofford were appointed to a committee charged with furnishing CPA speakers for such bodies as they deemed "advantageous to the work of the Society."[16] By the same token, bankers, credit men, and other business leaders were invited to address the Society at meetings. Scales once remarked that "wholesale credit men and bankers are the two groups of business men that can do more for the certified public accountant than any other class of individual in business. . . . If a banker says to an applicant for a loan, 'You must furnish me with a certified public accountant's statement of your business,' that applicant is going to comply."[17]

There was a prolonged though inconclusive discussion of the institutional advertising problem in 1924 at Houston. Speaking on the topic "Ethical Collective Advertising," Frank Rodgers supported the notion that the Society should publish an official organ that would go beyond the *Bulletin* just published by adding a "Tax Department" and a few "snappy jokes." Such a publication widely circulated, he said, would bring the profession before men in the commercial world. Should this suggestion prove unpopular, Rodgers was ready with another. The Society should take out page advertisements in the *Banker's Journal*

15. "Minutes . . . January 31, 1920," TSCPA.
16. "Minutes . . . May 22, 1920," TSCPA.
17. "Minutes . . . May 16, 1924," TSCPA.

and similar publications. Joseph Hutchinson, Sr., warned against the latter suggestion. "Straight advertising" in trade journals was tried "when we first started out," Hutchinson remarked, "but we dropped it very hastily." A better approach, he suggested, was to commission Homer Pace of Pace Institute to write a series of articles explaining the field of accountancy and to publish these in the Sunday editions of local newspapers. Along slightly different lines, Armistead argued that the objective of advertising should be to distinguish between the certified and the noncertified accountant. A bulletin doing this, he advised, should be sent to banks, municipalities, state government officers, and business concerns. Smith and Scales added that such a publication should include the names and addresses of all CPAs in Texas, not just members of the Texas Society.[18] The minutes of the meeting do not reveal it, but the decision was probably reached at the time to publish, in 1925, a narrow twenty-page booklet containing a short history of national accountancy, a syllabus of the Texas law, a warning against fraudulent credentials, and a geographical and alphabetical listing of CPAs in Texas.[19]

In 1928 William Aikman reported for a publicity committee that came back to Hutchinson's advice of four years earlier. Aikman recommended six monthly advertisements in fifteen newspapers around the state to acquaint the public with the services accountants were qualified to render. The cost of this program, he estimated, would be $8,000. The plan was not adopted. Discussion of it did lead Peter to urge the Society and local chapters to invite more business leaders to address their sessions and to have the speeches printed and distributed. This suggestion brought a retort from Harry Robertson that businessmen "would not read such articles but must be reached through the story form of advertising."[20]

The problem of institutional advertising was not settled in the 1920s. Suffice it to say the Society confined its activities in 1921 to the publication of three bulletins ranging in size from fifteen to twenty-seven pages. These contained reprints of speeches delivered at Society meet-

18. "Minutes . . . May 16, 1924," TSCPA.
19. *The Texas Law Relating to Certified Public Accountants and A Roster of Those Who Are Certified in Texas* (Houston: Texas Society of Certified Public Accountants, 1925).
20. "Minutes . . . December 1, 1928," TSCPA.

ings and articles aimed at persons outside as well as inside the profession. The bulk of the material, however, related to committee reports and Society business. Even more important, both in terms of public relations and professional advancement, was the inaugural issue of the *Texas Accountant*, which appeared in January, 1928. Appearing monthly, the *Texas Accountant* was designed to be "an open forum for the accountants of Texas."[21]

## Accounting Educators

A fairly close bond was established in the early years between the practitioners and the teachers of accounting. Jesse Buford, holder of certificate number 25, operated a commercial college in Dallas, and Jesse Nelson served for a time as dean of the YMCA School of Commerce in Dallas. Other practitioners were sometimes guest lecturers or special professors in hometown colleges and universities. After collegiate schools of business administration were organized in Texas—the University of Texas graduated its first class in 1919—faculty members were frequent speakers, guests, and sometimes members of the Society. At Fort Worth in 1927 eleven professors organized the Texas Association of University Instructors in Accounting. Seven different colleges were represented in this group: J. W. Ballard and Avery L. Carlson of Texas Christian University; A. W. Foscue, Jr., Laurence H. Fleck, and Frank K. Rader of Southern Methodist University; Monroe S. Carroll of Baylor; Tom W. Leland of Texas A&M; B. F. Condray, Jr., of Texas Tech; J. M. Dubray of St. Edwards; and Chester F. Lay and Henry J. Rehn of the University of Texas. Professors held their meeting one day in advance of the Texas Society and then remained as guests of the Society to participate in its programs. This established a pattern that continued for a number of years. In 1930 the Texas Society's committee on education was authorized to give a $50 prize annually to the student submitting the best thesis on accounting. Several other avenues were reported open, said the committee, by which the Society could be of service to educators. It was suggested that the Society help graduates find jobs, attempt to determine the effectiveness of accounting instruction, provide practice problems for students, and continue the joint sessions of the Society and Association of University Instructors.

21. *Texas Accountant* 1 (Jan., 1928): 1.

## Faltering Steps Toward Regulation

Any group that owes its existence in part to state law is especially sensitive to legislation. The legislative committee of the Texas Society, therefore, has always had a most important responsibility. No changes in legislation were mentioned in Society records until October, 1923. At that time a committee was instructed to help Texas credit societies get a bill through the legislature making it a felony for a merchant to make a false statement in a credit report. In 1924 some members suggested amending the accountancy law to make two years' experience a prerequisite for the certificate. Upleger, however, advised against any tampering with the law. Joseph Hutchinson, Sr., also reminded the members of the difficulty they experienced with small-town bookkeepers and rural legislators when the 1915 law was passed. Should the question be reopened, he argued, "we shall have to think of those same boys from the forks of the creek. The first thing we know we will not have any law at all worth having."[22]

In November, 1924, President Armistead came near to advocating legislation limiting the practice of public accounting to certified accountants only. Armistead sent letters to public officials urging them voluntarily to confine their selections of auditors to certified men, but he had not been too successful, he reported. A case in point was the awarding of the audit of Texas A&M College for that year to a noncertified firm. What made this such a cruel blow, he said, was the fact that the contract was awarded to the noncertified firm at the insistence of an A&M board member who just a few months earlier had addressed the Society in its Houston meeting on the "preferred serviceability of certified public accountants[!]"[23] Armistead did not press his case, however, and no action was taken supporting this type of legislation.

The next stirrings within the Society in regard to regulatory legislation came at the annual meeting in Fort Worth in 1927. A. E. Myles, Lee V. Brinton, and Joseph L. Block brought in a report calling for replacement of the 1915 permissive statute with a law similar to the recently enacted Florida and Louisiana statutes that defined public accounting and restricted practice to permit holders. The bill they proposed strengthened the certificate by adding three years' experience and

22. "Minutes . . . May 16, 1924," TSCPA.
23. "Minutes . . . November 15, 1924," TSCPA.

a high school education as prerequisites, but, to accommodate currently practicing noncertified accountants, they suggested that the State Board issue "certificates of authority" to noncertified public accountants of three years' or more experience who made application within one year of the enactment of the law. At the end of one year no further registrations would be accepted from noncertified accountants, thus making them a dying class. In time, therefore, only one class of accountants would remain to engage in the lawful practice of the profession—the certified public accountant. Unwilling to commit themselves fully at this time, the members nevertheless called upon the president to appoint a nine-man committee to study the problem more carefully and to incorporate in its report any changes and suggestions from the membership that were compatible with the principle of two-class regulation.

From 1927 until 1931 regulatory legislation was the most important single issue before the Society, and all signs pointed toward its acceptance by the membership. At San Antonio in 1928 careful plans were laid for a two-year program publicizing the merits of a new regulatory act. The following year, at Beaumont, the twenty delegates in attendance gave unanimous consent to proceed with drafting the bill in final form and circulating it among the membership. In his presidential report for 1929, J. R. Nelson acknowledged the question of legislation to be the most important assignment of his administration. Nine states, he remarked, had recently enacted legislation similar to the bill now being proposed in Texas. In 1930, Durand Springer, executive secretary of the American Society of Certified Public Accountants and one of the earliest advocates of regulatory legislation, addressed the meeting in Dallas. Later that same year a board meeting in San Antonio tried to wrap up the loose ends and prepare the bill for submission to the legislature in 1931. The board suggested that advocates of the bill hold rallies in key cities and solicit support from bankers, clearinghouse officials, trade association members, directors of chambers of commerce, and representatives of credit associations.

The years of work and effort that went into the preparation of the bill came to naught, however. A bill was introduced in the Texas State Senate that supposedly met all objections from practitioners, certified and noncertified alike. The measure died in the Senate committee, however, when divisions within the ranks of the accountants appeared. Opposition came from several sources. The American Institute of Accountants, generally recognized as speaking for the larger national firms, at that time opposed regulatory legislation. Some local men, Armistead and Phillips particularly, followed the institute's lead and turned against the bill. Phillips read a statement prepared by Armistead at the Senate committee hearings which argued that registration of noncertified accountants would elevate and unduly dignify this class and would also confuse the public, which was just coming to accept and understand the one class of licensed accountants.[24] Some national accounting firms, but not all, feared two-class legislation for these and other reasons, the most important being the restrictions such a law would place on the transfer of noncertified personnel into the state. When one national firm filed a complaint with the Dallas Clearing House Association protesting the support Dallas bankers had given the bill, the bankers withdrew their endorsement, to the embarrassment of Society officials and other supporters of the bill.[25] Even this opposition might have been overridden, however, had proponents of the measure been more diligent in lining up support. As Forrest Mathis noted in his presidential report a few months later, the bill failed to pass "not because of the efforts of its enemies but because of the inactivity of its friends."[26]

The defeat of regulatory legislation in 1931 temporarily checked the momentum the Texas Society had generated in the late 1920s. What should have been a well-attended gathering in Shreveport, Louisiana, of a joint meeting with the Louisiana, Oklahoma, and Arkansas societies in November, 1931, attracted instead the smallest number of members in over five years. All in all, much had been accomplished in these first fifteen years, however, and the Society and the profession prepared to mend their fences and move ahead.

## The Early Presidents

While information is lacking for some, the personal and professional backgrounds of the presidents who presided over the affairs of the Texas Society of Certified Public Accountants from 1915 to 1931

24. Jay A. Phillips to author, July 11, 1959.
25. Forrest Mathis, "History of the Texas Society of Certified Public Accountants to June 27, 1945" (unpublished MS in TSCPA), pp. 27–28.
26. *Texas Accountant* 5 (April, 1932): 1.

tell us much about the changing profile of the accounting profession in Texas.

Daniel Kernaghan and Marion Douglas, the first and third presidents of the Society, have been identified. After two terms (1915–1917), Kernaghan retired from Society office to devote full time to his Fort Worth practice. His association with Archinard ended in 1916, and for a brief time after World War I he practiced with Charles Bridewell. Kernaghan's practice was never very large; his staff seldom consisted of more than two men. His two sons, Daniel Harvie and William A. Kernaghan, followed their father in the profession. Kernaghan died in New Orleans in 1923. Douglas, the genial host of the meeting in 1911 that launched the profession in Texas, was elected president in 1921, but his tenure was cut short by his death on December 8, 1921. Both Kernaghan and Douglas also served on the Texas State Board of Public Accountancy.

Loyd Smith of Dallas, the second president of the Society, served during the trying period 1917 to 1920. Born in Bonham, Texas, on April 28, 1877, Smith attended Coles Military Academy as a youth and then gained business experience in the insurance and banking institutions of Dallas before associating with Joseph Hutchinson, Sr., in the practice of public accounting. Smith received one of the early waiver certificates issued by the new State Board in 1915 and shortly thereafter was elected vice-president of the Society. While serving as Society president, Smith was appointed to the Texas State Board of Public Accountancy in 1919, where he served until 1927, all but two of those years (1924–1925) as chairman. Smith's interest in professional matters extended to the American Institute of Accountants, his election to membership on its council in the middle 1920s making him one of the first persons from Texas to be so recognized. Following Hutchinson's death in the late 1920s, the firm Hutchinson and Smith was reorganized as Smith, Prince & Harris and remained so until Smith's death in April, 1938.

The Society's fourth president, Austin H. Cole, was vice-president at the time of Douglas's death in 1921. He served out the remainder of the 1921–1922 term and was then elected to a full term ending in 1923. Little is recorded about Cole's personal or professional life. It is known, however, that he was awarded Texas certificate number 79 by examination in May, 1920, and that on or before August 14, 1920, he was admitted to membership in the Society. He was associated with Jesse Nelson in Dallas for a short while in the 1920s, but thereafter he apparently practiced alone until his death in the middle 1930s. He is known to have had a number of Baptist schools and institutions as clients, and during the early 1930s he was associated with a Dallas real estate firm.

George Armistead of Houston, fifth president of the Society, served two years, 1923–1925. Born in Mississippi in 1870, Armistead moved to Arkansas at an early age and then to Texas, settling in Houston in 1897. His introduction to accounting occurred when he was employed in the accounting department of the Missouri Pacific Railroad. He later managed rice mills along the Gulf Coast and for a while served as president of the Texas-Louisiana Rice Millers Association. He began a public accounting practice in 1916 and was awarded Texas certificate number 66 by examination in November, 1918. During the World War I years he was an auditor for the Emergency Fleet Corporation of the U.S. Shipping Board, but after the war, Armistead returned to public accounting, and at the time of his election to the presidency of the Society he had one of the larger practices in Houston, which, upon his death in 1937, was taken over by Peat, Marwick, Mitchell & Co. Armistead also took an active part in American Institute of Accountants affairs, serving on its council for several years in the 1920s. Aside from holding office in professional societies, Armistead advised the Texas legislature on fiscal matters. He was chairman of the Texas Fiscal Survey Committee in the late 1920s and published a book, *The Texas Tax Problem*, that pointed up the need for a state auditing department and the establishment of better accounting systems for state agencies.

Luke Bunyan Garvin, president in 1925–1926, was born in Como, Texas, in 1886. Upon graduating from the local schools, Garvin enrolled in a business college at nearby Sulphur Springs. On June 18, 1907, his twenty-first birthday, he arrived in Dallas seeking employment. For the next ten years he worked in the accounting departments of a variety of businesses, ranging from railroads and hotels to the bursar's office of the newly opened Southern Methodist University. He augmented experience with correspondence courses, and in 1917 he joined the staff of Ernst & Ernst in Dallas.

Garvin remained in public accounting from 1917 until his death in 1953, except for two brief intervals in 1918 and 1921. In addition to Ernst & Ernst, he was with Schoolar-Bird & Co. (1918–1920) and

Barrow, Wade, Guthrie & Co. (1930–1931). In the 1920s, however, Garvin was associated with a Dallas tax lawyer, George S. Atkinson, first in the Dallas Income Tax Service (1920–1923) and then under the firm name of Atkinson & Garvin (1923–1929). On November 1, 1931, Garvin and Mary Ethel Welborn, the first woman to receive a certificate in Texas, formed a partnership under the name of Luke B. Garvin & Company. After World War II the firm name changed on occasion to reflect changes in partners, and at the time of Garvin's death it was Garvin, Welborn & McCulloch. In addition to a large volume of tax work, the Garvin firms did a substantial amount of auditing, particularly of Baptist institutions in Texas. Garvin qualified for CPA certificate number 109 in December, 1921, and two years later he joined the Society.

Arthur C. Upleger of Waco was elected president of the Society in 1926. Born in Mount Clemens, Michigan, in 1883, Upleger received his accounting education in the New York University School of Commerce, Accounts, and Finance, one of the first collegiate schools of accounting in the United States. Finishing NYU in 1910, he remained an additional year to take some law courses and then moved to Dallas, where two of his classmates, Harry Gordon and Dan McKeever, had come to practice and where, as previously noted, Upleger worked with the firms of W. P. Peter & Company and Hutchinson and Smith. On January 1, 1913, he moved to Waco and opened the office of Upleger & Falk, Inc., in association with a Denver accountant, Henry B. Falk, whom Upleger had also known at NYU. In 1925 the corporation was dissolved, Falk dropped out, and the firm name A. C. Upleger & Company was adopted. At one time in the 1920s Upleger had branch offices in Tyler, Corpus Christi, and Dallas, but these arrangements ultimately proved to be unsatisfactory and the offices were closed. While Upleger developed a diversified practice, his firm, later merged with Main Hurdman, became known for auditing fraternal organizations.

Upleger was on the steering committee in 1915 that engineered the passage of the Texas Public Accountancy Act, and from 1921 to 1925 he served on the Texas State Board of Public Accountancy. His Texas certificate, number 42, was awarded in 1916, and he later held CPA certificates from Louisiana, Ohio, and New York. Upleger became a member of the American Institute of Accountants in 1918, but he dropped out of the institute in the early 1920s in favor of the new American

Society of Certified Public Accountants. Following his tenure as president of the Texas Society, Upleger was elected president of the American Society in 1928. When the American Society and the American Institute of Accountants merged to form what later came to be the American Institute of Certified Public Accountants, Upleger automatically became a life member of the AICPA Council and was recognized as a past president of AICPA. Upleger also helped organize the Southern States Accountants Conference, was a member of the advisory board of the International Accountants Society, was a charter member of the National Association of Accountants, and, from 1908, was a member of the Alpha chapter of Alpha Kappa Psi. In addition to his professional duties, Upleger was a pronounced advocate of accountants' taking a leading role in civic and community affairs. By the time of his death in 1969, Upleger had served in leadership roles in Waco's Community Chest, Civic Music Association, public library, and Red Cross and in the affairs of the Episcopal church.

Bouldin Shivers Mothershead came to the presidency of the Texas Society in 1927. A graduate of the University of Texas in 1919, he enjoyed the distinction of being the first accounting graduate of the first collegiate school of business in Texas to enter the profession. Mothershead was born in Fort Worth in 1896. His early years were spent there and in San Benito, where he graduated from high school in 1913. His studies at the University of Texas were interrupted by World War I, but he returned to Austin to complete his academic work in 1919. He received CPA certificate number 100 in 1920. Mothershead worked one year on William Aikman's staff in San Antonio before returning to Fort Worth, where he practiced independently for a time and then in partnership with Charles Scales. Following Scales's death in 1926, Mothershead remained in Fort Worth but rejoined Aikman in the firm of Aikman, Griffin, and Mothershead. In 1931 he moved to Harlingen to take over the firm's practice in the Rio Grande Valley, then virtually an accounting frontier. At no time during the 1930s were there more than three CPAs living south of Corpus Christi. The manpower crisis of World War II caused Aikman and Mothershead to dissolve their partnership, but Mothershead remained in Harlingen and at the time of his death in August, 1977, was senior partner in the firm of Mothershead, Hamilton, Day & Mayo. Like Upleger before him, Mothershead was a strong proponent of the American Society of Certified Public Accountants and from 1929 to 1931 he served as a director of that organization. He also served six years on the Texas State Board of Public Accountancy, two of those years as chairman.

In 1928 the presidency of the Society went back to Dallas with the election of Jesse Ray Nelson, the first of two brothers to head the organization. J. R. Nelson was born in 1885 in the small East Texas community of Clayton in Panola County, where his father farmed, operated a mill, and was county surveyor. Nelson finished high school in 1903 and moved to Dallas, where he enrolled in the Metropolitan Business College. His first job, in 1905, was as bookkeeper for the Texas Seed and Floral Company. Three years later he went to work in a similar capacity with the Anheuser Busch Company. It was here that he first came into contact with professional accountants, one of whom advised him to continue his education if he expected to rise in the profession. Accepting this advice, Nelson went to New York University's School of Commerce, Accounts, and Finance. He returned to Dallas in 1910 and entered public accounting in the employ of Charles Byers. Byers's clients included several cotton textile mills, cotton oil mills, the Dallas Cotton Exchange, and several Dallas cotton firms. Two years later Nelson and Charles Snyder formed a partnership that lasted until the end of World War I. In 1920, Snyder and Nelson parted, and J. R. Nelson took his younger brother, H. Tracy Nelson, into the Nelson Audit Company. Later the firm name was changed to Nelson and Nelson, with each of the brothers bringing sons into the firm. Nelson, who died in 1971, held Texas certificate number 22, dated July 29, 1915.

The Society elected C. W. Wittman, Jr., president in 1929, the first time a president was chosen from a national accounting firm. Wittman had moved to Houston in 1925 to take charge of the local office of Mattison and Davey, a New York–based firm with thirteen offices throughout the United States specializing in accounting and taxation matters relating to the petroleum industry. Wittman was born in 1895 in Baltimore, Maryland, where his father was engaged in the real estate business. He attended Baltimore City College and the Johns Hopkins University before serving in the U.S. Air Service during World War I. His career in accounting began immediately after the war, when he was employed in the Baltimore office of Haskins & Sells. Wittman joined the firm of Mattison and Davey in 1921 and rose to partner shortly thereafter. Upon moving to Texas, Wittman qualified for CPA certificate number 220 by examination and joined the Society. He left Texas in 1931, moving at that time to San Francisco, where he established his own firm, and in 1953 he merged with Arthur Young & Company. Wittman died in 1967.

William M. Aikman, elected president of the Society in 1930, was born in Indiana in 1877 and died in San Antonio in 1964. Illness restricted his formal education to the third grade. He read widely, however, and in 1896 became an apprentice to an "expert accountant" in Indiana. Much of his early experience was auditing municipalities to check for defalcations. Undaunted when he failed to secure the contract for proving defalcations, Aikman made his services available to the lawyers defending the accused. In a short period of time he established a reputation for defeating accountants' reports! This work brought Aikman into close contact with the legal profession, whereupon he read law and was admitted to the Indiana bar.

In 1911 Aikman moved to San Antonio, a victim of the "white plague." He hoped to continue the mixed practice of law and accounting, but he soon gave up the law. Upon arrival in Texas, Aikman joined in the Galveston conference that led to the formation of the Texas Society of Public Accountants, and he was an active supporter of the 1915 CPA law. He received waiver certificate number 15 on July 29, 1915. Until it dissolved in 1943, the firm Aikman, Griffin and Mothershead provided accounting services in San Antonio and for much of the lower Rio Grande Valley.

Forrest Mathis, president of the Society in 1931–1932, came into the accounting profession from an earlier career in banking. Mathis was born on a farm four miles south of Tyler, in 1882. He attended Summer Hill Select School at Omen during the summer of 1898 and secured a temporary teacher's certificate, but a shortage of teaching jobs that fall led him instead to become assistant bookkeeper for L. L. Jester and Co., Bankers, of Tyler. A year and a half in this bank and nine years with the Citizens National Bank of Tyler prepared him for the position of auditor of the Commonwealth National Bank of Dallas, which he took in May, 1909. Mathis retired from banking in 1916 and returned to his farm near Tyler. During the war years he served as executive secretary of the War Savings section of the Liberty Loan drives in Texas. In 1920 his wife's failing health brought him back to Dallas.

Upon his return to Dallas, Mathis joined the public accounting firm of Schoolar, Bird & Company, where he remained with one brief interruption until 1928. Mathis secured CPA certificate number 189 in December, 1924, and he joined the Society in November, 1925. In that same year, he was assigned to audit a highway construction firm under investigation by Texas Attorney General Dan Moody. This brought Mathis into contact with Moody, who later, as governor, appointed Mathis to the Texas State Board of Public Accountancy. The assignment also brought Mathis into close association with W. D. Prince, who was working on a similar audit of another construction firm. This association ripened into a more formal one in 1928 when Mathis joined the newly reorganized firm of Smith, Prince & Harris, successor to the firm of Hutchinson & Smith. Except for a brief period from 1936 to 1938 when he represented trustees in the reorganization of the American Liberty Pipe Line Company, Mathis remained with Smith, Prince & Harris through its several changes and ultimate merger with Arthur Young & Company.

# 4

## *The Texas Society Achieves Strength and Purpose*

THE decade and a half from 1931 to 1946 might well be called the mid-passage of professional accountancy in Texas. It was also a transitional period in the Texas economy. Recovering from the depression of the early 1930s, the state's business and commercial development was spurred by the production and refining of petroleum products. The once overwhelmingly agricultural economy acquired more balance with new industry and commerce. World War II brought heavy government and private investments in aircraft manufacturing and chemicals, which served as catalysts to an industrial revolution already in the making. By the end of 1945 Texas stood poised on the brink of what will probably be remembered as the era of its most significant industrial expansion.

### Growth of National Firms in Texas

The complexion of the accounting profession in Texas also changed during this period. Local firms grew stronger, and by 1945 the larger national firms had offices in Texas, in many instances having merged with well established local firms. National firms tended to upgrade public practice. While local firms with good reason staunchly defended the proposition that the caliber of work done by local and national firms was not materially different, the national firms did enhance the prestige of the profession in the eyes of the businessman and the public. Partly because of this, the national firms were able to command higher fees and thereby open the way for local firms to follow suit. This provided some balm for the local firms, as did the fact that the accounting profession as a whole was undermanned and there was usually enough work for all, even when the national firms took on local clients. Within the state society there was never an open cleavage between national and

local firm men. Noteworthy, though, is the fact that only three presidents from 1915 to 1951 were with national firms, an indication that
Society membership preferred leadership from local firms.[1]

## Toward a More Representative Membership

The Society and the profession became more nearly one in the late
1930s. In 1933 only one out of three Texas resident certified accountants eligible for membership belonged to the Society. The following
year, however, Theodore W. Mohle spearheaded a membership committee that netted seventy new members. With 53 percent of the state's
resident CPAs now members, the *Texas Accountant* announced that the
Society was "fully representative of the profession." Those CPAs still
outside the ranks fell into one of three groups, the editor asserted. First,
there was a "considerable number . . . not engaged in public practice,
and . . . who do not have as great an interest in . . . the profession."
Second, there were the new young men "who have not had time to
understand the nature of the needs of the profession." Third, "there are
the few who let purely personal reasons stand in the way of their con-
tributing to the advancement of the profession."[2] Accompanying this
article was an interesting breakdown of the membership by cities. Fort
Worth led the four larger cities in percentage of accountants enrolled as
members, with fifteen out of twenty-two (68 percent). Dallas followed
with forty out of seventy-one (56 percent), Houston with thirty-five out
of sixty-seven (52 percent), and San Antonio with sixteen out of thirty-
three (49 percent).

The Society's prerogative to speak for all professionals grew stronger
as the years passed. In 1938–1939 a record high of 120 new members
were enrolled. Walter C. Burer, chairman of the membership committee that set this record, received a parchment scroll for his distinguished
service.[3] Burer, an employee of Sugarland Industries and the first Society president to come from private industry (1939–1941), was also a
leader in breaking down much of the reserve and stiffness of the mem-

1. C. W. Wittman, Jr. (1929–1930) with Mattison and Davey; T. W. Mohle (1937–
1938) then with Lybrand, Ross Brothers and Montgomery; and Joseph C. Cobb (1942–
1943) with Barrow, Wade, Guthrie and Company.
2. "Our Membership," *Texas Accountant* 7 (May, 1935): 1–4.
3. "Minutes . . . October 6–7, 1939," TSCPA.

bers and the mistrust accountants still held toward one another, substituting instead a spirit of conviviality at chapter and state meetings. The result of this new and lighter touch was quickly discernible. By 1941 approximately 80 percent of the resident Texas certificate holders were on the roll books. The total membership of the Society in June, 1941, was 482, or 65 percent of the 739 resident and nonresident Texas certificates in force at the time. The rate of growth fell off slightly during the war years, though an average of forty-five new members a year was a healthy showing and demonstrated that the Society had won the respect and support of the state's CPAs.

Two important constitutional changes in 1935 regarding membership had some bearing on the increase in Society rolls.[4] The first lifted the ban on fellow membership previously placed on Texas certificate holders not engaged in public practice. This ban had put "an unnecessary restriction on fellow membership," proponents of its repeal said, "evidently inspired by the thought that those accountants not in public practice might come to dominate the Society. We believe no such danger exists and that the section is an affront to those in private practice." The second change incorporated a suggestion made as early as 1932 that associate membership, previously restricted to Texas certificate holders, be opened to CPAs "of any State or Territory of the United States . . . or of the District of Columbia." It was successfully argued "that no harm should come . . . from this since requirements for certificates are now more or less uniform."[5]

In the middle 1930s opposition appeared to the selection of the Society's Board of Directors by district rather than statewide elections. District elections guaranteed geographic representation, but they also favored accountants in the more sparsely settled areas and limited the Society membership in choosing the best qualified officers. Representation by district allegedly gave "disproportionate representation to certain sections of the state" and tended to "solidify controls of the Society and its appeal to the profession within narrow limits." In view of the Society's limited membership, it was argued further, the members' choice of directors "should be restricted only by the known qualifications of

4. The constitution and by-laws as amended in October, 1935, are printed in *Texas Accountant* 9 (Jan., 1937): 1–4.
5. These arguments were advanced three years earlier. See "Report of the Committee on Constitution and By-Laws, September 30, 1932," TSCPA.

the candidates."[6] No analysis of the vote on this proposed change was made, but accountants outside the four principal cities of the state were probably responsible for its defeat. Only slight modifications were made in the hierarchy of the Society during this entire period. In 1945 the office of second vice-president was created, terms of directors were increased to two years, and a standing Committee on Nominations was established. The latter was composed of the immediate past president as chairman, and four other members, each of whom came from a different district.

## Annual Meetings and Finances

The economic depression and the low professional morale of Texas accountants in the early 1930s is clearly evident in the financial records of the Society. Not only was membership low but many of those whose names were carried on the roster were a year or more behind in the payment of their dues as well. Receipts for 1933, for example, were $827.60, but $1,583.33 in delinquent dues were outstanding. Forty members were two years or more behind in their obligations. In 1934, after a concerted effort had been made to collect back dues, the most delinquent members, including one director, were dropped from the rolls. The situation gradually improved as economic recovery set in, though as late as 1937, the secretary-treasurer, Cyril F. Milledge, cautioned the Board of Directors that if the by-laws were rigidly enforced and members dropped after seven months' arrearages in dues, the Society would have "very few members."[7] Suffice it to say, a lenient policy in regard to delinquents was followed until the war years.

There was reason for optimism regarding Society finances by 1938, however. A finance committee reported in September of that year that estimated receipts would be $2,600. Disbursements were budgeted in the following fashion: salary for secretary-treasurer, $900; salary for editor of the *Texas Accountant*, $300; travel expenses for officers, $500; printing costs, $420; convention expenses, $250; office supplies, stationery, and the like, $230. Remarking that the membership had increased from 105 to 274 in the past six years, the committee laid down

6. "Report of the Committee on Constitution and By-Laws, October 5, 1933," TSCPA.
7. "Minutes . . . November 22, 1937," TSCPA.

the challenge that 75 additional members could be added "if proper effort is put forth." The dues collected from these new members, the committee advised, would allow the Society to provide travel expenses for committee members, retain a representative in Austin during legislative sessions, expand the publications program, allow the president to travel more widely around the state, and build up an emergency fund. As an incentive to join, the initiation fee, already waived for a person who joined the Society within one year from the time he received his certificate, was waived for others as well.[8]

As has already been pointed out, membership did increase—in fact, more rapidly than anticipated. The financial report for 1944–1945 reflected a relatively prosperous society. The budget for that year was just under $5,000. Major disbursements, which stopped roughly $500 short of the expected income, were $1,920 in salaries for the secretary and editor; $900 printing costs for the *Texas Accountant* and *Yearbook*; $1,000 for travel expenses; $250 for convention costs; and the remainder for stationery, office supplies, and services. The cash balance that had been accumulating over the years was $2,895.67 on June 30, 1945.

Attendance at annual meetings tended to rise with the membership. A good attendance in the middle 1930s was 50 to 60 persons. By the early 1940s, however, annual meetings attracted around 125 registrants. Even the 1943 meeting held in San Antonio in the midst of the war was attended by 85 persons. The following year, 169 gathered in Houston for a joint meeting with the Wartime Accounting Conference sponsored by the American Institute of Certified Public Accountants.

The programs at the annual meetings changed little from the pattern established in the 1920s. Members carried out the bulk of the speaking and discussion chores, officials of the American Institute of Accountants and the American Society of Certified Public Accountants frequently appearing as guests. The theme of cooperation with other professions brought bankers, lawyers, and internal revenue service personnel before the meetings. It was not part of the permanent record, so we do not know for sure, but the address Charles Schoolar's wife made in 1932, entitled "How Accountants May Cooperate with Their Wives," must have carried this theme to an uncomfortable extreme! Proceeding

8. "Report of the Chairman of the Finance Committee, September 16, 1938," TSCPA.

at a relaxed tempo, the annual dinner at the October, 1934, meeting consisted of an informal supper and dance with "no speeches of any kind."[9] A feminine note was also struck in 1934 when a "rising vote of welcome" was extended Mary Ethel Welborn, "the only lady in Texas holding a State Certificate and membership in the State Society."[10]

After several years of discussing the point, members changed the time of the annual meeting in 1940 from the fall to late spring. The change brought the Texas Society in line with most other state societies and also gave new officers time to formulate plans "during the dull season following tax season." Another advantage of the May or June meeting was that newly elected officers could attend the AICPA meeting in their official capacity. Appropriately, the first spring meeting, June, 1940, commemorated the Society's "Silver Jubilee."

## Merger of the American Society and the American Institute

In many respects the most notable meeting of this fifteen-year period was held in Dallas in 1936 in conjunction with the merger of the American Institute of Accountants and the American Society of Certified Public Accountants. The institute complimented Texas accountants, of course, by announcing that its first meeting in the South would be held in Dallas. The selection of Dallas also recognized the contribution George Armistead, the first southerner to hold the office, made as president of the institute in 1934–1935.[11] The event took on historic

9. "Minutes . . . June 23, 1934," TSCPA.

10. Mary Ethel Welborn was born, reared, and taught school for ten years in Kaufman County, Texas. She enrolled in the LaSalle Extension University to study accounting and worked in the Treasury Department, Washington, D.C., from 1919 until 1921. In Washington she took a YMCA accounting course. She qualified for North Carolina CPA certificate number 185 in 1921, at a time when residence in that state was not a requirement. She returned to Texas in 1922 and was employed by Judge A. S. Walker, a Dallas lawyer who had a large volume of tax work. She practiced on her own from 1924 until 1931, when she entered a partnership with Luke Garvin that continued until Garvin's death in 1953. She continued to practice under the firm name of Garvin, Welborn & McCulloch. Miss Welborn qualified for Texas certificate number 219 by examination on November 14, 1925. The certificate is lettered in gold in recognition of its being the first one issued to a woman in Texas.

11. After the merger, past presidents of the American Society of Certified Public Accountants were recognized as being past presidents of the American Institute. This, of course, would give Arthur C. Upleger recognition as an earlier past president, as he was president of the American Society in 1928.

proportions, however, when the American Society met in Fort Worth immediately preceding the institute gathering in Dallas and several years of negotiations leading to a merger of the two organizations were successfully concluded.

Members of the Texas Society were pleased to host these meetings. The merger had been the subject of much discussion at Society meetings. In 1933, presidents of the New York Society of Certified Public Accountants and the institute appeared before the Texas Society convention in Houston to discuss the problems involved. They agreed that a merger was logical. The next year in San Antonio the Society heard William D. Morrison of Denver, president of the American Society, speak on the same subject. The membership in Texas then went on record recommending the merger, providing the name of the new organization include the words "Certified Public Accountant" and that only CPAs be admitted to membership in the future. Texans also stipulated that the new society's governing council be chosen in district elections rather than at large, and that an advisory board consisting of the presidents of the respective state societies be created.[12] This resolution put the Texas Society on record favoring the American Society in the merger negotiations, as the American Society had insisted upon excluding noncertified men from membership and checking the power of eastern accountants through district representation.

With regard to other meetings, the combined meeting of the Louisiana, Arkansas, Oklahoma, and Texas societies in Shreveport in 1931 was not repeated in subsequent years. Luke Garvin, chairman of the Committee on Cooperation with Other Accounting Societies in 1932, reported that word had been received from the neighboring societies that they would be unable to meet again that year in joint session. "And our Committee was accordingly left with an immense amount of leisure," Garvin added.[13] In 1938 this committee, through its chairman, Arthur Upleger, reported on the organization of the Southern States Accountants Conference in Memphis, Tennessee. Upleger, along with T. W. Mohle, Tom W. Leland, Frank L. Wilcox, Joseph Hutchinson, Jr., and Francis E. Keeple, attended the first conference meeting. "In the future," Upleger advised, "there will be no necessity for the ap-

12. "Minutes . . . October 10–11, 1935," TSCPA.
13. "Report of the Committee on Cooperation with Other Accounting Organizations, October 5, 1932," TSCPA.

pointment of a committee on cooperation with state societies. The new program provides that a representative of our Society will act with representatives of the other twelve Societies in furthering inter-state relations."[14]

The Society's public relations effort was hit-and-miss during the 1930s. The favorable publicity the Society received through the reporting of the 1936 merger of the institute and the American Society helped advertise the profession. Three years earlier, however, the Society secretary informed the *Texas Weekly* that the Society had decided to forego a proposed institutional advertising program "due to lack of necessary funds."[15] A monthly tax calendar suitable for printing in newspapers was suggested at the Society board meeting in Galveston in 1937, but nothing was done with the suggestion. In 1940, however, the Society decided to sponsor several fifteen-minute radio programs dealing with the history of the profession and the services it rendered. Charles Sparenberg presided over the committee responsible for the project. These programs, thirteen in number, were produced in cooperation with the University of Texas radio workshop and cost the Society only $390. The Texas State Network played the records as a public service at no expense to the Society. The series elicited favorable comments and brought requests from other state societies to use the records.[16] Another project the Public Relations Committee undertook was the circulation of a questionnaire to all Texas accountants asking that they list subjects on which they felt qualified to speak to business and professional groups. Five speaking engagements had already been filled, the committee reported in 1941, and more were pending. The war, however, curtailed this program.

## The Emergence of Chapters

Chapter work during the 1930s and early 1940s was only moderately successful. The *Texas Accountant* noted in April, 1934, that the only active chapters in the state at that time were Houston and Dallas, though San Antonio was organizing. A committee to encourage chapter

14. "Report of the Committee on Cooperation with Other State Societies, August 31, 1938," TSCPA.
15. "Minutes . . . December 16, 1933," TSCPA.
16. "Minutes . . . June 29, 1940," TSCPA.

organizations suggested that the Society director in each of the Society's seven districts take the initiative in setting up a chapter in his district's larger city. A minimum of five programs was suggested for the year, with topics ranging from bidding, fees, legislation, and technical accounting subjects to social programs and open meetings to which bankers, businessmen, and others would be invited.

Three years later the subject of chapter meetings was again a source of concern. Walter Burer gave out the secret that made some of the Houston chapter meetings notable. A good speaker was just one factor, he said. "The biggest meeting we had was when we served beer and sandwiches." Tracy Nelson suggested accountants follow the example of the Dallas bar, of which he was a member. The lawyers had informal suppers at the country club with an interesting nontechnical speaker. Fred Alford seconded the idea of nontechnical speakers. No one liked to hear a technical paper after having wrestled with similar problems all day along, Alford complained. J. Glenn Bixler of El Paso added that perseverance was needed. "We formed a chapter a year and a half ago," Bixler said. "We had a very nice meeting and elected a chairman and officers' board, and we never had another one." Harry Robertson, whose home town of Amarillo had no chapter at that time, observed that the "main thing you have got to overcome . . . is petty jealousies."[17]

Evidently some of these suggestions fell on fertile ground, for chapter activities soon showed promise. By 1941 or 1942 formal reports of chapter activities were made a part of the Society records. Money for the chapters was a problem, however, for the Society denied chapters permission to charge dues and refused to allot any of its meager budget for chapter expenses. Finally, in 1945 Society dues were raised from $10 to $15, with some of this money diverted into chapter coffers. This solution proved cumbersome, however, and in 1947 chapters received permission to collect their own dues independently of the Society.

## Professional Ethics and Competitive Bidding

Events within and without the profession dictated changes in the code of ethics first adopted at Beaumont in 1929. Exactly ten years

17. "Minutes . . . November 22, 1937," TSCPA.

after the first code was adopted, the Committee on Rules of Professional Conduct, headed by N. O. Richardson, overhauled the code and brought it more nearly up to date.

The rule against contingent fees, hotly debated at Beaumont in 1929, was frequently violated and came under even heavier fire during the 1930s. Recognizing that the public interest would be amply protected in tax cases by Treasury Department rules, and searching for a Society rule "that will be observed," members agreed to permit contingent fees in "cases such as those involving Federal, State or other taxes, in which the findings are those of the Tax or other similar authorities, and not those of the accountant."[18]

There were other changes in the code. One prohibited affiliation with "any corporation engaged in the practice of public accountancy." Another ruled against an accountant's permitting the use of his name "in conjunction with . . . estimates of earnings contingent upon future transactions in such a manner which might lead one to believe that the accountant could vouch for the accuracy of the forecast." Still another rule prevented an accountant from certifying to the "financial statement of any enterprise financed in whole or in part by the public distribution of securities" in which he had an economic interest.[19]

No conclusion, however, was reached on competitive bidding, perhaps the most perplexing of the ethical problems confronting the Society. The arguments against competitive bidding were as old as the profession. Frederick H. Hurdman, addressing the Society in 1941, quoted extensively from a paper delivered in 1907 by Joseph E. Sterrett alleging that competitive bidding lowered the quality of work and thereby diminished the public's respect.[20] Many Texas accountants felt they were confronted with a fact rather than a theory, however, and in 1932 the Society passed the following resolution condemning an American Institute of Accountants proposal against competitive bidding: "Inasmuch as there are many assignments of considerable import in Texas, where to be considered for the assignment, it is necessary that an estimate be submitted and in many cases a flat fee be named, and in those cases it

18. "Minutes . . . October 6–7, 1939," TSCPA. See also "Report of the Committee . . . ," *Texas Accountant* 11 (Dec., 1939): 1.

19. Ibid.

20. Frederick H. Hurdman, "Ethics of the Accounting Profession," *Texas Accountant* 13 (Nov., 1941): 1–6.

is expected that many reputable accountants will submit proposals, Be It Resolved That the Texas Society . . . go on record as opposing the resolution proposed by the Committee on By-Laws of the American Institute."[21] Even George Armistead, in many respects the personification of high ethical conduct, suggested that competitive bidding was "not altogether nor invariably an ethical question."[22]

As the years passed, however, pressure mounted for a stand against bidding. In 1934 the institute passed a resolution against it and about a year later supported state societies seeking to curb competitive bidding by declaring that institute members doing work in a state where such a rule was in force would have to respect the rule. In October, 1937, Henry J. Miller of New Orleans spoke to the Texas Society on Louisiana's newly adopted rule against bidding. After the speech, the delegates supported a resolution condemning the practice by a three-to-one majority and instructed the Committee on Professional Conduct to draft an amendment to the code putting these sentiments into effect. This was not done, however, and in 1939, when the code was being overhauled in other respects, another effort was made. Bidding was most prevalent in "municipal, quasi-municipal and bank work," it was pointed out, and "there is every possibility that . . . the practice will become as widespread in commercial work." Texas, it was urged, should join with the eight states and the District of Columbia having already adopted such a rule. A motion to this effect was presented. The vote was 23 to 18 in favor of the new rule, but the closeness of the vote indicated enforcement would be extremely difficult. Consequently, the vote was rescinded and further action put off a year.[23] In the meantime, accountants asked the Texas attorney general whether a bid was mandatory for city, county, and school district work. The Society was advised on May 10, 1940, that bids were not required.

A poll conducted late in 1939 showed Texas accountants 76 to 49 in favor of a stand against competitive bidding, but the Society seemed no nearer committing itself in 1940 than it had been in 1939. A majority committee report read by Fred Alford "condemned" competitive bidding, while the minority report read by N. O. Richardson sought to prohibit the practice altogether. When both reports were merely ac-

21. "Minutes . . . October 13–15, 1932," TSCPA.
22. "Report of the Committee on Professional Ethics, October 13, 1932," TSCPA.
23. "Minutes . . . October 6–7, 1939," TSCPA.

cepted and filed with the board, it was apparent that no decisive action would be taken. There was one bright spot in the meeting for those who wanted a strong stand against bidding, however. Jay Phillips told how Houston accountants had agreed among themselves not to bid for the city of Houston audit, city officials finally relenting and awarding the work on a noncompetitive basis.[24]

The issue came up before the Society again in 1943. Roy L. Pope advised the annual meeting in his report for the committee on the audit of government units that the legislature was "audit-minded." He referred specifically to the county fiscal control bill requiring auditors for each county, and to another bill calling for public audits of each independent school district. Both these measures failed in 1943, but Pope predicted their passage in the near future. He then warned his fellow practitioners that they must reach an understanding on minimum specifications and competitive bidding, and not "just fight it." "Sooner or later we are going to have to act or someone is going to act for us," he said, in which case the action taken "might be hostile to our interest." Pope's advice was not acted upon at that time, however, and restraints on competitive bidding had to await a later date.[25]

The enforcement of a code of ethics is just as important as its adoption. The first steps upholding the code were taken in the middle 1930s. Charges of practices that were defined merely as "highly unethical" were filed against a Houston accountant in 1936. Apparently this brought on a reprimand from the Society, but no further punishment. Four minor infractions were brought to the Board of Directors' attention in November, 1940. Two involved members working for incorporated accounting firms. Another concerned an honorary member of the Society who had notice of his honorary membership printed on his business letterhead. What at first appeared to be more serious charges were filed against a fourth member. These concerned irregularities in work for the Texas Highway Department, but they were dropped after an investigation proved they were "not wilful and intentional."[26] In 1942 the board of directors responded to an informal complaint lodged by one Houston accountant against another charging negligence in an in-

24. "Minutes . . . June 13–15, 1940," TSCPA.
25. "Minutes . . . June 15–16, 1943," TSCPA.
26. "Minutes . . . November 29, 1940," and "Minutes . . . March 29, 1941," TSCPA.

58    TEXAS SOCIETY OF CERTIFIED PUBLIC ACCOUNTANTS

dependent school district audit. The accountant whose work was attacked submitted a 336-page brief in his defense, but the entire matter was dropped when no formal charges were made. The most flagrant violation of the Society's ethics code to that time was uncovered in 1945 when the commissioner of the Securities and Exchange Commission reported that a fellow and honorary member of the Texas Society had signed an audit report without making the audit. On December 13, 1946, the board accepted the accused person's resignation.[27]

Very close to the problem of ethics was the question of whether a public accountant who acts as an advisor and counselor to a client can then objectively and independently audit that client's business record. "Accountants generally agree," Tom Leland editorialized in the *Texas Accountant* in January, 1943, "that the public accountant loses his professional and independent status with a *given client* when he accepts responsibility for the preparation of entries, keeping of books, prescribing accounting policies, and internal check systems and controls of the *same client*." Citing a recent case before the SEC in which an auditor had made and posted entries in a company's books and had then audited those records, Leland agreed with the commission that the accountant had "taken upon himself the function of bookkeeping as well as auditing." While the manual work of the accountant was emphasized in this case, Leland asked the disturbing question: "If the decision in regard to entries for transactions is made by the outside auditor, do we not have the same situation irrespective of what person made the entry?"

This editorial brought comments and protests from several quarters. Clifton Morris, chairman of the Texas State Board of Public Accountancy, took sharp exception to it at the next Society Board of Directors meeting. Morris noted the chief accountant of the SEC had cited Leland's editorial and that he, Morris, was in receipt of a letter from Samuel J. Broad, vice-president of the American Institute, suggesting the Society take action making it clear this statement was not Society policy.[28] A committee was thereupon created to reply to the editorial.

27. "Minutes . . . December 14, 1945," and "Minutes . . . December 13, 1946," TSCPA.
28. "Minutes . . . July 23, 1943." The case Leland referred to was *In the Matter of Interstate Hosiery Mills, Inc.*, 4 SEC 706, 717 (1939). Leland was willing to accept the clarifications which upheld the right of the independent accountant to suggest entries to correct or improve the client's accounts and which established the fact that indepen-

Appearing in the December, 1943, issue of the *Texas Accountant*, the statement recognized "many ways" in which an independent accountant can serve a company and its stockholders. Moreover, it was "the duty of the public accountant to consult with his client on accounting methods and systems of internal control and to suggest improvements therein. . . . it is also his duty to suggest entries in the books when he believes such entries are necessary to correct or improve the client's accounts." It was unanimously agreed by the Society's Board of Directors, the statement concluded, "that a public accountant can render these services and still retain his independence and in every way be qualified to audit the books of his client. . . ."

Thus it was amid lively but dignified controversy over matters within the profession that members concluded this period of the Society's history. All in all, the Society had rallied well from the debilitating effects of the Depression years and the trying period of World War II. The problems generated by contacts with other professions and the need for revising the public accountancy law in 1945, however, called for responses of a different sort.

---

dence is a state of mind and attitude on which it is difficult to make rules. He retained his belief, however, that a CPA cannot audit his own accounts. (Leland to author, Oct. 5, 1959.) The ethical problem which Leland raised was discussed fully in a contemporary article: Andrew Barr, "The Independent Accountant and the SEC," *Journal of Accountancy* 108 (Oct., 1959): 32–37.

# 5

## Relations with Other Professions and the Accountancy Act of 1945

DURING the 1930s and early 1940s, accountants were drawn into closer and sometimes more difficult relations with groups outside their profession. Contacts with lawyers, bankers, and governmental agencies became more frequent as the profession matured and demands for accounting services increased. The Texas Society also maintained close contact with instructors in the collegiate schools of accounting, who, if not outside the profession, were nonetheless involved in a work different from the practitioner's. In fact, the interests Society members exhibited in recruiting and training young people for the profession and in beginning to think about the need of continuing education for the practitioner were harbingers of things to come.

The Texas Association of University Instructors in Accounting, whose membership included some members of the Texas Society, continued to meet in the same city just before the Society's annual meeting, remaining to attend Society functions later. Monroe S. Carroll of Baylor University, president of the academicians in 1938, thanked the Society for its hospitality and noted that the instructors had organized "especially to afford an opportunity . . . to contact leading CPAs of the state." That purpose was served admirably. So also was the Society served by the professors. They frequently read papers at the technical sessions. More important, Tom Leland of Texas A&M was the long-time editor of the *Texas Accountant* and president of the Texas Society for two terms (1933–1935), and Laurence Fleck of Southern Methodist University was elected president in 1945.[1]

In other ways, practitioners evidenced interest in the education of

1. Monroe S. Carroll, "Accountancy Education in Texas," *Texas Accountant* 10 (April, 1938): 1. The year Carroll made this observation, Leland was elected secretary-treasurer, a post he held for sixteen years.

future accountants. In 1940 Arthur Upleger headed a committee that organized groups of CPAs to visit the larger collegiate schools of accounting and describe to students opportunities the profession offered. This was "the most constructive action ever taken by the Society in the matter of education," according to some educators.[2] Unfortunately this activity, which had important recruiting value for the CPAs as well as instructional value for the students, had to be called off for the duration of the war.

## Raising Educational Requirements

Concern was expressed during the 1930s and early 1940s over the low formal educational requirements demanded by the 1915 accountancy law. C. Aubrey Smith, professor of accounting at the University of Texas, spoke for the Committee on Legislation in 1937 recommending that a graduate from an accredited college with twenty-one hours in accounting be credited with three of the five years' experience needed for certification. The most important reason for this proposal, Smith said, was that a five-year experience requirement without credit for college training seriously handicapped college graduates in accounting. They would either go into some other profession, Smith predicted, or the accounting firms would individually have to set up their own training schools where students could gain experience and training at the same time. The latter alternative, he added, was a financial burden most accounting firms could ill afford. Smith also recommended approval of the committee report as a major step in the direction of establishing the college diploma as a prerequisite for certification.[3]

The committee's proposal met with little enthusiasm in 1937. A year later, Leland editorialized in the *Texas Accountant* regarding the trend nationally toward higher educational standards. New York, Pennsylvania, and New Jersey required a college diploma for certification. The American Accounting Association, the national professional organization for accounting instructors, recommended thirty-nine hours of accounting as a minimum for CPAs. "But as a matter of current policy," Leland said, he did "not favor the introduction . . . of any bill to change

2. "Minutes . . . June 12–14, 1941," TSCPA.
3. *Texas Accountant* 10 (April, 1938): 6.

the requirements for the CPA certificate until such time as it becomes certain that the proposed changes have the approval and the support of a very large per cent of practicing accountants. . . . Since at the present time this support is doubtful, it would be folly to introduce any bill modifying educational or experience requirements."[4]

There the matter rested until the drive for regulatory legislation in 1944 gave proponents of higher educational requirements their opportunity. Speaking before the Houston Chapter in November, 1944, Smith argued that a high school diploma might have been sufficient in 1915 when the Texas law was enacted but that it was far from adequate thirty years later. More people finished college in Texas in 1940, he pointed out, than finished high school in 1915. More than that, the demands of modern accounting made formal instruction imperative. He then made an embarrassing comparison between the statutory requirements of other professions and accounting. Medical doctors were required to take two years of premedical and four years of medical school training, lawyers had to have two years of college credit, and it was necessary for professional engineers to graduate from a four-year school of engineering. "How can we encourage the brightest minds of this and coming generations to elect professional accounting as a career," Smith asked, "when the practitioner tells our future accountant he needs no more educational background than is required to be an embalmer or a teacher in a barber college? How can we expect the public to take us very seriously professionally when they are told that while their lawyer, their dentist, and their engineer require collegiate training for their respective pursuits, accountancy is so simple and so lacking in basic knowledge as to have no need for formal training?" Smith went on: "How can we convince the courts we rightfully belong in the family of the higher professions when we profess that while our ethical, technical, and other professional standards have materially and continually improved during the past thirty years that educationally we are impervious to change and improvement?" This much said, Smith proposed that one year of college be a prerequisite for certification after 1947; two years after 1949; three years after 1951; and four years after 1953. Two years of the professional experience requirement should also be waived, Smith added, for those who completed thirty hours in accounting.[5]

    4. Ibid., p. 2.
    5. C. Aubrey Smith, "Education for the Professional Accountant," *Texas Accountant* 16 (Dec., 1944): 1–6.

Smith and his supporters won only half a loaf. The high school diploma remained the statutory minimum in the 1945 law. However, one year of the four-year experience requirement was waived for persons who graduated from a junior or senior college or university. Three years of the experience requirement were waived if twenty hours of accounting and at least ten additional hours of business, finance, or economics courses were taken.

At the other end of the educational spectrum, Laurence Fleck reminded his fellow members in 1938, the accountant's education did not cease when he qualified for the certificate, nor did the Society's obligation in regard to education apply only to recruits and apprentices. The Society needed to sponsor institutes and short courses for the practicing accountant, he advised, just as it encouraged undergraduate training.[6] Technical sessions at the state and local chapter meetings together with papers of a similar nature published in the *Texas Accountant* were about all the Society did for its members in this respect, however, for over a decade to come.

Somewhat related to the emphasis on education for those entering the profession was the establishment of the John Burnis Allred Merit Award. At a meeting of the Board of Directors in December, 1941, Allred, secretary of the Texas State Board of Public Accountancy at the time, offered to present an award to the applicant making the best showing on the CPA examinations of the year just ending. Allred asked that, in making the award, the Society consider attainment in the face of difficulty and overall achievement along with excellence on the examinations.[7] The Society accepted the offer and in 1943 made the first award to Stanley W. Smith, recipient that same year of the Elijah Watt Sells Gold Medal given by the American Institute.

## Relations with Bankers

Cooperation with bankers and officials of credit agencies continued to be a matter of concern to accountants during the 1930s and early 1940s. A pamphlet entitled "Preparation of Audit Reports for Credit Purposes" was prepared and widely distributed in 1941 by a committee led by Jesse Nelson. Bankers had epitomized their thoughts on this

6. Laurence H. Fleck, "Educational Activities of the Texas Society," *Texas Accountant*, 10 (April, 1938): 1.
7. "Minutes . . . December 13, 1941," TSCPA.

subject earlier by simply calling for "more audits, more detailed audits, better audits!"[8] but accountants were now depending less and less on bankers for business because of the increasing volume of tax work and preparation of financial statements for the new Securities Exchange Commission. One clear indication of this independence was the suggestion made by Frederick H. Hurdman of New York, a former president of the American Institute of Accountants (1928–1930), that banks might profit by independent audits just as other businesses did. Speaking to a Texas audience in the Depression days of 1935, Hurdman suggested that banks, having just lost millions of dollars in depositors' and stockholders' money, might owe it to these groups to have independent audits made. He asked if the reluctance of bankers to require of themselves what they required of others was "because the banker believes . . . the accountant is qualified to assist all other types of business . . . except a bank? Is it because he thinks that the present examination by governmental departments furnish him with everything he should have or might get from the professional accountant?" The New Yorker continued: "Is it because he hesitates to add one more item of expense even though that item might produce . . . larger profits? Is it because he fears the result of a full disclosure of the bank's affairs though he always demands such a disclosure in relation to borrower's?" Hurdman added that the only type of examination bankers asked for themselves was the kind which called for "a minimum of time and cost the least amount of money."[9]

## Controversy with Lawyers

A conflict developed between lawyers and accountants during the 1930s. The issue was not as acute in Texas as it was in some other parts of the nation because of the willingness of leaders on both sides to discuss the problems involved and to try and reach an amicable settlement. Among accountants, William Aikman deserves major credit for keeping friction to a minimum.

The root of this difficulty went back to the very early days of the income tax law, when the taxpayer's only recourse in appealing deci-

8. "Minutes . . . October 13–15, 1932," TSCPA.
9. Frederick H. Hurdman, "Need for Examination of Banks by Accountants," *Texas Accountant* 7 (March–April, 1935): 1–4.

sions of the Internal Revenue Service was to pay the tax and sue in the federal courts for a refund. This procedure was cumbersome and costly to taxpayer and government alike. A new and less expensive means of reviewing controversies of this type was inaugurated in 1924 when the Board of Tax Appeals was formed. As originally constituted, the Board of Tax Appeals was not intended to be, or even resemble, a court of record; rather it was to be an independent agency of the executive branch of the government. Practice before the board was open, therefore, to both CPAs and lawyers without examination and to such other persons as the board, by examination, might admit. Accountants were pleased at this recognition of their profession. They also envisioned the board as an informal body that would be composed mostly of nonlawyers who would cut quickly to the substance of a tax case. "The complex bedevilments of legalism should be kept as far as possible from the path of taxation," the *Journal of Accountancy* editorialized. "Sometimes it may be well to vary the procedure by introducing a little of the direct and effective manner of the market place."[10] It was admitted that some tax questions would be pure law, some would be a mixture of law and accounting, but most, it was presumed, would be pure accounting.

This optimism was short-lived. The Board of Tax Appeals became, in effect, a court of record in 1926 when the board adopted the rules of procedure and evidence of a federal district court. Furthermore, cases on appeal from the board went directly to the U.S. Court of Appeals, where only evidence previously submitted to the board was admissible. The name of the board was retained, however, as well as the rules pertaining to admission to practice. Many CPAs became wary at this point. They usually advised their clients to call in a lawyer to guide the case through the complex rules of evidence and procedure, even though this imposed an additional financial burden on the client. In many instances, however, cases were settled after a petition was made to the Board of Tax Appeals to hear the case but before it was actually heard. The accountant's right to file petitions, therefore, gave him and his client a valuable instrument with which to force a settlement before the need for a lawyer actually arose. Consequently, there was not too much concern in the ranks of accountancy during the late 1920s and

10. "Practice Before Board of Tax Appeals," *Journal of Accountancy* 41 (June, 1926): 449.

1930s. A total of 7,298 accountants had been admitted to practice before the Board of Tax Appeals by 1942.[11]

By World War II several things had happened that changed the picture. Most important was the fact that more and more questions of law were being introduced into tax controversies. At the same time, the overcrowded legal profession, which had long shunned tax practice, came to look upon it as a lucrative field. Some accountants were also skating on the thin edge of professional ethics by preparing semilegal and legal business documents for their clients, thereby laying the profession open to charges of unauthorized practice of law on other than tax matters.

Almost unnoticed by the accounting profession, the Revenue Act of 1942 changed the name of the Board of Tax Appeals to the Tax Court of the United States and the title of the court's members to "Judge." The court was still technically designated "an independent agency of the executive branch of the government." However, the wording of the 1924 and 1926 statutes designating lawyers and CPAs as equally qualified to practice before the Board of Tax Appeals was omitted. In its place, the law merely read that "no qualified person shall be denied admission to practice before such Court because of his failure to be a member of any profession or calling." The matter was thus left up to the court to determine who would be qualified to practice before it.

Accountants urged the court to continue allowing CPAs to represent their clients as they had for almost two decades. The court ruled, however, that while persons registered to practice before the Board of Tax Appeals prior to January, 1943, would be privileged to continue their practice before the new court, new applicants would be required either to hold a law license or successfully pass an examination administered by the court.[12]

The court quickly revealed the nature of the examination. Whether by accident or design, only twelve CPAs passed the examinations given from January, 1943, to 1949.[13] The net effect of the 1942 ruling, there-

11. "The Bill . . . to Make the Tax Court a Court of Record . . .," *Journal of Accountancy* 88 (Sept., 1949): 256–60.

12. "Practice Before Tax Court," *Journal of Accountancy* 75 (March, 1943): 194–95.

13. "The Bill . . . to Make the Tax Court a Court of Record . . .," *Journal of Accountancy* 88 (Sept., 1949): 256–60.

fore, was to make CPAs a dying class insofar as trying cases before the tax court was concerned. Later, from 1948 through 1951, lawyers unsuccessfully sought further changes in the law denying accountants the right of even filing petitions with the tax court. As 50 percent or more of the tax cases appealed to the court are settled before trial, blocking the CPA out of this part of tax practice would have constituted a hardship on the profession. Even more important, it would have imposed a greater financial burden on the client.

As part of the campaign against accountants in tax practice, lawyers also brought a number of suits against individual accountants, some of whom were noncertified, on charges of unauthorized practice of law. This practice soon brought a rebuke to the legal profession from Dean Erwin N. Griswold of the Harvard Law School. The dean admonished both lawyers and accountants to recognize a legitimate overlapping of the two professions in tax practice where free competition should exist. But he then added that "within very wide limits, lawyers are not protecting the public if they seek to prevent certified public accountants from engaging in tax practice. They are protecting themselves; and that is not a legitimate basis for using the weapon of unauthorized practice of law."[14]

While no full-scale fight broke out in Texas, local accountants were certainly aware of the conflict between the two professions centering on tax work. In 1935 Charles M. Trammell of the U.S. Board of Tax Appeals advised members of the Texas Society to associate with a lawyer versed in rules of evidence and procedure in the presentation of a case before the board, because the record made before that court was all that could be appealed to the U.S. Circuit Court of Appeals.[15] This was a moderate proposal indeed, however, compared with the suggestion some lawyers made: that CPAs be denied the right to practice at all before the board. For example, officers of the Texas Society spent considerable time in August, 1936, discussing a letter from the American Institute which alleged that lawyers were trying to shut account-

14. Erwin N. Griswold, "Lawyers, Accountants, and Taxes," *Journal of Accountancy* 99 (April, 1955): 33–41. The key cases cited by Dean Griswold were *Matter of New York County Lawyers Association* v. *Bercu* (1948), *Gardner* v. *Conway* (1951), and *Agran* v. *Shapiro* (1954).

15. Charles M. Trammel, "The C.P.A. Before the Board of Tax Appeals," *Texas Accountant* 7 (Jan., 1935): 1–4.

ants out of tax work, "which lawyers claim constitute a practice of law."[16] And a member of the Wisconsin Bar Association's Committee on Unauthorized Practice urged annulment of all CPA laws and the denial of permits to practice to all accountants except those admitted to the bar.[17]

Representation of clients in tax matters was not the only source of friction between lawyers and accountants. In response to demands of the legal profession, the Texas legislature in 1937 prohibited CPAs from preparing and filing domestic charters, applications for permits of foreign corporations, and similar instruments filed in the office of the secretary of state. Lawyers also disputed the right of accountants to prepare and file franchise tax returns, routine work which the accountant was many times as well qualified to do as the lawyer. There were signs that wholesale prosecution of accountants was in the immediate offing.[18] According to C. Aubrey Smith, chairman of the Committee on Legislation in 1937, the president of the American Bar Association that year appointed a San Antonio lawyer "to watch the activities of public accountants in Texas for evidence of illegal practice of law."[19]

To prevent an open and unseemly fight between the two professions, particularly on ground disadvantageous to the accountants, a committee headed by William Aikman sought to ease tensions. Being a lawyer as well as a CPA, Aikman sponsored a local meeting of San Antonio lawyers and accountants in which some points "were crystallized." Then early in 1938 he was invited to meet with the Committee on Unauthorized Practice of Law of the Texas Bar Association. At this meeting Aikman argued that the most constructive approach to the problem would be to educate both lawyers and accountants in their

16. "Minutes . . . August 8, 1936," TSCPA.
17. *Texas Accountant* 10 (May, 1938): 2.
18. Ibid., p. 5.
19. "Minutes . . . July 24, 1937," TSCPA. One casualty of the strained relations between lawyers and CPAs was the work accountants performed in the field of bankruptcy. Rather than calling in lawyers to liquidate receiverships, the courts often appointed accountants to operate them. In many cases, court administrators found that operating receiverships usually paid for themselves, to the benefit of creditors and bankrupts, while liquidating them was costly to both parties. As relations between the two professions became less cordial, however, this activity subsided. Arthur C. Upleger to author, Aug. 22, 1960.

proper and respective fields and thereby eliminate professional encroachment by either group.[20]

These conciliatory moves were temporarily set back in 1939, however, when the Board of Directors of the Texas Society protested a proposal from the Council of the American Institute discouraging institute members from trying cases before the Board of Tax Appeals without an attorney. The action of the board was taken "not with the idea that it was advisable for accountants to try cases without association with an attorney, but rather because such resolution might invite further steps by the American Bar Association to prevent accountants from representing clients in tax matters."[21]

During World War II relations between lawyers and accountants improved. A National Conference of Lawyers and Accountants was organized in May, 1944, and laid the foundation for the statement of 1950. In Texas, events moved a bit faster. A Texas State Conference of Lawyers and Certified Public Accountants was convened, and a "Statement of Policies" was accepted by the boards of directors of both professional bodies in 1945. Aikman, Phillips, Ben F. Irby, and Harry H. Roberts represented the Society in these negotiations.[22]

The "Statement of Policies" began with the generalization that matters involving legal questions should be handled by lawyers and matters involving accounting should be handled by accountants. More specifically, it advised "contracts, deeds of trust, trust agreements, wills, articles of incorporation and the dissolution of corporations, partnership agreements and other legal documents . . . should be prepared under the advice of and by the lawyer." It was further agreed, although the Society expressed some reservations on this point, that in "matters before the Securities and Exchange Commission the accountant should not appear except to give expert opinions in matters relating to accounting." Either the lawyer or the CPA could prepare income tax returns, although in returns that "have a legal implication," the lawyer should be consulted. Accountants conceded "the preparation of cases for trial

20. William M. Aikman, chairman, Committee on Cooperation with Attorneys, to T. W. Mohle, Sept. 16, 1938, in "Society Records, 1937–1938," TSCPA.

21. "Minutes . . . May 20, 1939," TSCPA.

22. "Statement of Policies . . . December 14, 1945," *Texas Accountant* 18 (Jan., 1946): 3.

and the trial of cases before the United States Tax Court belongs primarily within the province of the lawyer." Estate and inheritance tax returns, it was also agreed, should come under the direction of the lawyer. Local chapters of accountants and local bar associations were then encouraged to hold joint meetings to familiarize their members with the limits of each and to encourage a "closer relationship." All in all, the "Statement of Policies" seemed to bear out Frank Wilbur Main's advice to the Dallas Chapter of the Texas Society in a speech he made on this subject in December, 1939. Urging closer cooperation between the professions, the Pennsylvania accountant closed with the thought that "the legal profession is more firmly established and entrenched than is the accounting profession. The legal profession has the oversight and protection of the judiciary. Our profession covers a very wide . . . range, and if there is to be any giving in any particular close question as between the law and accounting, I am certain that we are the ones who should give the most. We should be very careful . . . not to tread upon the toes of our legal brethren."[23]

Legislation was a constant concern to the Texas Society from 1931 to 1945. Occasionally a fight had to be made against bills in the legislature deemed contrary to the best interests of the profession. "Credit goes to the Houston Chapter," the *Texas Accountant* reported in February, 1937, "for taking the lead . . . in opposition to House Bill No. 171. . . . This bill, in its definition of the term 'practice of law' appeared to invade the field of accountancy."[24] On occasion an Austin attorney was retained by the Society to keep close watch on all bills introduced and report those felt to be unfriendly to the profession.

On another front, the Society mustered support for bills stimulating practice. The Legislative Committee in 1933 endorsed state legislation requiring audits of state, county, and city governments and supported national legislation calling for audits of national banks and other members of the Federal Deposit Insurance Corporation.[25] Later, during the war, the committee advocated legislation requiring audits of independent school districts. A member wrote the Board of Directors in May, 1939, expressing the novel idea that nonresident accountants en-

23. Frank Wilbur Main, "Cooperation of Accountants and Attorneys," *Texas Accountant* 12 (March, 1940): 1–5.
24. *Texas Accountant* 9 (Feb., 1937): 4.
25. "Minutes . . . December 16, 1933," TSCPA.

gaged in temporary work be taxed on the fees they earned in Texas. The suggestion was voted down for several reasons. First, it was feared other states might enact retaliatory laws against Texas CPAs. Second, there was the danger that such a tax on outsiders might in time be expanded into a general occupation tax on domestic accountants. Finally, in view of strained relations with lawyers, the board thought it would be dangerous to open up any accountancy legislation "at this time."[26]

## Public Accountancy Act of 1945

By all odds, the most pervasive legislative issue involved efforts to enact two-class regulatory legislation. The defeat of the regulatory bill in 1931 kept the issue down for a year or so. In 1932 Loyd Smith, chairman of the Legislative Committee, took a dim view of reintroducing the bill in 1933 because of the "chaotic condition of politics in Texas." When and if another try were made, Smith added, it would be "of paramount importance" to line up the accountants themselves "because if we do not as a group want the law, most assuredly no one else can be expected to be interested in it."[27]

In 1934 Henry J. Miller of New Orleans, a past president of the American Society of Certified Public Accountants, spoke on the merits of the Louisiana two-class law. Encouraged by this message, the Society voted to get a bill before the legislature immediately, and President Tom Leland appointed Luke Garvin to chair a Legislative Committee composed of Aikman, Mathis, Clifton Morris, and Upleger.[28]

The committee first sent out a questionnaire to determine the sentiments of the rank-and-file Society members. Returns indicated members were 150 to 22 in favor of change and 143 to 20 in favor of regulation. Asked if they would pledge active cooperation and support to secure passage of the legislation, the answer was 133 to 5 in the affirmative. Highly encouraged by this response, the Society prepared a bill in 1935 that was introduced in the legislature by Representative J. C. Duval of Fort Worth. Garvin's report in the June, 1935, issue of the

26. "Minutes . . . May 20, 1939," TSCPA.
27. "Report of the Committee on Legislation, October 11, 1932," TSCPA.
28. "Minutes . . . October 12–13, 1934," and "Minutes . . . November 24, 1934," TSCPA.

*Texas Accountant* explained what then happened. "In due time notice was given . . . that a hearing would be had on the bill. At this hearing the Committee . . . presented the bill, with no special comment. The committee did not attempt in any way to stampede sentiment for the bill." However, Garvin added, "it was apparent from the beginning that the opposition was well prepared. It consisted of an organized minority of Certified Public Accountants together with a few noncertified public accountants, and was successful in blocking the bill approved by the majority of our membership."[29]

Little was done in regard to regulatory legislation for a decade. Meeting in June, 1940, the board directed the Legislative Committee to draft a new law "within six months," but no action was taken.[30] In the 1944 annual meeting in Houston, however, there was strong sentiment for change. Victor H. Stempf, president of the American Institute, indicated that the institute, formerly hostile to regulation, was now neutral on the subject and that he personally supported the measure. The Society, he added, should take "early action" on the matter. Roy Pope, chairman of the retiring Legislative Committeee, Upleger, C. H. Cavness, Fred Alford, Frank Rodgers, and Joseph Hutchinson, Jr., also spoke in favor of the change. Pope said noncertified accountants would support the bill for the immediate advantages recognition would bring to them. However, the long-run advantages would be realized by the certified accountants because the law would make the public accountants a dying class. Rodgers was in favor of submitting the bill in 1945 unless "dangerous opposition should arise." The regulatory bill, he argued, would "strengthen the position of accountants in relation to lawyers in tax work." Alford and Hutchinson sponsored a motion authorizing the Society to raise $3,000 from individuals and firms to defray expenses attendant to adoption of the bill.[31]

The best indication that this legislative campaign might be successful where others had failed was the new stand taken by Jay Phillips, who, with the late George Armistead, had led the opposition in 1931 and 1935. Phillips now reversed himself, declaring he "had no fear of a two-class regulatory bill and no fear of amendments contrary to the

29. "Report of the Committee on Legislation," *Texas Accountant* 7 (June, 1935): 3–4.
30. "Minutes . . . June 29, 1940," TSCPA.
31. "Minutes . . . April 21–22, 1944," TSCPA.

interest of the profession in Texas." He even consented to head up the legislative committee charged with the bill's passage.

The committee moved quickly. September 15, 1944, was the target date selected for turning the preliminary draft of the bill over to legal counsel for formal drafting. Care was taken to secure the endorsement of a large number of noncertified accountants. When the bill was introduced, Leland, then serving a one-year tour of duty as educational director of the American Institute, came to Austin to help with its presentation. All these efforts were rewarded on June 4, 1945, when the Texas legislature formally approved the bill and on June 6, 1945, when Governor Coke Stevenson signed it into law.[32]

The Public Accountancy Act of 1945 defined public accounting and public accountants in the following terms: "A person engages in the 'practice of public accountancy' within the meaning of this Act who, holding himself out to the public as a public accountant, in consideration of compensation received or to be received by him, offers to perform or does perform, for other persons, services which involve the auditing or examination of financial transactions, books, accounts, or records, or the preparation of, or the reporting over his signature on, financial, accounting and related statements." So defined, the practice of public accounting was now restricted in Texas for the first time to CPAs and licensed public accountants who held annual permits to practice. The requirements for certification as a public accountant remained essentially the same as stipulated in the 1915 law except that the four-year experience requirement was reduced to one year for junior- or senior-college graduates with accounting majors and to three years for graduates without formal accounting courses. Noncertified accountants who had practiced public accounting during three of the preceding ten years were also eligible for permits to practice if they registered with the Texas State Board of Public Accountancy by November 1, 1945. After that date, the licensed public accountant became a dying class, and the law anticipated a day in the future when only CPAs could engage in public practice.

Though perhaps not fully appreciated at the time, the 1945 act greatly enhanced the responsibility and authority of the Texas State Board. The composition of the State Board remained, for the moment,

32. For a copy of the law see *Texas Accountant* 17 (July–Aug., 1945): 1–7.

as before; five CPAs serving two-year terms. But the board now had the sole power to admit persons to the practice of public accounting, and it also received authority to promulgate rule of professional conduct that would protect the public and maintain "high standards of integrity in the profession of accounting." The promulgation of professional rules of conduct depended upon the approval of a majority of permit holders, and to that extent the rule-making authority was still shared with the great body of certified and licensed public accountants, but given wise leadership the State Board was in position to assume a dominant voice in the development of the profession.

## Presidents from 1932 to 1945

At the time of his death in 1977, Jay Phillips was acknowledged by most to have made the most sustained contribution to the profession in Texas during his lifetime. Phillips was born in Holland, Texas, in 1892, the son of a Central Texas tenant farmer. He graduated from high school in Moody and attended Draughon's Business College in Waco, this being the extent of his formal education. He worked for a short time in a general store in Moody and a bank in Pendleton before taking a position with the Texas state comptroller's office in 1913. There his experience in accounting broadened, and in 1918 he joined the Ernst & Ernst staff in Dallas. He received CPA certificate number 87 in 1920. Phillips managed Ernst & Ernst in Houston until 1925, when he formed his own firm, which, in 1963, merged with Deloitte, Haskins & Sells. Before and after his term as Society president in 1932–1933, he was a member, and most of the time chairman, of the Texas State Board of Public Accountancy for almost eighteen years. In 1952 he was elected president of the American Institute of Certified Public Accountants. In addition to his own professional attainments, Phillips brought recognition to the accounting profession through his wide acquaintance with business and community leaders in Texas. He served terms as president of the Houston Club, Houston Kiwanis Club, and the Better Business Bureau; he was for twenty years on the board of governors of the Jefferson Davis City-County Hospital, and he was chairman of the board of Scott and White Hospital in Temple. Appointment to the Texas State Securities Board in 1957 was further recognition of his standing in the Texas business community.

Thomas W. Leland, president of the Society for two terms, 1933–1935, was the first accounting professor—and the first nonpractitioner—elected to serve in that office. Leland was born in Oskosh, Wisconsin, in 1895. He attended Oskosh State Normal for two years and then the University of Wisconsin, receiving the bachelor's degree in 1921 and the master's degree one year later. He joined the Texas A&M faculty in 1922, the second year the college offered accounting courses, and in 1926 became head of the Department of Accounting and Statistics. In 1928, Leland qualified for CPA certificate number 295 and immediately joined the Texas Society and the American Institute of Accountants. Leland was instrumental in bringing members in national and local firms as well as those in public practice and private employment into closer relationship within the Society, resulting in significant gains in membership and increased chapter activity. Perhaps as important as his accomplishments while president were the duties he performed as secretary-treasurer and editor of the *Texas Accountant* from 1938 to 1953. Leland, who died in 1963, also served as educational director of the American Institue of Certified Public Accountants in 1944–1945 and was a long-time member of the American Institute's Board of Examiners.

Frank G. Rodgers, of San Antonio, the fifteenth president of the Texas Society, was born in Pontotoc County, Mississippi. He prepared for a teaching career at the State Normal College of the University of Mississippi, but after one year of teaching he enrolled in the Queen City Business College of Meridian. Upon completion of an eighteen-month course, he went to work in the lumber business. For five years he lived in Georgia and Tennessee before moving to San Antonio and accepting employment with Wm. B. Lupe & Company, Investment Bankers. In the early part of 1918, Rodgers entered public accounting through association with William Aikman. In 1920, the same year he received CPA certificate number 78, Rodgers established his own firm in San Antonio. In the wake of the oil boom, Rodgers opened a second office in San Angelo in 1927, and the next year he added a Fort Worth office. The San Angelo practice was disposed of in 1933, before his presidency, and the Fort Worth office was closed in 1943. As president of the Society in 1935–1936, Rodgers had the unique distinction of welcoming both the American Society of Certified Public Accountants and the American Institute of Accountants to Texas when the two organizations met in Fort Worth and Dallas, respectively, preparatory to their merger. Active in a variety of civic and community endeavors, Rodgers also served on the Texas State Board of Public Accountancy for ten years. Rodgers died in 1966.

In 1936 the presidency of the Society passed to H. Tracy Nelson, younger brother of Jesse Ray Nelson. Tracy Nelson was born in Clayton, Texas, in 1895 and graduated from the local public schools. He attended Southwest Texas State Teachers College in 1912–1913 and taught school in his native Panola County for two years after that. In 1915 Nelson moved to Dallas, entered the Metropolitan Business College, and worked part time for his brother's firm, Nelson and Snyder. His schooling was interrupted by World War I and overseas service in the army air corps. After the war, Nelson worked briefly as field agent in Dallas and auditor in the Washington, D.C., office of the Internal Revenue Service, leaving the IRS to join his brother in organizing Nelson Audit Company, later Nelson and Nelson. Tracy Nelson qualified for Texas certificate number 242 in 1926 and joined the Society the same year. In addition to his accounting studies, Nelson finished Jefferson Law School in Dallas in 1930 and was admitted to the State Bar of Texas.

While serving as seventeenth president of the Texas Society, Theodore W. Mohle also managed the Houston office of Lybrand, Ross Brothers and Montgomery. Thus he became the second national firm accountant to lead the Society. Born and reared in Lockhart, Texas, Mohle attended Texas A&M and graduated from Tulane University. He also took accounting courses at Columbia University where, in 1923, he joined Lybrand's New York office staff. He later moved to the Dallas office and in 1927 acquired Texas certificate number 251. From 1931 to 1941 Mohle managed the firm's Houston office, forming his own local firm in 1941. Upon retirement, Mohle moved back to Lockhart, where he died in 1981.

Joe C. Harris, born in West, Texas, in 1892, had finished public school and nearby Trinity University at Waxahachie by age nineteen. After three years of office and construction work with Texas Power & Light, Harris enrolled in the Eastman College of Poughkeepsie, New York, one of the better accounting and business schools in the East. Upon completing the program at Eastman, Harris moved downstate for a year of accounting and law studies at Columbia University Graduate

School. In New York City he worked as a junior accountant for Lybrand, Ross Brothers & Montgomery for a short period in 1917. World War I intervened and Harris served as a first lieutenant. During his army career he met Edward Hunter, a member of the first Texas State Board of Public Accountancy, who prevailed upon Harris to return to Texas and work for his San Antonio firm, the Alamo Auditing Company. In 1920, Harris qualified for CPA certificate number 88 and moved to Dallas and the firm of Hutchinson and Smith. His election into the Society in 1920 was made easy by the fact that the annual meeting of the Society that year was held in the Hutchinson and Smith offices in Dallas with all twelve members present! In 1925, Harris became a partner in Hutchinson, Smith, Prince and Harris and, following subsequent changes over the years, the firm of Prince, Harris & King merged with Arthur Young & Company in 1953. Harris died in 1962.

At the time of his two-term presidency in 1939–1941, Walter C. Burer was controller for Sugarland Industries and had the distinction, therefore, of being the first Society president elected from the ranks of CPAs in industry. Burer was born into the family of a Washington County tenant farmer in 1900. He finished Brenham High School in 1917 but lacked the funds to attend college until 1920, when he enrolled at Texas A&M for one year. Later, he attended a six-month course in general business at Tyler Commercial College and got a job with the Texas Company in Port Arthur. Upon the advice of his sister-in-law, a secretary in the Dallas Ernst & Ernst office, Burer applied for a position with the firm's Houston office managed by Jay Phillips. This led to an association with Phillips lasting over two decades. Burer went with Phillips when the latter organized his own firm in 1925, and in 1930 Phillips sent him to Sugar Land on a "temporary assignment" that lasted eleven years. In 1941 Burer returned to the Phillips firm until 1945, when he and T. W. Mohle formed a partnership. From 1948 until his death in 1962, Burer practiced alone. Through a combination of practical experience and self-study, Burer qualified for CPA certificate number 290 in 1928.

Fred F. Alford, president of the Society at the beginning of World War II, was born in 1899 on his father's 800-acre farm in Van Zandt County. He was graduated from Wills Point High School in 1916, thereafter attending Texas A&M for two years and the University of Texas for one year. Later, he enrolled in Tyler Commercial College for an introduction to accounting and then moved to Dallas and the staff of Ernst & Ernst. He acquired certificate number 313 in 1929. By the time of his presidency, Alford had formed Alford, Meroney & Company. The firm became one of the state's largest regional firms before merging with Arthur Young & Company in 1980. Shortly after World War II, however, Alford retired from public practice and spent the years until his death in 1964 attending to personal business interests.

Like Alford, Joseph C. Cobb, president 1942–1943, was born on an East Texas farm and attended Tyler Commercial College. Cobb was born in 1893 and finished public schools in Elkhart. He followed up on his studies at Tyler Commercial College with correspondence work in accounting from the University of Texas, LaSalle Extension University, and the Hamilton Institute. He moved to Houston and gained public accounting experience with J. Austin Smith & Co. and with Main and Company. In 1929 he was awarded CPA certificate number 303, and the following year he joined the staff of Barrow, Wade, Guthrie & Co. Two years later he was made resident manager of the Houston office and was serving in that capacity at the time of his death on April 25, 1945.

Economic necessity prevented Lyle R. Sproles, president 1943–1944, from completing his formal education. Born in 1893, Sproles was only eight years old when his father died and the family moved from Warrenburg, Tennessee, to Greenville, Texas, to be near relatives. Later, two years short of completing high school, Sproles became a clerk and bookkeeper for a cotton exporting firm. After service in World War I, he joined the staff of W. O. Ligon & Co. in Oklahoma and qualified for Oklahoma certificate number 144 in 1923. In the mid-1920s the Ligon firm was reorganized, and Sproles became a partner in the new firm of L. E. Cahill & Co. He was placed in charge of the Wichita Falls, Texas, office. He later moved to Fort Worth in a similar capacity. In 1933, the same year he qualified for Texas certificate number 449, Sproles organized his own firm in Fort Worth. The firm Sproles, Woodard, Laverty & McGee came to specialize in petroleum accounting, the bulk of its clients being independent oilmen. Sproles died in 1972.

Cyril Frederick Milledge was the first president of the Society to have come from England, the country to which professional accountancy owes so much. Born in Shrewsbury, England, in 1893, Milledge was educated in the public schools of England and studied for a year and a half at Kings College in London. In 1911 his family moved to Dickinson, Texas. The move to this country ended Milledge's formal education, aside from some correspondence work from the University of Texas. Except for a four-year interruption (1915–1919) for volunteer military service in the British Expeditionary Armed Forces in World War I, Milledge was employed by the Santa Fe Railroad in Galveston and Winslow, Arizona, from 1912 to 1920. He joined the accounting department of Humble Oil and Refining Company in June, 1920, remaining there until 1925, when he became a staff auditor for Mattison & Block in Houston. He qualified for his CPA certificate in 1926 and that same year opened his own firm in Houston.

# 6

## The First Decades of State Regulation, 1945–1965

JOHN L. CAREY expressed cautious optimism in addressing delegates to the Texas Society's first postwar meeting. "No one could blame certified public accountants if they were found, in this year of 1946, to be enjoying a sense of security," the executive director of the American Institute of Certified Public Accountants declared. The profession had acquired status, minimized friction within its ranks, strengthened standards, established cooperative relations with related business and professional groups, and, last but not least, built up the fee structure to a point commensurate with other professions. On the other hand, Carey cautioned, there were problems ahead. The profession's right to determine acceptable accounting principles and auditing standards was threatened by the national government's insistence upon uniformity in auditing reports filed with the Securities and Exchange Commission and other federal agencies. Carried to the extreme, Carey said, such a policy would reduce accountants "to the status of clerks filling out government forms." Public accountants also faced competition from government auditors, tax lawyers, and management engineers, Carey added, while the certificate as the hallmark of the profession was under attack from the National Society of Public Accountants, organized in 1945.[1]

These remarks were drawn primarily from Carey's national experience, but they applied as well to Texas. There were also additional opportunities and problems peculiar to the local scene. The demand for accounting services increased even more rapidly in Texas after 1945 than in the nation at large. The profession was understaffed in 1946, when there were roughly 1,000 Texas certificates in force; it was still

---

1. John L. Carey, "The Uncertain Future," *Texas Accountant* 18 (Sept., 1946): 1–6.

understaffed in 1965 when there were over five times as many Texas certificate holders. A postwar business and industrial boom created a heavy demand for accountants' services, as did the state government's tendency to require independent audits of an ever-increasing number of public and semi-public institutions: school districts, insurance companies, and business corporations under the jurisdiction of the Texas State Securities Board.

## Adjusting to the New Law and Public Accountants

The accommodation of certified and licensed public accountants to the 1945 regulatory act and the two groups to each other took some time and effort. More than 3,500 noncertified accountants initially registered under the 1945 law. An extension granted by the legislature in 1947 brought the cumulative total to 4,254 in 1948 and resulted in CPAs being outnumbered roughly four to one. In time, approximately 500 of the licensed accountants qualified for the certificate and became CPAs. But in an address to the Southern States Accountants Conference in June, 1947, Jay Phillips reviewed the efforts noncertified accountants were making in several states, Texas included, to water down professional standards. According to Phillips, these included attempts to abolish the designation "certified public accountant," leaving only "public accountants"; to substitute individually prepared state examinations for the AICPA uniform examination; to reopen registration for public accountants and perpetuate the two-class system; to provide for equal representation of certified and noncertified public accountants on state boards; to liberalize provisions for granting waiver certificates; and to broaden the definition of public accounting to include bookkeepers, tax preparers, and government employees. Directed by the National Society of Public Accountants, these efforts had already borne fruit in New York, where the passage of the Oliver bill authorized waiver certificates for accountants over forty years of age with fifteen or more years' experience "in the intensive application of accounting and auditing procedures." Closer to Texas, Phillips noted New Mexico public accountants had succeeded in amending their state law to provide continuing registration of noncertified public accountants.[2]

2. Jay A. Phillips, "State Legislation," *Texas Accountant* 19 (July–Aug., 1947): 1–5.

Those attuned to the situation in Texas needed no alert from Phillips to know relations between certified and noncertified accountants were deteriorating. Feelings between the two groups were cordial at first, but when the Society refused to reopen associate membership to noncertified accountants, many licensed public accountants joined the newly formed Texas Association of Public Accountants (TAPA). The admission of licensed accountants to associate membership might have been a good move politically, but the Society viewed the return to two-class membership which existed prior to 1928 as misleading to the public, lessening the prestige of membership in the Society for CPAs, and being harmful even to the noncertified accountants cast in the role of second-class members.[3] Friction increased further when the TAPA supported attacks against the AICPA leveled by the National Association of Public Accountants. Alleging that the institute, working through the state societies, constituted a national monopoly of the accounting profession, NAPA demanded a return to "professional states' rights" by discontinuing the use of AICPA uniform examinations and the designation "certified public accountant." Those familiar with the history of the accounting profession in the United States recognized an inaccuracy in these charges. A battle had been fought within the profession along these lines, but it was won in the 1930s, not by the institute, but by those who championed control of the profession at the state level through state boards issuing state certificates.[4]

The TAPA's exaggerated charges against the AICPA prompted over one hundred of its members to split off and form the Texas Society of Accountants (TSA). The Texas Society of Certified Public Accountants helped TSA organize, securing as speakers for its early meetings the president of the AICPA, E. B. Wilcox, and AICPA secretary John L. Carey.[5] However, because many members of TSA were working toward a certificate and membership in the TSCPA, the ranks of the organization gradually dissipated.

Critics of the 1945 accountancy law made their first concerted legislative attack on the measure in 1947. Three amendments to the law were introduced, one of which proposed to abolish the Texas State Board of Public Accountancy. As finally passed, however, House Bill 589

3. "President's Report, June 11, 1947," TSCPA.
4. See above, pp. 51–52.
5. "President's Report, June 11, 1947," TSCPA.

only extended the registration period briefly for qualified accountants out of the state during the first registration. As the bill did not reopen registration permanently, it was not contested by the Society.[6] This political skirmish, however, dampened relations between the Society and the TAPA. Roy Pope, chairman of the committee on cooperation with other state and national organizations, advised the Society to adopt an attitude toward the TAPA that would be "dignified, friendly, but not ingratiating," and to "encourage registered public accountants to sit for CPA examinations."[7]

The events of 1947 were merely a prelude to 1949. Senate Bill 118, introduced that year on behalf of the TAPA, proposed the liberal granting of waiver certificates to many registered public accountants, licensing bookkeepers as public accountants, and giving credit for experience to offset failing grades on the CPA examination.[8] The bill was beaten down in the legislature only with considerable expenditure of time, effort, and money. The fight convinced many CPAs of the need for a broad educational program aimed at state legislators to help them understand that the standards CPAs were fighting to uphold were more in the public interest than they were in the narrow interests of practitioners. If and when this education could be accomplished, it was felt, the TAPA's efforts would collapse.

With the 1951 legislative session approaching, both sides jockeyed for position. Hatcher Pickens, chairman of the Society's Legislative Committee, reported to the board in August, 1950, that the TAPA had approached his committee on the feasibility of placing one or more public accountants on the Texas State Board of Public Accountancy. The Society board firmly opposed any concessions. However, on October 22, 1950, the Society and TAPA legislative committees met together in Mineral Wells and hammered out a compromise. TAPA first demanded sweeping changes in the accountancy act, including, on the one hand, a licensing board and status entirely independent of CPAs, and, on the other, liberal credit for experience in passing the CPA examination. Advised that the Society would strongly oppose these changes, both committees then agreed to support legislation giving licensed pub-

6. "President's Report, June 11, 1947," TSCPA.
7. "Digest of Committee Reports, 1947–1948," TSCPA.
8. "Minutes . . . January 30, 1949," and Harry Hopson, "President's Message," *Texas Accountant* 21 (Feb., 1949): 1.

lic accountants representation on the State Board, initial credit for passing a single subject on the examination, and a more acceptable definition of public accountancy. The TAPA board of governors, by a vote of 8 to 6, later rejected the compromise, holding out for a completely separate licensing board for public accountants.

When the legislature met in 1951, however, the TSCPA, joined by the Texas Society of Accountants and individual TAPA members from Fort Worth, Amarillo, and Austin, successfully amended the accountancy act along the lines of the Mineral Wells compromise.[9] Four public accountants were added to the Texas State Board, increasing the membership to nine, though the public accountant members had no jurisdiction over applicants or the certificate holders. Another change, made retroactive to 1915, awarded credit to persons having passed one but not two parts of the examination previously required to receive initial credit. This "credit by amendment" resulted in more than eight hundred applicants' receiving one or more credits for parts of the examination a few of them had passed as far back as the 1920s. Five persons received credit for all four parts of the examination and were thus awarded certificates. The law, as amended, also lowered examination fees and provided that, upon request, unsuccessful candidates be supplied the correct answers to the parts of the examination they failed.[10]

For the time being, the Society had successfully resolved its differences with licensed public accountants. Phillips, as close to the legislative problem as anyone, remarked that the amendments of 1951 "gave promise of ending the controversy."[11] The next year at the annual meeting in Waco, the Committee on Cooperation with Other Organizations reported, "there has been a marked improvement in the feelings between the public accountant and the Certified Public Accountants of Texas since the low ebb reached in the spring of 1949."[12]

Membership in the TAPA dwindled rapidly after 1950. By 1956 only 250 names were reported to be on its mailing list. The TSA had 125 members and numbered several CPAs among its membership. TSA

9. "Minutes . . . December 16, 1950," TSCPA.

10. *Texas Accountant* 23 (June, 1951): 8–9.

11. "Minutes . . . June 10–12, 1951," TSCPA.

12. "Report of the Committee on Cooperation with Other Organizations, 1951–1952," TSCPA.

President Hugh B. Hackney was also a member of the TSCPA. Seeing little likelihood of any new attacks from either of these societies, the TSCPA Committee on Cooperation with Other Organizations requested through its chairman, Lod Allison, permission to establish a closer liaison with the noncertified accountants. Much good could be accomplished, Allison said, if CPAs would join with the noncertified accountants in taking action against bookkeepers and tax service people who "are coming into the accounting field through the back door." Encroachment from these quarters had not bothered the larger accounting firms, Allison contended, but the smaller CPA firms and public accountants deserved the protection that only the larger firms could provide. In this connection, a Committee on Unauthorized Practice of Accounting was established in 1955. Its activities were seriously limited, however, when cases of unauthorized practice referred to the Texas State Board of Public Accountancy for prosecution were returned with the explanation that the board had jurisdiction only over persons registered with it. Thus, as Allison explained, protection against encroachment by nonregistered persons was squarely the responsibility of the Society, or of individual practitioners who would take the trouble of going to the courts.[13] Meanwhile, the Society extended the olive branch a little further in 1957. Local chapters were urged to invite noncertified accountants to attend their technical sessions. Technical bulletins and the *Texas Certified Public Accountant* were made available to members of the TAPA and the TSA, and the three societies were urged to cooperate in reporting to the Texas State Board of Public Accountancy permit holders guilty of performing substandard work.[14]

At the same time these constructive accomplishments were being made, there was a flare-up in 1956 and 1959 of the criticism first heard in 1949 and 1951. It started when a delegation from the TAPA attended a meeting of the Society's legislative committee in December, 1956. To the astonishment of some of his own group, one of the guests read a prepared statement bitterly attacking what he termed the American Institute's domination of accounting in Texas and demanded the repeal of virtually all of the 1945 act. The statement was so vitriolic that it even

13. Ibid., 1955–1956. See also the committee's report for 1959–1960.
14. "Minutes . . . December 6, 1957," TSCPA.

criticism from Ward P. Westbrook of Jasper, president of the A.[15] In spite of threats that such a bill would be introduced in the legislature, the session passed without incident. The attack was renewed in 1959, however, to the surprise of officials of the Society. It had been generally understood that further changes in the law would await the outcome of a proposed July, 1959, meeting of the TSCPA, the TAPA, the TSA, and the Texas Association of University Instructors in Accounting. This schedule was upset, however, by a TAPA bill calling for the replacement of the AICPA uniform examinations with one prepared by the Texas State Board of Public Accountancy and a provision under which liberal credits would be handed out on the basis of experience. The bill was badly drawn, however, and died in committee even before CPAs had an opportunity to speak against it.

Beginning with a joint meeting of the Executive and Legislative committees in Austin on February 28, 1959, the Society abandoned the defensive posture it had adopted following 1945 and laid plans to revise the accountancy law in 1961. A special committee composed of Ludwell Jones, Charles T. Zlatkovich, and Bouldin Mothershead, chairman, drafted the general objectives to be achieved. These included giving the State Board broader enforcement powers and upgrading the educational requirements for the certificate.[16]

The Society won most of its objectives in 1961 when Governor Price Daniel signed into law Senate Bill 100. As amended in 1961, the Public Accountancy Act of 1945 omitted the definition of public accountancy previously included in section 2 of the act, but it spelled out in much greater detail in section 8 the prohibitions against practicing without a permit. New amendments also gave the State Board subpoena powers and authority to seek court injunctions and enjoin persons from engaging in the unauthorized practice of public accounting. Educational requirements for the certificate were raised to the bachelor's degree level, though an "Abraham Lincoln" provision permitted persons with six years' experience to sit for the examination with only two years of college training. Experience requirements for holders of baccalaureate degrees were set at two years; master's degree holders, one year. Applicants were also allowed to take the complete examination as

15. "Report of the Committee on Legislation, 1956–1957," TSCPA.
16. "Minutes . . . February 28, 1959," and "Summary of Proposed Amendments to the Texas Public Accountancy Act . . . May 28, 1960," TSCPA.

soon as they satisfied the educational prerequisites rather than waiting until the experience requirements were met before attempting the practice part. All in all, Walter Flack, chairman of the 1960–1961 Committee on Legislation, looked back upon the 1961 amendments as a "major victory."[17]

Flack's optimism and sense of victory seemed accurate enough as the Society approached its fiftieth anniversary in 1965. For instance, shortly after the 1961 legislative session ended, the Texas Society was asked to comment on negotiations between the AICPA and the National Society of Public Accountants concerning the need to recognize "tax practitioners" and "public bookkeepers" as a second class of "accounting practitioner" qualified to render all accounting services except the attest function. Society President Kenneth Hurst reported to the Executive Committee in September, 1963, that even leaders of the TAPA in Beaumont expressed opposition to the proposed AICPA-NSPA statement and denied as well any affiliation with the NSPA.[18] The committee on long-range planning for legislation responded more formally to the AICPA proposal in December, 1963. Recognizing approximately one thousand unlicensed "technicians" in Texas who offered some form of accounting or public bookkeeping services, the committee observed the public interest did not require their identification and control. Moreover, the committee argued, somewhat naively in light of future events, "there is no evidence that the bookkeepers and tax return preparers have made any effort in Texas to obtain legislation favorable to their position."[19]

## Relations with Bankers and Lawyers

The success the Society achieved in its legislative program between 1945 and 1965 was only partly matched in some other areas of professional development and in the profession's relations with nonaccounting groups. Work with bankers to develop a credit form acceptable to banker, accountant, and client yielded only modest rewards. A study in 1953 by C. Aubrey Smith and Robert G. Standlee revealed that only 32 out of the 146 banks responding to a questionnaire required

17. "Report of the Committee on Legislation, 1960–1961," TSCPA.
18. "Minutes, Executive Committee, September 20, 1963," TSCPA.
19. "Mid-Year Report, Committee on Long Range Planning for Legislation, 1963–1964," TSCPA.

audits for loan purposes. Some bankers were critical of short-form reports that did not present as much detail as the banker desired; others
objected to statements prepared without audit. Still others pointed to
substandard work by the accountant. The third criticism, of course, was
one that the profession was as anxious to correct as the banker. The
other two criticisms, however, more nearly represent an underestima-
tion and a misunderstanding on the banker's part of the value of the
statement and short-form report.[20] To improve this situation, beginning
in 1959 one issue each year of the *Texas Certified Public Accountant*
was devoted to the mutual problems of accountants and bankers. Local
chapters were encouraged to arrange a yearly meeting with bankers as
guests and participants on the program. Even more to the point was a
survey of CPA audit reports for credit purposes, begun in 1960 by Dan
Davis of the Southern Methodist University faculty. This study was
sponsored jointly the the Society and the Texas Chapter, Robert Morris
Associates. The first of its kind, it was followed with national interest
and promised to dispel many doubts and misunderstandings.[21]

After 1946 lawyer-accountant relations in Texas were consistently
more cordial than they were in some other states. The statement issued
by the Texas State Conference of Lawyers and Certified Public Accountants in September, 1945, did much to create and maintain a friendly
spirit between the two groups. The next year the full memberships of
the San Antonio Bar and the San Antonio Chapter of the Society met
jointly in one of the first meetings of its kind in the country. Further
evidence of good feeling came in 1947, when the chairman of the Texas
Bar Association's grievance committee joined accountants in opposing
legislation aimed at watering down the 1945 public accountancy act.[22]
Then, in 1950, the Texas Bar Association set up a standing committee
to represent it in relations with accountants. This act removed the stigma
accountants formerly bore in dealing only with the committee on unauthorized practice of law. Two years later a joint state board of lawyers
and CPAs was appointed. This was done partly at the suggestion of the

20. An analysis of this report is found in Lee W. Branch, "Cooperation Between
Bankers and Certified Public Accountants Subject of Growing Interest," *Texas Accountant* 25 (Nov., 1953): 5.
21. See *Texas Certified Public Accountant* 32 (Jan., 1960), and "Report of Committee on Cooperation with Bankers . . . 1959–1960," TSCPA.
22. "President's Report, June 11, 1947," TSCPA.

National Conference of Lawyers and Certified Public Accountants in 1951. E. Roy Body, Marquis G. Eaton, and Frank L. Wilcox were the first accountants on the Texas committee. The joint state board held its first meeting October 15, 1955.

Texas accountants were not immune to the quarrel with lawyers going on in other states, however. They took note of the New York Supreme Court's 1947 decision in the *Bercu* case in which the court ruled a CPA could legally give advice on tax law but could not lawfully perform research or give advice on problems involving a knowledge of the law aside from the tax law itself. The court also warned accountants that in the preparation of income tax returns they could not lawfully pass on such questions as legal domicile, the validity of a marriage, the construction of a will, a deed of trust, or any other legal document upon which tax liability might on occasion depend.[23] Also in 1947, the Texas Society joined the American Institute in registering a vigorous and successful protest against a measure in Congress, sponsored by the American Bar Association, that would have had the effect of restricting accountants in their practice before federal agencies. This resolution (HR 2657) called for the creation of a credentials committee composed of four government officials and one lawyer empowered to issue certificates of admission to practice before federal administrative agencies. Lawyers would have been given certificates without question, but non-lawyers would have been subjected to such tests of competence as the committee saw fit to give.[24]

The next year, 1948, accountants objected a second time to legislation pending in Congress. This time a bill (HR 3214) proposed to change the tax court from an independent agency of the executive branch of the government to a court of record. One immediate consequence of such a move would have been to bar CPAs from practicing before the court and even from petitioning the court to hear cases. As a matter of course, most CPAs had long since given up appearing without a lawyer in the trial of a case. But in view of the fact that fully 50 percent of the cases appealed to the court were settled before trial, accountants took the position that they should be permitted to handle the case until trial actually began.[25]

23. See above, p. 67.
24. "Report of the President, June 11, 1947," TSCPA.
25. "Minutes . . . May 31–June 1, 1948," TSCPA.

Texas accountants, having pioneered in setting up joint lawyer-CPA committees, applauded the move of the AICPA and the American Bar Association in 1950 in reconvening the 1944 National Conference of Lawyers and CPAs.[26] The "National Statement of Principles Relating to Practice in the Field of Federal Income Taxation" that issued from this meeting, however, was endorsed with some reluctance by the Texas Society. A major stumbling block was paragraph five of the statement, which prohibited CPAs from designating themselves as "tax experts" or "tax consultants." The statement included the provision that lawyers were similarly "prohibited by the canons of ethics of the American Bar Association . . . from advertising a special branch of law practice," but there was no such proscription in the ethics of the Texas Bar Association, which led some accountants to fear that lawyers in Texas might avail themselves of this opportunity to make further inroads on tax work. It was also pointed out the ban on advertising did not apply to noncertified accountants and that substantial tax work might go to this group by default if CPAs tied their own hands. Underneath these specific objections was the feeling that the American Institute had not taken a firm enough stand in these negotiations because the large national firms, prominent in the affairs of the institute, were more interested in audit work than tax business, whereas, in Texas "the most important part of public accounting . . . is in connection with tax work." These objections were finally overcome after considerable persuasion by William Aikman and other members of the Society's Committee on Cooperation with the Bar.[27] At the annual meeting in Galveston in June, 1951, the Texas Society ratified the statement.

The feeling that accountants had come off second best in their negotiations with lawyers came to the surface again in 1953. Mark Eaton, chairman of the Committee on Cooperation with Lawyers, reported to the Board of Directors on the eve of the annual meeting in June that CPAs were still divided on the statement. One group, he said, was encouraged that no punitive action against accountants had been taken since the national statement was ratified and that nothing should be done to upset the arrangement. On the other hand, there was a strong feeling, which his committee shared, that the statement was inadequate

26. A copy of the "National Statement of Lawyers and CPAs" and a copy of the 1945 "Statement" issued by the Texas State Conference of Lawyers and Certified Public Accountants is found in *Texas Accountant* 24 (Jan., 1952).

27. "Minutes . . . June 10–12, 1951," TSCPA.

as a point of reference for tax practice. It imposed limitations on the CPAs and it lacked a statement outlining and justifying the CPAs' proper place in tax practice. Owing to this state of affairs, a considerable number of CPAs believed that in carrying out their tax engagements they were to some extent actually practicing law. Claiming a "strong undercurrent of events is running against the CPA in the tax field," Eaton added: "This group is alarmed by the continuing fee suits in which unauthorized practice is plead against the CPA; at the comments of a militant nature that continue to be made by lawyers in bar journals and elsewhere; at the new practice of bar associations of distributing the Statement of Principles to meetings of lawyers without an accompanying document which justified the CPA's position more clearly; and by the attitude of some state bar associations when they sit down to deal with CPAs at that level."

All efforts to have the American Institute formulate a more positive statement for accountants had failed, Eaton observed. Therefore, he recommended that the Texas Society draft a unilateral statement to "explain and justify the CPA's position in tax practice . . . and dispel in the minds of any CPAs who had such opinions, any notion that in performing their traditional tax work they are engaged in the practice of law." Such a document would also "serve as evidence to non-CPAs that the certified public accountant has something to say for himself in support of his present position." His committee, Eaton emphasized, did not "suggest that lawyers be asked to approve it nor do we think such approval is necessary."[28]

The extent to which the committee reflected the views of the membership of the Texas Society is not known. It must be surmised, however, that most members were reluctant to press their case, for no further action was taken on the committee's recommendation.

The Texas Conference of Lawyers and CPAs, appointed in 1952, was not called into its first session until October 15, 1955. By that time, the tensions over federal tax practice had subsided and Frank L. Wilcox, spokesman for the CPAs, reported that the bulk of the conference's time was taken up with discussing problems relating to the employment of attorneys by accounting firms, the employment of CPAs by attorneys, and the status of the person who was both lawyer and CPA.[29]

28. "Report of the Committee on Cooperation with Lawyers, 1952–1953," TSCPA.
29. "Report of the Committee on Joint Conference of Lawyers and CPAs, 1955–1956," TSCPA.

## Public Relations

Strained relations with the legal profession and persistent efforts by noncertified accountants to water down the provisions of the public accountancy act led the Texas Society membership to look upon its public relations activities in a new light. If the profession was to defend itself successfully in the political arena and possibly in the courts, it needed much greater acceptance and approval by the general public. John Carey, speaking for the Council of the American Institute in 1947, stated the problem in this manner: "The profession is faced with conflicts and critical attitudes which may seriously impair its opportunity to be of maximum service . . . if it does not have the support in legislatures and in other influential circles which can come only from public confidence."[30]

To this end, Hatcher Pickens and the Public Relations Committee argued in 1948 that the profession's "Challenge No. 1" was to "inform a public that doesn't know." "We need a public," Pickens said, "which has a clear knowledge of the scope of our essential work, and which will realize that a future restriction of that scope will not be for the general good. We need a public which believes that the CPA's thorough education, training and experience in his field have qualified him to know when it is to the client's benefit to call for the services of representatives of other professions, and that he never hesitates to do so when the requirement is indicated." The Fort Worth accountant then added: "We need a public which . . . will take a strong stand for us in situations where our own statements may be discounted to some extent on the ground of self-interest." Finally, he made it clear that the profession must avail itself "of every effective, dignified medium of contact with those whose attitudes affect the profession's future. And that includes the man on the street."[31]

Taking the lead in gaining the public's confidence and support, the American Institute prepared a series of institutional advertisements explaining the profession's role in the modern economic order. State societies were then invited to sponsor and underwrite the expense of pub-

30. John L. Carey, "Institutional Advertising of Public Accounting," *Texas Accountant* 19 (Nov., 1947): 8.
31. Hatcher Pickens, "The CPA's Challenge No. 1," *Texas Accountant* 20 (April, 1948): 5.

lication within each society's jurisdiction. Carey recognized an "intuitive antipathy to paid advertising on the part of many accountants," but the "trend of recent events" outweighed the criticisms and justified the "use of the quickest and most direct means of communication to the public." "There is nothing unethical in institutional advertising," he advised, "which does not attempt to sell the services or attainments of any individual or group of individuals, but rather attempts to convey information which it feels is beneficial to the public to have."[32]

This explanation did not satisfy some Texas accountants. Percy W. Pogson, CPA since 1909 and a Texas certificate holder since 1918, felt such an advertising program would wipe out the gains of thirty or forty years' work in which the profession had tried to build on the basis of "honesty, ability and conscientious work." "I suppose I am out of tempo with modern times," Pogson added, "but I do worry a little about our professional future if its success must depend on advertising as though we were selling soap or cigarettes."[33]

Pogson represented a minority point of view. The Society, convinced of the dignity and value of the project, set a goal of $15,000 to defray the costs of running six full-page advertisements in state newspapers and trade journals. Although it was difficult to measure the effectiveness of institutional advertising, the results seemed to be very discouraging. A poll showed few people read the advertisements.[34] The Society did not repeat this form of public relations for three decades.

The failure of the institutional advertising program brought the Public Relations Committee back to its more traditional moorings. Under the chairmanship of Fladger Tannery in 1951–1952, the committee laid down a number of long-range objectives. The program was in two parts: the education of members, and the education of the public. For members, the committee recommended one chapter meeting of the year be used to acquaint accountants with the philosophy and meaning of good public relations and to outline the ways and means by which individual members could make their own contribution in this field. It was suggested a public relations professional be secured to speak and direct the discussion on this occasion. The committee also advised

32. Carey, "Institutional Advertising."
33. Letter from Percy W. Pogson reprinted in *Texas Accountant* 20 (April, 1948): 5.
34. Hatcher A. Pickens to author, Dec. 19, 1958.

chapters to devote fewer of their monthly meetings to technical subjects and more to programs that would "create a closer working relationship with business men, government officials, and members of other professions."[35] A statement entitled "The CPA and Public Relations" was also distributed to the Society membership, and a six-page brochure entitled "The CPA in Texas" was prepared as the foreword in the 1952–1953 Society directory.

For the education of the public, the Society distributed copies of a booklet entitled "Some of the Big Problems of Small Business." Plans to send out reprints of a *Kiplinger Newsletter* on the subject "What Accounting Can Do For You" were abandoned when local chapters showed little interest.[36] The committee further advised accountants to take a leading role in their local Community Chest drives and to contribute articles to trade and professional magazines. In addition, the chairmen of the chapter committees on public relations were urged to secure speaking engagements for CPAs, particularly during the tax season months of January and February. Finally, local chairmen were informed that the American Institute had available a program on taxation suitable for broadcast over local radio stations.

## Expanding Opportunities for Service

Both cause and effect of the unparalleled growth of the profession in Texas was the manner in which the state legislature turned to accountants for help in solving some of the pressing problems of governmental administration. In 1957 the Committee on Cooperation with State and Legislative Officials reported the passage of three separate bills which increased the demands upon accountants. One bill reorganized the Texas Insurance Commission and provided that the commission could use either its own examiners or "any holder of a permit . . . in public practice" to examine the financial condition of insurance companies operating in this state. The second required school districts to file a detailed financial statement with the State Board of Education. The third established the State Securities Board, which required information from Texas business corporations similar to that collected from

35. See "Public Relations Program for 1951–52," *Texas Accountant* 23 (Oct., 1951): 5–N9.

36. "Report of the Committee on Public Relations, 1951–1952," TSCPA.

national concerns by the SEC. In the case of each of these measures, special committees of the Society met with the appropriate state agency to give advice on implementation of the law. The magnitude of the job facing the profession was illustrated by the advice Don C. Chorpening passed on in the mid-year report of the committee in 1957–1958; accountants were asked to be patient with school districts, since only three hundred of some eleven hundred independent school districts in the state had ever submitted professional audits![37] The very important role the profession played in setting up the State Securities Board was recognized by the appointment of Jay Phillips to the board. "Prospects are," said Albert W. Caster, chairman of the Committee on Cooperation with State and Legislative Officials in 1956–1957, "that our Society may be called upon more and more to furnish aid to various state agencies in the improvement of their accounting procedures."[38]

## Responding to the Texas Insurance Crisis

In a class by itself was the extraordinary demand thrust upon the profession on December 29, 1955. For some months before that date the Texas insurance business had been rocked by a number of scandals. Public confidence in this industry had declined almost to the vanishing point, as company after company failed because of mismanagement or fraud. In action similar to that of Franklin D. Roosevelt in 1933 when a banking holiday was declared until all banks could be examined and the solvent ones permitted to reopen, the Texas Insurance Commission appealed to the profession to help in the emergency by conducting an independent audit of every Texas chartered insurance company. On January 3, 1956, Tannery, president of the Society, along with Chorpening and W. Boone Goode met with commissioners in Austin to set plans in motion implementing the commission's request. A special committee, headed by J. Raymond Jordan, prepared a bulletin entitled "Examination of Texas-Chartered Insurance Company Financial Statements by Independent Certified Public Accountants." This bulletin, released on February 15, 1956, served as a guide for the work ahead.

37. "Mid-Year Report of the Committee on Cooperation with State and Legislative Officials, 1957–1958," TSCPA.
38. "Report of the Committee on Cooperation with State and Legislative Officals, 1956–1957," TSCPA.

Forums were also held in Fort Worth, Dallas, Houston, and San Antonio to familiarize some 350 certified and noncertified accountants with the material. Texas accountants were then asked to examine over twelve hundred insurance companies chartered by the state.

The insurance examination program was not altogether successful.[39] It would have been difficult to complete under the most desirable conditions. These did not exist, Tannery said later, noting it "was an emergency measure conceived in an atmosphere of disturbed public sentiment. . . . The insurance industry as a whole did not accept it. . . . The Texas Insurance Department was not organized for such a program, and contrary to our advice . . . the commissioners attempted the program without qualified manpower to direct it and to analyze and appraise the significance of the opinions expressed by the accountants." These circumstances "encouraged the use of 'short cut' methods and subterfuges in complying with the directive." As a result, some opinions were filed by persons without legal authority to practice public accountancy in Texas, and others by accountants who were directors, employees, or stockholders of the insurers and therefore unqualified to render an independent opinion. Over the Society's specific protests, the commissioners accepted "affidavits of accountants" in lieu of the accountant's opinion. A number of opinions were prepared under conditions suggesting the absence of "sufficient information to warrant the expression of an opinion."[40] On the whole, however, the spirit in which the profession entered into this program even under trying conditions was commendable. And in spite of these almost inevitable shortcomings of a crash program, Tannery was awarded a special plaque in recognition of his leadership in the emergency.

## Professional Ethics and Society Discipline

Both the insurance audits and the reports filed with the Texas Securities Board unearthed evidence of substandard work by Society members. A number of statements were prepared in which unprofessional terminology was used. Certain desirable auditing standards were

39. J. Raymond Jordan expressed the view that the program was "not as successful as the profession had hoped" (Jordan to author, Dec. 3, 1958). Curtis H. Cadenhead described it as "definitely not a success" (Cadenhead to author, Dec. 29, 1959).

40. "Report of Special Committee on Accounting Legislation Terminology for Legislative Drafters, June 3, 1957," TSCPA.

not observed in others. On one occasion, a statement was changed by the accountant after inquiry by the commission. Still worse, reports were filed by accountants who were officers or directors of the reporting corporation.[41] The revelation of this kind of accounting work performed by CPAs led the Committee on Long-Range Objectives and Planning to observe that it was "the opinion of many that the heaviest brake on our professional progress is the vast amount of sub-standard work being performed in Texas. Too many CPAs lack either the knowledge of or the will to live up to present day standards of practice."[42]

These deficiencies involved perhaps no more than 1 or 2 percent of the membership of the Society. The Society moved promptly, however, to discipline those who were wilfully violating this cardinal rule of professional ethics and to impress upon all others the need for maintaining proper standards. President Robert J. Hibbetts made "professionalism" the theme of his administration in 1957–1958. An even more salutary effect was achieved when the Committee on Professional Ethics began to enforce the rules more rigorously. Twenty-four members were called before the committee in an investigation of the insurance reports alone. In most cases, the committee discovered, the mere act of pointing out the deficiency to the guilty party was enough to correct the situation. Eight cases were carried to the trial board, however, resulting in penalties that ranged from reprimands and short suspensions to the expulsion of three members of the Society.[43] This pattern of enforcement continued into the early 1960s and began to attract attention outside professional and financial circles. The widely publicized collapse of the Billie Sol Estes financial empire focused attention on improper auditing by a Texas Society member, and the difficulties of the Farnsworth Chambers construction company in Houston involved a Society member who, as a corporate official, filed false and fraudulent corporate income tax returns. In all, eight members of the Society were expelled between 1957 and 1963.[44] The willingness to keep its own house in order through proper discipline was one of the Society's most signifi-

41. "Minutes . . . July 14, 1957," TSCPA.
42. "Report of the Committee on Long Range Objectives and Planning, 1958–1959," TSCPA.
43. See "Mid-Year Report of the Committee on Professional Ethics, 1957–1958," and also *Texas Certified Public Accountant* 20 (Feb., 1958).
44. "Report of the Committee on Professional Ethics, 1958–1959," and "Report of the Trial Board, 1958–1959, 1959–1960," TSCPA.

cant achievements and a factor, no doubt, in the state's escaping some of the trauma associated with the problems of the profession nationally in later years.

The gravity of the problems involving substandard and unethical practices prompted President Kenneth Hurst to propose in 1963 that, as an educational program, applicants for membership in the Society take an examination on professional ethics. After considerable discussion, the Society worked out a cooperative plan with the Texas State Board of Public Accountancy whereby the State Board, beginning in the spring of 1965, distributed a questionnaire on professional ethics to successful candidates for the state certificate immediately following their completion of the examinations. When returned to the State Board, the questionnaires were reviewed by an ad hoc committee of the State Board and the Society, and in those cases where the new CPAs scored low on the questionnaire, members of the Society undertook the burden of visiting with and bringing the new members up to date on the ethics of the profession.

## New Directions in Education

The ethics questionnaire was but one evidence of the interest the Society has had in professional education. The inauguration of the annual tax institute in 1954, the formation of the Educational Foundation in 1957, and the creation of the Professional Development Council in 1964 amplified that concern and provided a preview of the dramatic support the Society provided preprofessional and continuing professional education in more recent times.

The idea of a tax institute was first broached in 1949, but five years elapsed before the first program, under the chairmanship of Raymond Jordan, was held in Houston in 1954. Even then, the Society as a whole lagged a year behind the East Texas Chapter, which, in 1953, invited CPAs from Texas and neighboring states to an institute in Tyler. Under the direction of Robert Knox, the Tyler event attracted more than 500 participants and spurred the state society into action. The next year more than 700 persons registered for the institute on the campus of the University of Houston; the high enrollment encouraged Society officers to make it an annual affair.[45] The university continued to serve as host

45. "Institute on Taxation: Report . . . December 4, 1954," TSCPA.

through 1963, when the attraction of better facilities downtown prompted a move. Gradually declining attendance at the Houston location also led the Society in 1964 to conduct identical sessions in Dallas at the conclusion of the Houston meeting. The result was an upswing in attendance, from 275 in 1963 to 540 in 1964.

The Educational Foundation, created to make loans from a revolving fund to worthy college students in accounting, got underway with Mothershead serving as the first president and Phillips as the chairman of the initial fund-raising committee. With relatively little fanfare, the foundation accepted its first application for a loan from Ervin C. Moore in December, 1959. While formal loan procedures were still being worked out, Walter Flack and Kenneth Hurst each advanced Moore $75, enabling him to pay his overdue tuition bill at Stephen F. Austin State College.[46] By April, 1963, thirty-one students had received loans, the total amount exceeding $17,000. Over the next two years an additional thirty students qualified for assistance. The foundation's fund balance exceeded $30,000 at that time, reflecting the fact that twenty-two of the loan recipients had repaid their loans in full. Pleased and encouraged by the response to the loan program, trustees in April, 1965, embarked upon a campaign to publicize the foundation's activities and to liberalize its loan policies. The success of the campaign was immediate; within three months, twenty-eight new applications, double the number received the preceding twelve months, were under review, and the need for additional funds was apparent. At the request of foundation president Stanley Scott and his fellow trustees, the Society authorized a new fund-raising program and readily agreed temporarily to underwrite the student loan program with Society funds until the foundation could catch up with the new demands being placed upon it.

The Texas Society's Professional Development Committee encouraged members to attend AICPA-sponsored programs on technical and professional subjects in addition to the tax institute and the technical sessions at annual state meetings. President Scott in December, 1961, pointed out that Texas led the nation in 1960 with 288 members attending AICPA programs. The next year the number dropped to 152, and California, with 517 attendees, took the lead. Scott interpreted the Cali-

---

46. Kenneth W. Hurst, president of the foundation in 1961, to Heloise Brown Canter, Dec. 18, 1961, copy in possession of author.

fornia Society's surge of participation to the presence of a full-time professional development director on its staff. He encouraged the Texas Society to do the same, adding that the California experience indicated that the costs of the program could be supported from course fees and therefore not be a drain on the state society's budget. The Executive Committee approved Scott's request, whereupon he appointed Homer Luther to chair the committee that selected Forrest R. Black to be the Society's first professional development director.[47]

Forrest Black was a native of Florida with a bachelor's degree from Duke University and master's degree from Columbia University School of Business. He had been a naval officer for three years and had worked for Mississippi Power and Light in advertising and public relations and, most recently, for Air Reduction Company in sales and marketing. He reported for work in December, 1962, spending the first several days of his employment in New York becoming acquainted with the professional development staff of the AICPA.

The level of professional development activity picked up noticeably after Black's arrival. A year-end report to the Executive Committee in June, 1964, noted a total of 52 professional development courses attended by 1,796 persons in the fiscal year just ended, a budget surplus instead of the predicted financial deficit, and a claim that Texas again led all other state societies in the presentation of AICPA courses.[48]

Meanwhile, earlier in March, outgoing President Hurst and incoming President Gordon George put into operation the Professional Development Council, which for more than a decade set professional development policy for the Society. As formally approved by the Board of Directors in June, 1964, the Professional Development Council consisted of six members, each serving three-year terms, who were responsible for the development, promotion, presentation, and administration of all Society activities in this area, including the tax institute, state conferences, workshops, and seminars. Chaired by Erwin Heinen, the first council included Glenn A. Welsch, Lionel E. Gilley, Mothershead, James F. Dunn, Jr., and Scott. The good work of the council was reflected in its first annual report in June, 1965: sixty courses, a record high number, generated $85,000 in course registration fees.[49] Also of

47. "Minutes . . . Board of Directors, December 2, 1961," TSCPA.
48. "Minutes . . . Executive Committee, June 19, 1964," TSCPA.
49. "Minutes . . . Executive Committee, June 18, 1965," TSCPA.

special note, the tax institute drew 553 registrants at the combined Houston and Dallas locations. The fact that each chapter in the state sponsored at least two seminars during the year gave further evidence of the membership's broad-based interest in professional development activities as the Texas Society concluded its first half-century.

# 7

## Internal Problems of a Maturing Society, 1945–1965

THE growth in the number of CPAs in Texas during the first two decades after World War II provided the Texas Society a pool of prospective members that allowed for steady expansion. In 1945, the Society counted 640 members, a figure that more than doubled by 1950 (1,485) and was approximately four times as large (2,420) by 1955. Active membership committees advanced the percentage of certificate holders belonging to the Society from roughly 70 percent in 1945 to 80 percent twenty years later. The hoped-for goal of "5,000 in '65" was not attained until 1967, but the membership base achieved during the 1950s and early 1960s permitted the Society to put into place an administrative structure and professional staff that responded effectively to the challenges of the moment and has stood the Society in good stead in more recent times.

### Development of the Society Staff

The rate at which the Society grew after 1945 and the additional pressures to which the profession was subjected created a need for a full-time executive director. Even with additional office help, it became increasingly clear that Tom Leland, secretary-treasurer from 1938 to 1954, could not do justice to both his teaching responsibilities at the A&M College and to the Society. As early as June, 1949, the Board of Directors heard a resolution from the Austin Chapter that a person be employed full time to run the Society office. Coming at a time when CPAs were under heavy attack in the legislature from noncertified accountants, the resolution specified the Society office be located in Austin, where "additional time and effort should be given to maintaining legislative contacts and relations."[1]

1. "Minutes . . . June 5, 1949," TSCPA.

This matter was discussed for several years, President Curtis H. Cadenhead (1951–1952) supporting it with great vigor throughout his incumbency. Reports from the chapters in December, 1952, reflected renewed interest and enthusiasm.[2] In June, 1953, a special committee headed by Frank Wilcox recommended that the post be created and offered to Leland, who, if he accepted, could maintain his office either in College Station or Austin. Should Leland decline the offer, the committee suggested a person with some public relations experience be hired. A $30,000 annual budget based upon a dues structure ranging from $7.50 to $17.50 was deemed adequate to finance this expanded operation.[3] The stamp of approval was placed on this report, and it fell the lot of the Mark Eaton administration to put the plan into operation. Leland removed himself from consideration for the post, stating that he preferred to remain on the faculty of the A&M College. The Board of Directors then met in Dallas on July 11, 1953, decided that Dallas should be designated the "headquarters city," and directed the executive committee to proceed with the selection of personnel. On October 1, 1953, Dan Dansby, Jr., took over as the Society's first executive director.

Dansby, whose background ranged from professional stage work to organizational and personnel work with trade associations, came to the Texas Society from the post of field director for the National Tax Equality Association. Born and reared in North Texas, he attended the University of Texas and was graduated from East Texas State Teachers College. He was selected primarily for his ability to organize and coordinate the housekeeping functions of the Society, to keep lines of communication open to all members, to edit the *Texas Accountant*, and in sundry ways to see that the Society offices functioned properly. These services he performed well. Facing a new and difficult assignment, he deserved much credit for the contribution his management of Society affairs made to its progress over the next four years. He spent several months in College Station becoming familiar with Society operations before the offices were moved to the Mercantile Commerce Building in Dallas.[4]

Dansby remained with the Society until June, 1957. By that time

2. "Minutes . . . December 13, 1952," TSCPA.
3. "Report . . . Committee on Appointment of Full-Time Director, May 4, 1953," TSCPA.
4. Dan Dansby to author, April 18, 1959.

the initial problems of organization were solved, and some members felt that an accountant should direct Society affairs, whereupon the executive committee chose Lod C. Allison to succeed Dansby. Allison was born and reared in Corsicana, Texas. He attended the University of Texas for two years and studied accounting at Dallas College and from LaSalle Extension University. His accounting experience began when he was employed by the Lone Star Gas Company and then, in 1940, as deputy collector in the IRS. He remained with the IRS until he passed the CPA examination in November, 1949. Shortly thereafter he went into public practice and opened a Dallas office for the Fort Worth firm of LaRue, Lawrence, Wood & Kelly. He became active in Dallas Chapter and Texas Society affairs and was appointed chairman of the Committee on Cooperation with Other Organizations by President Fladger Tannery in 1955.[5] In this role Allison demonstrated an ability to work with people and a good sense of public relations. These qualities as well as his experience in private, government, and public accounting commended him for the position, which the executive committee offered him in December, 1956, and which he assumed six months later.

Allison remained executive director of the Texas Society for three years. He resigned to reenter public practice in August, 1960. A careful search to name his successor resulted in the selection of thirty-four-year-old Clifton W. Fichtner in June, 1961. A veteran of the naval service in World War II, Fichtner came to the Society from the National Association of Accountants (NAA), where he served as manager of the member relations division. In that capacity, he led the membership activities of a national organization with fifty thousand members and 175 separate chapters. Prior to his experience with the NAA, he was the western division manager of National Sales Executives, experience that also prepared him for his duties with the Texas Society. Fichtner was born and reared in Arkansas and attended Ohio Wesleyan and Oberlin before graduating from Harvard in 1948.[6]

Fichtner inherited an office staff that consisted of himself, two other permanent employees, and a part-time student helper who operated the addressograph and mailing machines. Compared with other state societies, the Society was woefully understaffed. Texas ranked third behind

5. Lod C. Allison to author, April 18, 1959.
6. Clifton W. Fichtner to author, Nov. 1, 1961.

New York and California in society membership, but New York, with a membership of 11,524 and a staff of eighteen, had a staff-to-member ratio of 1 : 640, and California, with 5,500 members and fifteen staff, had a ratio of 1 : 367. Texas, with a membership of 3,681, had a ratio of 1 : 1,227. Impressed with these statistics, the Society leadership authorized four new staff positions over the next eighteen months; Forrest R. Black was designated director of professional development and Dorothy R. Smith, office manager. Fringe benefits that included medical insurance and a pension plan were also established for staff employees by December, 1964.

Meanwhile, Fichtner resigned his position in June, 1964, to return to a higher job with the NAA. Outgoing President Hurst named an ad hoc committee of six former presidents to recommend Fichtner's successor, and on August 12, 1964, President George appointed William H. Quimby to the position. Thirty-three years of age, Quimby came to the Society from a twelve-year career in county government and chamber of commerce work. His most recent position had been assistant general manager of the Fort Worth Chamber of Commerce. Quimby was born in New Hampshire, but he was reared in New Mexico and graduated from Stanford University with a BBA degree.

Quimby and Black, who left the Society in 1976 and 1975, respectively, and Smith, who has remained, were staff leaders during a decade of rapid growth and great change. Quimby and Smith were elected honorary members of the Society in recognition of their services.

## Debate over Location of Society Offices

Coincident with Dansby's departure in 1957, there occurred the first of several attempts to move the Society offices to Austin. The support some South Texas chapters gave the move created overtones of a tug-of-war between Houston and Dallas accountants. Unable to reach a decision in June, the Board of Directors instructed the new Executive Committee to make a recommendation in December at the mid-year board meeting. There, with only eight members, the committee reported that it was hopelessly deadlocked, whereupon the pros and cons were debated by the full board.

Austin, it was argued, had the advantage of being more centrally located than Dallas and of being the home of the Texas State Board of Public Accountancy and several other state bureaus and commissions with which the accounting profession had close contact. Austin was also the location of the University of Texas, which had the state's largest department of accounting. The legal and medical professions maintained headquarters there. It was neutral in any rivalry that might exist between Houston, Dallas, San Antonio, and Fort Worth, the four large cities in the state. The cost of maintaining an office, it was alleged, would be less expensive in Austin than in Dallas. Finally, some feared the "big firm" and "big town" ideas and policies of Dallas accountants would dominate Society affairs if the offices were not removed.

Dallas supporters noted the ease and convenience with which that city could be reached from all sections of the state. As a principal business and financial center, Dallas was home for a large number of accountants, from those who were running single-member firms to those staffing the city's nine national firms. The great number of Society members living in Dallas, it was pointed out, would make it easy for Society officers to find help in performing emergency jobs. Furthermore, Dallas held the headquarters for the Texas Bankers Association, the regional office of the Bureau of Internal Revenue, and the office of Eleventh Federal Reserve District, agencies as vital to the welfare of accounting as were the political offices located in Austin. It was argued that the Society would become less deeply involved in lobbying if located in Dallas; yet if it became necessary for Society officers to appear before legislative committees, they would be more effective coming to Austin from out of the city. Finally, other state societies with similar problems supported the contention that Texas Society offices should be located in the midst of professional rather than political activity.[7]

The vote was cast and Dallas won. Houston accountants took their defeat gracefully. When the Society moved to larger quarters in the Tower Petroleum Building in 1959, Homer Luther, a Houston accountant then serving as president, signed the five-year lease for office space.

## Expanding the Board of Directors

A number of administrative changes, other than the hiring of a full-time executive director, were made in the wake of the rapid in-

7. "Minutes . . . October 12–13, 1958," and "Minutes . . . December 7–8, 1958," TSCPA.

crease in members and duties of the Society. The most significant change occurred in 1952, when the Board of Directors was overhauled to provide proportional representation from the chapters. As reconstituted, the board consisted of the immediate past president, the four current officers (president, two vice-presidents, and secretary-treasurer), the presidents of each of the chapters, and five directors-at-large chosen at the annual meeting. In addition to the chapter president, each chapter was also entitled to one directorship for the first seventy-five members and one more directorship for each additional two hundred members. Two years later, in 1954, three more directors-at-large and all past presidents were added to the board.

With an initial membership of seventy to eighty persons—and committed to expansion as Society membership increased—the new Board of Directors found it difficult to act between annual meetings in an executive fashion. After two years the Society restructured the Executive Committee and empowered it to function in about the same way the old board performed in the 1930s. Composed of five members at the time (past president, president, two vice-presidents, and secretary-treasurer) and limited to powers specifically delegated to it by the Board of Directors, the Executive Committee was expanded to eight persons in 1954. This was accomplished by splitting the office of secretary-treasurer into two positions and adding two members from the Board of Directors chosen by the directors at their first meeting. In later years, the Executive Committee added two more vice-presidents (1959 and 1961) and the president elect (1961) and replaced the past president with an additional board member (1963). The addition of a fourth board member in 1979 raised the membership to twelve. Meanwhile, in 1959 the Executive Committee was empowered to act for the Board of Directors between board meetings.

## Strengthening the Chapters

Local chapters and the state society entered into a new relationship soon after the end of the war, chapters achieving a degree of independence in 1947 when the Society gave them permission to charge and collect local dues. More significantly, chapters were allowed to incorporate in 1959 and thereby contract for office space, hire secretarial help, and carry on other duties necessary to service a large and active membership. The Houston Chapter was the first to avail itself of this opportunity to incorporate in 1961, followed by the Dallas Chapter in 1967. By 1965 the Houston and Dallas chapters each listed 1,344 and 1,034 members, respectively, with the other chapters ranging downward in size as follows: Fort Worth (300), San Antonio (293), Austin (152), Panhandle (133), Permian Basin (133), East Texas (131), Lubbock (127), Corpus Christi (125), El Paso (115), Beaumont (80), Abilene (69), Central Texas (68), Rio Grande Valley (67), Wichita Falls (51), Victoria (37), and San Angelo (29).

While the Society granted chapters more latitude in the conduct of some of their affairs, it also put new emphasis on the coordination of chapter activities. Reporting for the Committee on Chapter Coordination in 1953, Homer Luther remarked that in recent years chapter bylaws had achieved uniformity, chapter boundaries were more clearly defined, fiscal years for the chapters were made identical with that of the Society, and chapter elections were brought into line with the annual meeting of the Society.[8] As noted above, chapter presidents became board members in 1954, and two years later Fladger Tannery inaugurated a president's conference to which all chapter presidents were invited. Later, when committee chairmen joined the group, it became a coordination conference.

The importance of chapter activities—and especially the key role the chapter president was coming to play in Society affairs—came under the scrutiny of the Long-Range Objectives and Planning Committee in 1959. Acknowledging that the "face of the profession is presented to the public at the chapter level," Society leaders assigned one of the vice-presidents to be full-time chapter coordinator. "Your job is to motivate, but not irritate!" the committee told Robert Knox in 1960, explaining further that he was to assist the chapters in improving their organization and operation and at the same time to coordinate chapter efforts to carry out the total Society program.[9]

Both the need for and the results of this special effort were reflected in Knox's first annual report in 1961. Reflecting upon the fact that when he began his assignment in 1960 several chapters had no programs planned for the coming year, most had never invited public accountants and state legislators to be guests at monthly meetings, and

8. "Report . . . Committee on Chapter Coordination," TSCPA.
9. Quoted in "Chapter Coordination Annual Report, 1960–1961," TSCPA.

eight of the chapters had held no more than two professional development seminars, Knox was pleased to report that during the intervening twelve months chapters held a total of 170 monthly meetings attended by 7,497 members and 1,875 guests. More importantly, chapters put on approximately fifty professional development seminars and meetings.[10] The momentum generated in 1960–1961 continued under Gordon George's coordination efforts in 1961–1962, chapters reporting approximately seventy professional development seminars that year. "Let us recognize that the chapter presidents are indeed the key men in this Texas Society," George wrote, "the men that hold this Society together and have the greatest part in implementing the program, aims and objectives of the Society, as conceived by its officers and committees."[11]

## Realigning Committees

With thirty-five to forty standing and special committees functioning within the Society by the mid-1950s, supervision of their activities, as with the chapters, became a major problem—even when, as Mark Eaton did on one occasion, the chairman makes a "full report of the extent to which this committee has not performed its duties."[12] A manual on committee structure and functions adopted in 1958 brought about some order by grouping committees under five headings, each group responsible to a coordinating officer from the Executive Committee. In 1963–1964 a distinguished Committee on Long-Range Objectives and Planning, chaired by Robert Hibbetts and composed of nine past or future presidents of the Society, recommended the clustering of twenty-four senior committees into four groups, as follows: Directive Group (Executive, Legislation and Long-Range Planning, Long-Range Objectives and Planning, Professional Ethics); Professional Development Group (Professional Studies, Accounting and Auditing Procedure, Taxation, Management Services); Relations Group (Bankers, Bar, Educational Institutions, State Administrative Officials, State Securities Board, Other Organizations, Public Relations); and Administrative Group (Admissions, Annual Meetings, Awards, By-Laws, Committee Appointments, Editorial Advisory, Membership, Members Insurance,

10. Ibid.
11. "Chapter Coordination Annual Report, 1961–1962," TSCPA.
12. "Digest of Committee Reports, 1947–1948," TSCPA.

Resolutions). It fell to Presidents Kenneth Hurst and Gordon George to implement these changes, which were accomplished by 1965.

While streamlining the committee structure for better internal communications, the society also changed its publications program to improve lines of communication with the rank-and-file membership. The *Texas Accountant*, renamed the *Texas Certified Public Accountant* in 1954, became a technical bimonthly publication in 1959, and a companion piece, the *Texas CPA News Bulletin*, appeared on alternate months. A formal history of the Society published in 1962 also gave perspective to its activities.

By 1965 the Society had established a number of honors and awards by which it recognized achievement and contributions to the profession. The oldest of these was honorary membership, reserved for persons outside the regular membership who distinguished themselves within the profession. In 1938 the Society inaugurated the order of honorary fellow for Society members who distinguished themselves within the profession and their community. An award for Meritorious Service to the Public Accounting Profession in Texas first appeared in 1953. In 1958, the Society established the Distinguished Public Service Award for members actively engaged in community, charitable, and civic activities that reflect favorably on the Society and the profession.[13]

As the Society approached its fiftieth anniversary, it became necessary to update its original articles of incorporation, which were due to expire in 1965. This was done at the annual meeting in June, 1964. It would be unfair to the original founders of the Society to read too much into the amended charter, but it is suggestive of the growth and maturity of the Society to note that in 1915 the purposes of the Society were described as "educational, literary and scientific," whereas in 1964 they asserted: "The Texas Society of Certified Public Accountants is established to promote and maintain high professional and moral standards; to advance the profession of accountancy by research and cooperation with other organizations of professional accountants; to protect the interests of its members and of the general public; and to act in a representative capacity for the profession." While the amended articles left unchanged the names of the Society's five original founders, they did extend the life of the Society into perpetuity, change the "place of

13. See Appendix B.

business" from Fort Worth to Dallas, increase the minimum number of directors to "not less than twenty-five," and list as "resident agent" Stanley Scott, whose name was used in place of Executive Director Clifton Fichtner, who had just resigned.[14]

## Presidential Leadership, 1945–1965

Confronting the problems of a rapidly expanding organization, presidents of the Texas Society between 1945 and 1965 came to appreciate in a special way the comments retiring president Mark Eaton directed to his successor, Hatcher Pickens, at the annual meeting in 1954. Eaton complimented Pickens on the high honor the Society had paid him, but he warned there were a "few small duties" that came with the office. The job actually began "six months ago," Eaton explained, "when the nominating committee brought in your name." After that, Pickens was put in the channel of Society correspondence, Eaton told the audience, and began to spend long hours with an advisory committee on appointments. Now that he was installed in the office, he was told that "your Texas Society mail can be handled in two or three hours a day, and will require no more than two-thirds of the time of a stenographer." The mail must be kept up with "or you will not see the top of your desk again during your term of office. This . . . will make it impossible for you to take a vacation," Eaton commented, "but we know you will be glad to forego that pleasure until next year."

Eaton gave Pickens carte blanche authority to use his own judgment when novel situations arose. "Some of us will be pretty mad at you sometimes. Don't pay any attention to this. Just go ahead and do what we would tell you to do if we knew what we were talking about." In the event of a conflict between Society business and his own practice, Pickens was admonished: "We want to be particularly clear on this point. The Society cannot be successfully operated by officers who neglect its business to take care of their own. You simply must make some arrangements to keep your own business from distracting your attention." There was "one more point," Eaton said. "There will be some trifling expenses for travel, stenographic help, postage, long-distance calls, entertainment, etc. Our budget contains no provision for such

14. "Minutes . . . Board of Directors, June 20, 1964," TSCPA.

expenses. We feel sure that you will want to relieve us of any embarrassment on this score by cheerfully absorbing your own costs. We offer no estimate of what the total may be. It will be best, perhaps, if you acquire this information gradually." Pickens was then left with this comforting thought: "You may feel that you won't enjoy any part of your term of office. But you will, Mr. Pickens, you will. In fact, you may never enjoy anything as much as you will the conclusion of your term of office."[15]

The first postwar president of the Texas Society, Laurence H. Fleck, was born on a ranch near Red Cloud, Nebraska, in 1898, but reared in Greenville, Michigan, and graduated from the University of Michigan in 1919. After two years of graduate study at Michigan, which included work with William P. Paton, Fleck joined the faculty of Southern Methodist University, where he developed the program in accountancy. A product of his own CPA coaching course, Fleck earned his certificate in 1926 and became active in Society affairs the following year. Also in 1927, he helped organize the Texas Association of University Instructors of Accounting. The year he was president of the Texas Society, he was appointed dean of the School of Business Administration at Southern Methodist University.

Fleck's successor, Roy L. Pope, worked part time for the Texas State Treasurer during the four years he studied engineering at the University of Texas. Within striking distance of his academic goal, he decided in 1927 against engineering as a career and turned instead to business management and accounting, most of his early accounting knowledge coming later from his experience as an officer with the Southwest Engraving Company and from university extension courses. In 1935 he passed the CPA examinations and in 1938 he began public practice in San Antonio in association with Eugene Howard, a noncertified practitioner. The firm developed a strong practice in municipal auditing. Pope, who died in 1973, was born in 1904 in Troup, Texas, but he graduated from nearby Tyler High School and took courses at Tyler Commercial College before enrolling in the University of Texas in 1924.

Clifton H. Morris, president in 1947–1948, first arrived in Fort Worth in 1916, twenty-two years of age and recently graduated from

15. "Minutes . . . Annual Meeting, June 20, 1955," TSCPA.

the University of Texas, where he studied accounting, only to be told by Daniel Kernaghan and Edward Archinard that he was "too young for public accounting." Thus rebuffed, Morris worked in the family retail lumber business in Marlin and served in the Quartermaster Corps during World War I. He returned to Fort Worth in 1920, however, and after working briefly with Roy M. Pitner and J. M. McTaggert & Co., he joined Y. Q. McCammon in 1922 to form what became one of the larger regional firms in the city. In 1961 the firm merged with Arthur Young & Company. Morris, who died in 1969, acquired CPA certificate number 191 in 1924 and later served six years on the Texas State Board of Public Accountancy.

Harry D. Hopson was born in Mart, Texas, in 1903, but he was reared in Fort Worth and graduated from the Fort Worth public schools. He worked for the city streetcar company and then a national construction firm, where he came to know a Scottish accountant, Tom McLaren, who later joined Peter & Moss in Dallas. Peter & Moss merged with Lybrand, Ross Brothers & Montgomery, and in 1931, through McLaren's influence, Hopson went to work in the firm's Houston office, which then was managed by T. W. Mohle. In 1935 Hopson successfully sat for the CPA examination and joined the Society. He left Lybrand's in 1940 and at the time he was president of the Society in 1948–1949, he was in partnership with J. G. Henslee. Later, in 1954, Hopson joined Phillips, Sheffield, Hopson, Lewis & Luther, now Deloitte Haskins & Sells.

In 1915, at age eighteen and a sophomore at the University of Oklahoma, Frank L. Wilcox moved to Waco, Texas, from his home state of Oklahoma to work as a bookkeeper for his uncle, the local office manager of a national brewery. Prohibition terminated that employment, and Wilcox worked at various jobs before joining Upleger & Falk in 1921. Largely by self-study and experience, Wilcox prepared for the CPA examination in 1923, receiving certificate number 141. He and N. A. Flood practiced together from 1923 to 1926, but thereafter Wilcox practiced alone until 1951, when Rowland D. Pattillo was admitted to partnership in Wilcox, Patillo & Company. Wilcox served on the Texas State Board of Public Accountancy from 1929 to 1939, and the year following his tenure as Society president he was elected vice-president of the American Institute. Wilcox died in 1977.

In 1950–1951, the Society turned again to one of the nonmetropolitan chapters for its president, fifty-five-year-old Ben M. Davis of Abilene. Davis, who died in 1981, was born and reared in the same Central Texas farming area south and west of Waco from which Jay Phillips came. Davis graduated from McGregor High School in 1911, then farmed and worked as a bookkeeper in Waco until 1917. He attended the army's first officers training camp at Leon Springs, served overseas during the war, and was discharged in 1919. In Dallas after the war, Davis worked in a nonaccounting job with the Veterans Bureau, but on the side he took the Pace Institute course and attended Laurence Fleck's CPA coaching course in order to pass the CPA examination in 1926. The following year he moved to Abilene and worked two years for a noncertified accountant before establishing his own firm, which is now a professional corporation, Davis, Kinard & Co., CPAs. Reading law on his own as he had studied accounting, Davis received a law license in 1934.

Curtis Cadenhead, president in 1951–1952, was born on a farm near Pittsburg, Texas, in 1904. He attended local public schools and secured a teaching certificate from East Texas State College in Commerce, after which he taught in and became principal of a rural school in Upshur County. After three years of teaching, but still in his early twenties, Cadenhead enrolled in the two-year accounting program at Eastman College in Poughkeepsie, New York, finishing in December, 1926. The following month he joined the Dallas office of Haskins & Sells, becoming a partner in the firm in 1948. Cadenhead delayed taking the CPA examination for ten years, receiving certificate number 606 in 1937, but once certified, he moved quickly into Society affairs.

John Raymond Jordan opened the Houston office of Price Waterhouse & Co. in 1938, and the year he was president of the Texas Society, 1952–1953, he became a general partner in the firm. Jordan was born in St. Louis, Missouri, in 1901, and he attended first St. Louis Academy and then St. Louis University, graduating with a degree in commercial science in 1924. He joined Price Waterhouse after college graduation and qualified for his Missouri certificate in 1928. His Texas certificate, number 666, was issued by reciprocity in 1938.

Few presidents made as lasting an impression as Marquis G. Eaton. His death in February, 1958, four years after his presidency of the Society and during the year following his presidency of the American Institute, cut short a productive and still-promising professional career.

Eaton was born in Hastings, Michigan, in 1898, but his family moved to Muskogee, Indian Territory, in 1900, and it was there he attended public school. He also attended Wentworth Military Academy before service in World War I, and following the war he enrolled in New York University School of Commerce, Accounts and Finance, lacking only eight credits of completing his degree. His business and professional career began first in the employment of former Oklahoma governor, Charles N. Haskell. He joined L. E. Cahill & Co. in Tulsa in 1928, moving to head the Oklahoma City office of Barrow, Wade, Guthrie & Company in 1931. While with Cahill, Eaton passed the CPA examination and received Texas certificate number 315 in 1929. He established his own consultation service in San Antonio in 1936 and in 1943 formed the partnership with Thornton C. Huddle that continued until his death. In addition to holding the profession's highest office, Eaton frequently contributed to professional journals, where he forcefully and effectively articulated the profession's position on major issues.

Hatcher Pickens, president of the Society in 1954–1955, was born in Lewisville, Texas, in 1898. His family moved to nearby Fort Worth in 1906, where Pickens attended public school. He took accounting courses at the University of Texas, but he graduated before the school had a formal major in accounting. He worked one year for a cotton firm and three years for Gulf Oil Corporation in Mexico before returning to Fort Worth in 1925. After a brief association with Ernst & Ernst, he joined the new firm of McCammon and Morris, becoming a partner in 1928 and joining the firm's merger with Arthur Young & Company in 1961. Receiving Texas certificate number 307 in 1929, Pickens later served as chairman of the Texas State Board of Public Accountancy and, in 1959–1960, vice-president of the American Institute.

Fladger F. Tannery was the first Society president to have an earned doctoral degree in accounting, the University of Texas having conferred the degree in 1940. Born in Birthright, Hopkins County, in 1905, Tannery was the son of a Methodist circuit-riding minister. He attended rural schools in North Texas before enrolling in Wesley College, a Methodist academy and junior college located in Greenville. He graduated from Wesley College in 1925 and then began teaching public school in West Texas during the year and attending Southern Methodist University and the University of Texas during the summer, receiving the BBA degree from the University of Texas in 1932. Tannery resided in Austin from 1933 until World War II, intermittently attending graduate school, working two years as first assistant state auditor, consulting for the State of Rhode Island and the Rockefeller Foundation, passing his CPA examination (1936, certificate number 532), and completing his doctorate. During World War II he headed up the Contract Audit Division of the U.S. Air Force and emerged from the service with the rank of colonel. In 1945, Tannery accepted the position of general auditor and then assistant controller of Humble Oil. He engaged briefly in the oil business on his own in 1952 but then joined the Dallas office of Arthur Young & Company. Following his term as Society president, Tannery became an executive with the Frito Company and, later, chairman of the board of Pepsico International.

The thirty-fifth president of the Society, Walter R. Flack of San Antonio, was born in 1908 and reared in Milburn, Oklahoma; he did not come to Texas until 1937. His educational background included a few prelaw courses at UCLA and the BBA degree from the University of Oklahoma in 1929. While a student at the university, Flack worked in the accounting operations of oil man Tom B. Slick. Following Slick's death, Carter Oil acquired some of the Slick interests, including Flack's services, but in 1937 Flack joined some of the old Slick group in forming Trans-Western Oil Company in San Antonio. Flack earned his Texas certificate number 766 in 1939 and thereafter moved gradually into public accounting, the break with Trans-Western being complete in 1944. Flack, who died in 1975, retained a strong interest in petroleum accounting, but he also expanded his practice into audit and tax work before merging with Alexander Grant & Company.

Robert J. Hibbetts of Amarillo was the first president elected from "the sparsely settled areas" of far West Texas, though the firm he represented, H. V. Robertson & Company, was one of the oldest in the state. Hibbetts was born in Mineola in East Texas in 1912, but he grew up in Austin and graduated from the University of Texas with BBA and MBA degrees during the depths of the Depression. Upon the recommendation of his professors, Hibbetts accepted a teaching position at Edinburg Junior College in 1934, and three years later he went to McMurry College in Abilene as assistant bursar and professor of accounting. He also had assignments with Ben M. Davis and Company in Abilene, and in 1938 he qualified for his CPA certificate. Hibbetts went to Canyon as professor of accounting at West Texas State College, where World War II interrupted his teaching career. Joining the U.S. Air Force in 1942, he was assigned to the Contract Audit Division commanded by Fladger Tannery. After the war, Hibbetts returned to West Texas and joined H. V. Robertson & Company, becoming a partner in the firm in 1948. Hibbetts's professional career began to turn full circle soon after he was president of the Society (1957–1958), as he became a charter member of the Committee of Accounting Faculty Associates of the University of Texas in 1959 and, upon his retirement from public accounting in 1978, returned to Austin to lecture in the University of Texas Department of Accounting. He also served a term on the Texas State Board of Public Accountancy from 1971 to 1977.

Homer L. Luther's father managed farm and ranch properties in several parts of Texas, which explains the fact that Luther, born in 1907 in the Central Texas town of Cleburne, began grade school at Goodnight in the Panhandle and finished high school at Palacios on the coast. He completed his formal education in 1929 with an accounting degree from the University of Texas. Luther's first job was in the accounting department of a mining company, followed in 1931–1937 by a staff position with Barrow, Wade, Guthrie & Co. During that time he earned CPA certificate number 465 in 1934. Luther became treasurer of an oil company in 1937 but returned to public practice in Houston in 1946. He merged his practice into Phillips, Sheffield, Hopson, Lewis & Luther in 1956, which firm, in turn, merged with Deloitte Haskins & Sells in 1963, where Luther practiced until his death in 1978. Luther was elected vice-president of the American Institute following his term as Society president.

W. Charles Woodard of Fort Worth, president in 1959–1960, was another in the long list of Oklahoma-born accountants who migrated to Texas. Born in Snyder, Oklahoma Territory, in 1904, Woodard attended local public schools and then worked in his father's drug store for four years before matriculating in the University of Oklahoma. He graduated in 1929 with a major in accounting and promptly joined the staff of L. E. Cahill & Company, where he became acquainted with two other future presidents of the Texas Society, Mark Eaton and Lyle R. Sproles. In 1933, Woodard joined Sproles in a new firm, currently Sproles-Woodard & Company, with offices in Fort Worth, Midland, and Odessa. Woodard received certificate number 786 in 1939. He was president of the Southern States Conference of CPAs in 1956–1957.

L. Ludwell Jones of Houston presided over the Society in 1960–1961. Jones was born in 1909 and, except for four years as a student at the University of Texas (1927–1931) and four years of professional experience in Austin early in his career, he has remained a resident of Houston. His first professional work was a year on the staff of the Texas state auditor in 1931 followed by three years in the Harris County auditor's office. He joined J. L. Block and Company shortly before he qualified for certificate number 697 in 1938. From 1940 until 1943, Jones was back in Austin as chief of the accounting division of the University of Texas auditor's office, but he returned to Houston in 1943 for two years with Arthur Andersen & Co. and, in 1945, a partnership in A. J. Farfel & Company, which carried over into a partnership in Peat, Marwick, Mitchell & Co. when the two firms merged in 1956. Jones also served on the Texas State Board of Public Accountancy from 1967 to 1974.

Stanley J. Scott, fortieth president of the Texas Society, 1961–1962, was born in San Antonio in 1918. His father was a Church of Christ minister who held pastorates in several parts of the state; Scott was living in Tyler at the time he graduated from high school in 1936. Encouraged by Tyler accountant Arthur Squyres, Scott enrolled in the University of Texas and received his BBA and MBA degrees by 1941. Having completed the course requirements for his graduate degree in December, 1940, Scott moved to Dallas and joined the staff of Fred F. Alford Company. While serving in the navy during World War II, Scott completed the requirements for the CPA and received Texas certificate number 966 in 1942. He rejoined Alford, Meroney & Company as a partner in 1946 and participated in the expansion of that firm to include offices in five Texas cities and one in New Mexico prior to its merger with Arthur Young & Company in 1980. Scott's professionalism also brought him the chairmanship of the American Institute in 1977 and appointment to the Texas State Board of Public Accountancy in 1981.

Jordan B. Wolf has the distinction of being the first graduate of Texas A&M University to serve as Society president (1962–1963). The college was well represented by faculty member Tom Leland during the Society's middle years, but Wolf, who studied under Leland and graduated in 1941, was the school's first alumnus to head the Society. He was also the first—and to date, the only—president chosen from El Paso, the westernmost city in Texas. Wolf was born in 1921 and reared in Lampasas. Upon graduating from A&M, he worked briefly with J. L. Block & Co. but within a year had begun a career-long association with Main & Co., now Main Hurdman. In 1945 his firm sent him on assignment to El Paso and three years later, in 1948, the same year he received his CPA certificate and joined the Society, the firm established an office in El Paso and named him a partner.

The East Texas Chapter furnished the next Society president, Kenneth W. Hurst of Tyler. Hurst, born in 1903, was originally from La Salle, Illinois, and graduated from the University of Illinois in 1926. He worked for private industry and a Chicago accounting firm, Requet, Bennington & Le Clair, until the end of the decade when, for health reasons, he moved to a drier climate in Oklahoma City. He practiced with H. E. Cole for two years before participating in a General Motors program of advising local dealers how to improve their auditing and management practices. The GM job took him in 1933 to Tyler, where, when the program terminated later that year, Hurst remained and began a public practice in association with Arthur Squyres and Co. He earned his CPA certificate in 1935 and thereafter became involved in Society affairs. Having taken ROTC in college, Hurst was called up for military service early in 1941. His wartime duties included extensive financial and auditing assignments and brought him into contact with Tannery and Hibbetts in the U.S. Air Force Contract Audit Division. Discharged a colonel in 1946, Hurst was called back in to military service during the Korean conflict and, except for a health problem, would have accepted a general's star and remained in the military. However, he returned to Arthur Squyres in 1952 and remained until 1956, when he became vice-president and controller of Brookshire Grocery Company. Holding this position in industry while Society president in 1963–1964, Hurst joined Walter Burer (1939–1941) as the first two members in industry to lead the Society.

The Texas Society ended its first half-century in 1964–1965 under the leadership of another army colonel, Gordon N. George of San Antonio. Born in 1918, George was the son of a noncertified public accountant who, in the 1920s, founded the San Antonio firm of George, Thrift and Cockrell. Having no intention of pursuing an accounting career, George majored in English and took one year of law at the University of Texas before accepting a commission in the army in 1940 that he held until 1965. Following extensive military service in Europe during World War II, George returned to civilian life and to college in 1946, enrolling for accounting courses first at the University of Texas and then finishing the BBA degree at St. Mary's in San Antonio. While enrolled at St. Mary's, George began work in his father's firm and then joined it full time. He earned his CPA certificate in 1955 and, as a partner in the firm, joined in the firm's merger with Ernst & Ernst in 1964. The following year he was made partner in charge of the San Antonio region, which included offices in Austin, Laredo, and Corpus Christi. In addition to his services to the Texas Society, George served eleven years on the Council of the American Institute before retiring from practice in 1978.

# 8

## *The Profession Under Attack: Standards, Education, and Ethics in the 1970s*

JOHN and Marlene Buckley, knowledgeable observers of contemporary accounting, wrote in the early 1970s that changes then occurring in the profession were as "significant as the emergence of record keeping in the fifth millenium BC, double-entry in the Renaissance, or corporate financial reporting and cost accounting as spin-offs of the Industrial Revolution over the past century."[1] Even allowing for an exaggeration of the importance of the immediate, it is nevertheless fair to say that urgent change was the most constant thing about accounting in the 1960s and 1970s.

During the 1940s and 1950s accounting optimistically assumed that time was on its side, but in the 1960s and 1970s the profession found itself under the gun, on the one hand from the courts and federal agencies, who criticized it for failing to eliminate negligence and sub-standard practice, and, on the other, from investors and creditors, who criticized it for failing to develop financial accounting and auditing standards that would give a comprehensive view of corporate practices and detect mismanagement. On yet another front, the Federal Trade Commission and the U.S. Department of Justice accused several professions, accounting included, of violating First Amendment rights and antitrust laws through their enforcement of rules of professional conduct restricting advertising and competitive bidding. A cross-section of leaders in 1978 noted the need for a responsible mechanism to address the profession's four most critical problems: setting accounting standards, maintaining auditor independence, improving the quality of accounting services, and defining the public accountant's role in mod-

1. John W. and Marlene H. Buckley, *The Accounting Profession* (Los Angeles: Melville Publishing Company, 1974), p. 127.

ern society. Once it reached a consensus on these matters, the profession could then handle subsidiary issues such as liability litigation, government intrusion into the setting of standards, the auditor's responsibility for detecting management fraud, the increasing concentration and dominance of national firms over regional and local practitioners, recruitment and retention of firm personnel, the recognition of specialties in accounting, and the accountant's need to reveal in financial statements and audits the impact of social and consumer legislation.[2]

The profession responded to its critics in several ways, holding firm in some areas but instituting changes in others. In their defense, accountants claimed that a consumer-oriented society unfairly expected information which audit reports and opinions were never intended to provide and that "strike" lawyers and uninformed juries harassed the profession with costly liability suits. Who was right and who was wrong was almost beside the point; the result was a rash of court cases accountants frequently lost or felt compelled to settle out of court, as well as a surfeit of newspaper reports and magazine articles unfavorable to the firms involved and to the profession as a whole.[3]

## AICPA Reports: Beamer, Wheat, Trueblood, and Cohen

While defending itself in court, the profession began a period of intensive self-study that produced three committee and one independent commission reports in the period 1969 to 1977. The first came in 1969 from the AICPA's Committee on Education and Experience Requirements for CPAs, chaired by Elmer G. Beamer. It called for increasing entry-level education requirements to include five-year collegiate programs in accounting with an emphasis on mathematics, statistics, communications, and computer technology. For practitioners already in the field, Beamer recommended a minimum continuing education program of forty hours per year. The second report emanated from a special

2. As reported in Part I of Stanley Charles Abraham, *The Public Accounting Profession: Problems and Perspectives* (Lexington, Mass.: Lexington Books, 1978), pp. 1–124.
3. See Abraham's references in ibid., pp. 157–63, for a sampling of the literature critical of accountants. More recently, Russell E. Palmer, managing partner of a national accounting firm, places events in the context of a revolt of the laity against all professions, not just accounting. See "Up in Arms Against the Professions," *Houston Chronicle*, Feb. 5, 1981.

committee established in 1971, chaired by Francis M. Wheat and charged with developing a new and faster method of setting accounting standards. Reporting in 1972, the Wheat committee prompted the establishment of a Financial Accounting Foundation funded by the profession and directed by a board of trustees which included lay members. The foundation, in turn, was charged with setting policy for the new Financial Accounting Standards Board (FASB), a permanent, professionally staffed successor to the Accounting Principles Board. The third committee, also established in 1971, was chaired by Robert Trueblood and charged with defining the objectives of financial reporting. While its recommendations, presented in 1973, involved no structural changes and was therefore less traumatic at the time, the Trueblood report attached great importance to social accounting and the need to design financial reports which provide a good basis for predicting future profitability.

Even after the landmark AICPA reports, criticism and confusion from within and without the profession persisted. In 1974, therefore, the AICPA invited Manuel F. Cohen, a former SEC commissioner, to head an independent Commission on Auditors' Responsibilities which would advise the profession and the public on such matters as the difference between accounting and auditing and the proper division of responsibility in preparing and publishing financial statements. Ranking with the Wheat report in importance, the Cohen commission report, released in 1977, represented a major step toward clarifying the profession's remaining problems.

## Congressional Inquiries: Moss and Metcalf

These reforms fell short of answering critics, however, especially when congressional committees chaired by Representative John Moss and Senator Lee Metcalf in the mid-1970s documented more than two hundred cases in which publicly held corporations made illegal kickbacks or questionable payments that went unreported by auditors. The charge by Moss and Metcalf was basically that accounting firms performing SEC work were more often client-oriented than they were concerned with protecting the public interest. To remedy the situation, they proposed that the federal government, through the SEC or a new regulatory body, impose "accurate" and "adequate" accounting standards and more closely oversee the activities of firms involved in SEC practice, oversight to include financial disclosures on the part of the firms. With its back to the wall, the AICPA in 1977 called for the division of CPA firms into two sections, one section mandated to include all firms practicing before the SEC and the other section made up voluntarily of firms in private practice. Once registered in either section, firms came under peer review and a quality-control program focusing on strengthened independence of auditors and professional staff development. The SEC section of firms also came under the scrutiny of an oversight board composed entirely of lay members who serve as watchdogs for the public.

By instituting these new measures—the division of firms, peer review, mandatory continuing professional education, and a public oversight board—the accounting profession demonstrated a good-faith effort to answer its congressional critics, and as a result, pressure for legislation declined. Meanwhile, by the end of the decade the AICPA rules of professional ethics relating to advertising and competitive bidding were first suspended and then repealed.

All in all, accountants weathered the traumatic 1970s rather well. While some are convinced accountancy is now more a business than a profession, most accountants were pleased to see the profession survive intact and free of federal control. They also felt that improvements in the formulation of principles and standards and the shoring up of technical standards, ethics, and work performance had largely restored public confidence in the independence of auditors and had clarified and enhanced the accountant's role in society.[4]

Whatever success the AICPA had in answering critics at the national level, the implementation of the Beamer, Wheat, and Trueblood committee reports and the division of firms depended, in varying degree, upon support from state societies, action by state boards, and, in the final analysis, acceptance by firms and practitioners. As the nation's third largest state accounting society, the Texas Society had an important role to play, and its response to the AICPA initiatives is a large part of the Society's recent history.

4. These sentiments, reflected in the professional literature, were also expressed to the author in his tape-recorded interviews with the past presidents of the Texas Society.

## Continuing Professional Education

The Texas Society anticipated the Beamer committee's recommendations concerning continuing education, having already in place a fulltime director and a Professional Development Council. Leading up to 1969, the Society developed a modest number of local programs, arranged to exchange programs with other societies, and shared the services of Forrest Black with the Louisiana and New Mexico societies. While attendance at professional development events leveled off at about three thousand persons in the late 1960s, this number was approximately 50 percent of Society membership, and the Board of Directors was informed in 1970 that only California—with an eleven-person professional development staff compared with two for Texas—had a more active and larger program. Directors were also assured that the program, budgeted at approximately $165,000, was operating at a "breakeven" level, allaying fears of some that fees were so high that the Society was making money at the expense of participants and the fears of others that the program was a drain on the Society. As President Miller Montag also noted on this occasion, the Society had begun to keep records of individual attendance at professional development seminars, primarily to aid Professional Development Council planning, but also to help the Executive Committee determine "whether we are educating the same or different people."[5]

The Beamer report and the AICPA's subsequent resolution of April, 1971, urging support for mandatory continuing education gave a new sense of urgency to the program in Texas. Beamer addressed the Society's annual meeting in June, 1971, after which President Frank Rea appointed Lloyd Weaver chairman of an ad hoc committee to (1) formulate an immediate response to the AICPA resolution and (2) develop long-range goals the Society should pursue in the whole matter of continuing education for CPAs in Texas. Serving with Weaver on the committee were J. Kenneth S. Arthur, Byron G. Bronstad, Willard L. Findling, John A. Killough, and Samuel H. Tannebaum.

The Weaver committee discharged its first obligation quickly. Unanimously endorsing the "concept of continuing education," the committee nevertheless thought the mandatory resolution was premature in view of the time—five to ten years—that would be required to

5. "Minutes . . . December 4–5, 1970," TSCPA.

change accountancy laws in the fifty states and to develop quality programs adequate to the increased demand. A voluntary program "with the expressed statement that it can be a prelude to a future required program would provide meaningful results in a relatively short period of time," the committee said. "Furthermore, such a program would provide a learning exercise in developing the machinery for required programs."[6]

The preparation of the long-range professional education goals for the Society took almost a year and involved the mailing of several questionnaires and the holding of public hearings in five cities around the state. Inquiries were also made into the actions of other states and into the continuing education requirements for lawyers and medical doctors in Texas. The evidence the committee collected from questionnaires revealed that virtually all CPAs thought well of continuing education, but only 57 percent favored manadatory requirements for Society membership, while only 48 percent thought it necessary for certificate renewals. At the public hearings, sentiment was two to one against mandatory education. Furthermore, it was reported, lawyers and doctors in Texas were not required to enroll in continuing education programs, and the experience of other states was discouraging to proponents of mandatory requirements. In pointed reference to the troubles of the times, the report noted "the extensive in-firm training programs and the professional development programs of the AICPA and the Texas Society are an indication of the positive approach taken to protect the public interest through education." But the committee saw "no connection between the rash of lawsuits against certain CPA firms and substandard work of a type which presumably would be corrected by continuing education requirements. Evidence available to the committee indicates that the major lawsuits against CPA firms have been against firms with the most sophisticated continuing education programs. The reason for these major lawsuits must, therefore, be found in areas other than in a form of incompetence which would be corrected by attending professional development courses." Taking a line from Alexander Pope: "Be not the first by whom the new are tried, nor yet the last to lay the old aside," the committee concluded, "mandatory education was nei-

6. "Interim Report of the Ad Hoc Committee on Required Continuing Education, July 14, 1971," TSCPA.

ther necessary nor helpful." It believed, however, the Texas Society "should ever continue to promote and expand its voluntary program of professional development," and also "should gather data on the voluntary continuing education undertaken by its members so as to make their accomplishments in this area more visible."[7]

The formal recommendations of the Weaver committee, adopted in June, 1972, called upon all members, in and out of public practice, to "voluntarily complete" and report twenty-four hours of acceptable continuing education course work beginning with the 1972–1973 Society year and to increase the number of hours to forty by 1974–1975.

Though Texas avoided mandatory continuing professional education during the 1970s, the voluntary program generated a surge of activity, from the 3,000 participants in Texas Society programs in 1973 to 5,700 in 1975; 10,000 in 1978; and 17,289 in 1982. Course offerings likewise expanded from 89 in 1973 to 174 in 1975, 271 in 1978, and 503 in 1982. The expenditures of the professional education program jumped from $180,000 in 1973 to $300,000 in 1975, $900,000 in 1978, and $2,843,000 in 1980. The expenditures for continuing professional education activities drew even with all other Society expenses about 1975; by 1982 they were twice as great. Little wonder then that Lawrence Pickens observed in 1978 that the Society's continuing professional education program might become "the tail that wags the dog."[8]

The Society accommodated the rapid growth of continuing professional education (CPE) but not without some stress and strain. Volunteer members of the council, renamed the Continuing Professional Education Council in 1975, continued to determine policy for the programs. In accordance with a mandate from the Society's 1976–1977 Board of Directors, an ad hoc committee on CPE structure, chaired by Carroll Phillips, proposed a tax-exempt foundation through which the Society's CPE activities could be conducted. As approved in June, 1977, the new CPE Foundation changed little in terms of control; that is, the Society's Board of Directors became the board of directors of the foundation, the Society's Executive Committee became the trustees of the foundation, and the CPE Council became the CPE Council of the foundation. The membership of the council was increased in size, however, from six to

7. "Report of the Ad Hoc Committee . . . April 24, 1972," TSCPA.
8. "Minutes 1977–78 Executive Committee Meeting, June 17, 1978," TSCPA.

thirteen. This was accomplished by increasing from six to nine the number of three-year appointees to the council, adding the CPE coordinators of the three most populous chapters on a year-to-year basis, and appointing one member of the Society's Executive Committee. The philosophy behind these changes was to reduce areas of conflict with chapters and their CPE activities, and to improve the liaison between the CPE Council and Society committees concerned with special aspects of professional development. The practical effect of creating the foundation was to save the CPE program an estimated $20,000 a year in postage and sales tax expense.[9] Meanwhile, the staff administering the CPE programs increased from two people at the beginning of the decade to eleven at the close. Director Forrest Black resigned in December, 1974, and was succeeded in March, 1975, by Don Weldon, who remained with the Society for four years and directed the programs through their period of most dramatic growth. Weldon was a native of Lubbock and a graduate of Texas Tech who came to the Society from Texas Instruments, where he was director of education programs for learning centers. Upon Weldon's departure in 1979, Julie Kirksey, an experienced employee of the Texas Society for nearly six years and assistant director of the CPE program after 1975, became director.

The burgeoning growth of CPE taxed the abilities of the Society and AICPA to develop and present courses in the quantity and quality that were demanded. College faculties helped some, either individually or through entities like North Texas State University's Professional Development Institute. A large number of private vendors also entered the market. The AICPA's 1976 Statement on Standards: Formal Group and Formal Self-Study programs also became the guide for the CPE Council in matters of quality control. According to a survey taken at the time the standards were adopted, the quality of Texas Society courses ranked above the national average in the four categories; effectiveness of discussion leaders, course material, contribution to professional competence, and the satisfaction of course objective.[10] However, another survey, undertaken by Larry Gene Pointer in 1978, revealed that the Society had not kept up with the demand for CPE courses relevant to the interests of members in industry and government. Complaining that current

9. "Committee of Continuing Professional Education Structure (Ad Hoc), Minutes of March 18, 1977 Meeting," TSCPA.
10. *Texas CPA News*, Nov., 1976, p. 13.

course offerings "were too slanted to individuals in public practice," accountants in the private sector called for more courses related to financial forecasting and the job of corporate controller.[11]

The Texas Society made a valiant effort to make the voluntary CPE program work, but nationally the tide ran strongly in the opposite direction. Even in 1973, the year in which Texas accountants first made their voluntary reports, three states had adopted mandatory professional education. By 1975 almost twenty states had followed suit, and the Texas leadership had legislation "ready for the hopper" in the event national events dictated such a move. But a poll of Texas Society members in 1977 revealed continued strong resistance, and a subcommittee of an ad hoc committee on continuing professional education advised against mandatory requirements.[12] As the committee spoke, however, the AICPA Division of Firms mandated continuing education, and two years later, with Texas Society approval, the new Texas Accountancy Act included a section authorizing the state board to impose mandatory professional education.

## Educational Foundation

At the other end of the educational spectrum, the Educational Foundation's student loan, awards, and fellowship programs made a significant contribution to the recruitment and support of promising newcomers to the profession and, at the same time, enhanced the image of the profession.

As noted earlier, the foundation gathered momentum in the middle 1960s with the successful launching of a $75,000 fund-raising campaign. Subsequent campaigns in 1970 ($100,000), 1973 ($175,000), and 1978 ($150,000), along with special memorial gifts and interest accrued on loans, built up a fund balance of over half a million dollars by 1980. In addition to these funds, the foundation received several gifts, one from Kenneth Hurst in 1975 in the form of a beneficial interest in a private trust, and one from Stanley Voelkel in 1980 in the form of land; the gifts, each valued at over $100,000, represent the largest single donations to the Educational Foundation. In appreciation of the

11. Ibid., March, 1978, pp. 12–13.
12. "Minutes . . . Board of Directors Meeting, December 2–3, 1977," TSCPA.

130   TEXAS SOCIETY OF CERTIFIED PUBLIC ACCOUNTANTS

Hurst gift, the trustees of the foundation in 1978 established the Kenneth W. Hurst Fellows Award, to be presented to individuals who contribute or cause to be contributed $5,000 to the foundation or who through service to the foundation merit this recognition. Wayne K. Goettsche, Byron G. Bronstad, Stanley H. Voelkel, Ford R. Hale, C. Tom Frazier, Carl S. Chilton, Jr., and Madie Ivy are Hurst Fellows to date. It should be added that the foundation's administrative and overhead costs are borne entirely by the Texas Society.

Like most Society activities, the student loan program grew most rapidly in the 1970s. During its first ten years, 1959–1969, the foundation made a total of 401 loans to 280 students in the amount of $196,000. Over the next decade, however, four times as many loans were made, and cumulative loan totals reached $500,000 in 1975, exceeded $1,000,000 in 1978, and stand currently at $1,527,000. Since the inception of the loan program, more than 1,900 loans have been made to 1,500 students. The maximum amount a student may borrow was raised from $4,500 to $6,000 in 1977, and the size of the average loan increased from approximately $500 in 1967 to $1,000 in 1980. Loans are repayable in installments beginning sixty days after graduation or termination of schooling, at interest rates competitive with other kinds of student loan programs.

The default rate on student loans was less than 1 percent as late as 1976, but, beginning with 1977, when the foundation first took legal action to collect thirteen seriously delinquent loans, the rate has edged up to 2.5 percent.[13] Still, foundation officials point with pride to the loss of only $29,000 out of $1,527,000 loaned over the lifetime of the foundation. They point with even more pride to the benefits, tangible and intangible, that have accrued from the program. By providing economic assistance when it was critically needed, the loan program permitted some students to complete their education. But even when the loan was not the difference between remaining in or leaving school, it was an expression of confidence in a person by the profession that he or she was preparing to enter which could only result in loyalty and pride in the profession.[14]

In 1970 the foundation inaugurated two new programs, one, an

13. "Report . . . Educational Foundation . . . May 31, 1977," TSCPA.
14. *Texas CPA News*, Aug., 1978, pp. 12–15; and *CPA 80*, May–June, pp. 39–40.

Accounting Excellence Award aimed at recognizing the top senior student in accounting in each of the state's senior colleges and universities, and the second, a series of fellowships for supporting promising graduate students. The annual Accounting Excellence Award consisted of a certificate and engraved memento from the Society along with the inscription of the student's name on a plaque displayed in the college. More than forty colleges in the state currently participate in the undergraduate awards program. The graduate fellowship program originated with the grant of one $3,000 fellowship in 1970, was changed to three grants of $1,000 each the following year, and then increased to five grants of $1,000 each in 1973. In 1975 the foundation named two of the fellowships in honor of Thomas W. Leland and Marquis G. Eaton. In subsequent years the remaining three were named for Jay A. Phillips (1978), C. Aubrey Smith (1978), and Arthur C. Upleger (1979). Also in 1979, foundation trustees voted to add one fellowship every other year to a maximum of ten. To date, Stanley Voelkel (1980) has been so honored.

In 1975 the Educational Foundation sponsored a one-day seminar for Texas accounting educators; the seminar developed into an annual affair reminiscent of the gatherings the old Texas Association of University Instructors in Accounting held in conjunction with annual Society meetings during the 1930s and 1940s. The educators had elected to change their meeting time in 1951 to a different date. The purpose of both the old meeting and the new seminar was to keep educators abreast of practitioners' interests and needs. The seminars have been held in Dallas each October and are attended by representatives from the nearly fifty colleges and universities that have accredited accounting programs, as well as a growing number of practitioners.

The most recently funded foundation activity, a CPA-in-Residence, is also reminiscent of the efforts some accountants made in the 1920s to acquaint students with the profession. In the 1978 reincarnation of the concept, the foundation supports the presence of a practicing CPA on a college campus for up to three days of dialogue with students and faculty.

A large number of prominent and dedicated Society members have devoted much time and effort to bringing the foundation to its present high level of achievement. They would all no doubt agree, however, that Dorothy Smith deserves equal credit for those achievements. From the time she joined the Society staff in 1962, she was directly charged with administering Educational Foundation affairs. Appreciation for what she has accomplished was expressed in 1977 when she was elected to honorary membership in the Society.

## Professional Schools of Accountancy

An important section of the Beamer report focused on the need for a five-year program in accountancy. The idea was not new. In 1961–1962 Robert Hibbetts brought before the Society Board of Directors a recommendation that the Texas Society endorse professional schools of accounting "within the colleges of business administration of the universities of Texas where such a program would be feasible and appropriate."[15] University of Texas Dean John Arch White expressed support of the idea, but no school was formed and there the matter rested for over a decade.

After the Beamer report was completed, the suggestion for professional schools was dusted off and Stanley Voelkel chaired an ad hoc committee charged with investigating the issue. After meeting with representatives from eighteen Texas universities and colleges in November, 1972, the Voelkel committee reported that five universities supported the idea, seven "were on the fence," and six expressed no interest whatsoever. The three schools most interested were the University of Texas at Austin, North Texas State University, and the University of Houston.[16] In June, 1973, the Society recommended support of professional schools and adopted a set of guidelines. Unfortunately, the three schools showing interest were all state supported and required approval of the Texas State Coordinating Board for new programs. The Coordinating Board was lukewarm and has remained so. North Texas State University did proceed far enough to secure internal university approvals, and the Texas Society in 1977 engaged the services of an Austin consulting firm to assist in getting Coordinating Board approval, but all to no avail.[17]

15. "Minutes . . . June 16, 1961," TSCPA.

16. "Minutes 1972–1973 Board of Directors Meeting, December 1–2, 1972," TSCPA.

17. See "Minutes 1976–77 Executive Committee Meeting, February 19, 1977," and "Report . . . Activities of the Committee on Programs and Schools of Professional Accounting, June 22, 1977," TSCPA.

### Changing Rules of Competitive Behavior

While the Texas Society was slow to adopt the AICPA position on mandatory CPE, it was even more reluctant to embrace the national organization's revised positions on competitive bidding, solicitation, and advertising. Few issues evoked the response that competitive bidding did in Texas, and few issues gave the Texas Society more the appearance of swimming upstream with relation to the profession nationally. The issue raised its head in April, 1966, when President Paul Cheatham alerted the Executive Committee to a motion pending before the AICPA Council to repeal Rule 3.03 of the AICPA code of ethics prohibiting competitive bidding. The Executive Committee urged all council members from Texas to oppose the motion. At the Society's June meeting, however, council member Ludwell Jones reported the council passed the motion to repeal Rule 3.03 on to the full membership meeting in Boston in October on the grounds that the rule was unenforceable in the courts and was confusing and unenforceable by the profession.[18]

The Texas Society responded to this news by forming an ad hoc committee chaired by Robert Hibbetts and composed of former Society presidents Charles Woodard, Hatcher Pickens, Jones, Bouldin Mothershead, and Walter Flack to oppose repeal and take the fight to Boston. There the Texas group passed out position papers and Hibbetts spoke from the podium; representatives from other sections of the country also joined in the opposition. Following the Boston meeting, mail ballots were distributed to the AICPA membership. Needing a two-thirds vote for approval, the amendment failed. The Texas victory had a hollow ring, however, for failing in its repeal, AICPA simply suspended enforcement of Rule 3.03.

There the matter rested until 1971, at which time the Justice Department filed suit against AICPA to force repeal of the competitive bidding rule and the advertising and solicitation rules as well. The institute agreed to drop the competitive bidding rule entirely if the Justice Department would relax its pressure on advertising and solicitation, and a consent decree to that effect was signed on June 2, 1972. The decree was broadly worded and seemed to apply to state CPA societies

18. "Minutes 1965–66 Executive Committee Meeting, April 22–23, 1966," and "Minutes . . . Board of Directors . . . June 18, 1966," TSCPA.

and state boards of public accountancy, even though the latter had not been parties to the suit.[19]

The ultimate success of the government's attempt to eliminate non-competitive bidding practices depended, in the last analysis, upon state boards' complying with the 1972 consent decree. As long as a state board, which many thought to be sheltered from antitrust laws, had rules against competitive bidding, repeal of Rule 3.03 by either state societies or AICPA would have no practical effect on the practice of accountancy within that state. The general terms of the consent decree were well known and anticipated before it was entered with the court in June; therefore, it was a matter of some significance that the Texas State Board announced in April its intention to continue enforcement of its Rule 14 of Professional Conduct, a rule that essentially restated the AICPA's and Texas Society's Rule 3.03.[20] Two weeks after the consent decree, the Texas Society held its annual meeting, the ball squarely in its court. Acting on legal counsel's advice that TSCPA, a voluntary organization like AICPA, had little chance of contesting the decree, but with full knowledge that the State Board would continue to enforce its own rule against competitive bidding, both retiring and incoming executive committees took steps to delete Rule 3.03 and advised the Professional Ethics Committee to forego any further action on cases involving competitive bidding.[21]

The task of deleting Rule 3.03 from the Society code of ethics fell upon the administration of President Jarman Bass. At the mid-year board meeting in Victoria in December, 1972, the Ethics Committee presented two amendments; one dropping 3.03 and the other deleting Rule 4.01, which by direct reference incorporated the State Board's rules into the Society's code and which, if left intact, would continue to expose the Society to court action. However, the wording taken out of 4.01 was placed in the preamble of the Society's code, thus restating indirectly, and presumably beyond the reach of the court, a matter of crucial importance.

Most of the two-day session in Victoria was given over to discussion of the amendments. Frank Rea summarized the arguments for re-

19. "Minutes 1971–72 Executive Committee Meeting, June 15–16, 1972," TSCPA.
20. "Minutes 1971–72 Executive Committee Meeting, April 24, 1972," TSCPA.
21. See J. A. Gooch to Jarman Bass, July 19, 1972 in "Minutes 1972–73 Executive Committee Meeting, August 11–12, 1972," TSCPA.

Many TSCPA members gathered in 1940 for the Society's twenty-fifth anniversary.

As presidents, these men guided the Texas Society in its formative years. *Front row (left to right)*: Arthur C. Upleger (1926–27), Bouldin S. Mothershead (1927–28), J. R. Nelson (1928–29), W. M. Aikman (1930–31), J. A. Phillips (1932–33), Frank G. Rodgers (1935–36), H. Tracy Nelson (1936–37), and Lyle R. Sproles (1943–44). *Back row*: C. F. Milledge (1944–45), Clifton H. Morris (1947–48), Harry D. Hopson (1948–49), Frank L. Wilcox (1949–50), Curtis H. Cadenhead (1951–52), Fladger F. Tannery (1955–56), and Robert J. Hibbetts (1957–58).

*Left*: Current successors of the founding fathers include Paul W. Hillier, Jr. (*left*), and Charles T. Zlatkovich (*right*). These presidents, in 1980–81 and 1981–82, respectively, were instrumental in the development of legislation, institutional advertising, and the curricula for continuing education. *Right*: Stanley J. Scott is one of only three Texans to serve as the top volunteer at the American Institute of CPAs. J. A. Phillips and Marquis G. Eaton also acted in this capacity. Arthur C. Upleger was president of the American Society of CPAs, one of the groups that merged to form AICPA.

*Left*: Miller Montag, Society president in 1970–71, has been active in other ways, too. He worked with the Educational Foundation for many years and has also served as a member of the Texas State Board of Public Accountancy. *Right*: Women are growing more visible in accounting. Johnnie Ray Seale was the first woman to serve on the Society's Executive Committee. She is also active on committees for CPAs working in industry and government.

*Left*: Lloyd J. Weaver; Dean Cobb, TSCPA legislative counsel; Don M. Lyda (*seated*); and Walter A. Bielstein discuss legislative activity and the accounting point of view. This is part of an ongoing effort by TSCPA members to protect the public interest. *Right*: Continuing professional education has been a rapidly expanding program in the last ten years. TSCPA supplied 218,000 hours of CPE in 1981–82.

TSCPA's Educational Foundation has helped more than two thousand students through college with its loan program and graduate fellowships. Some of the current trustees are: (*front row, left to right*) Betty Bell and Dorothy R. Smith, executive director of the Foundation; (*middle row*) Morris D. Johnson, Sammie L. Smith, and J. W. Giese; and (*top row*) C. H. Hamilton, Jr., vice-president, I. Lee Wilson, and Pat Thomas, president.

*Left*: The chief operating officer of the Texas Society is the executive director. William H. Quimby filled that post for more than ten years. He is currently serving as a public member of the Texas State Board of Public Accountancy. *Right*: Webster W. Sharp has held the position as TSCPA's executive director since 1977. Member growth and expanding programs have distinguished this period in TSCPA development.

Meritorious Service to the Public Accounting Profession in Texas is TSCPA's highest honor. Homer L. Luther (*far left*) was the first recipient of the award in 1952–53. Some other honored members are (*left to right*): Kenneth W. Hurst (1953–54), Jack E. Collier (1956–57), Louie B. Green (1957–58), Lionel E. Gilley (1958–59), and Gilbert F. Orcutt, Jr. (1959–60).

peal of Rule 3.03, and Robert Hibbetts, who saw "not one iota of difference" between what the Society fought for in 1966 and what it was now debating, marshaled the arguments for retention.[22] The board finally voted 46 to 22 in favor of submitting the proposed changes to the general membership in June, but upon petition from the San Angelo and El Paso chapters, a mail ballot was distributed in the spring with the votes to be counted and certified at the annual meeting. Along with the ballot, the Executive Committee prepared a ten-page statement of reasons for and against the proposed changes. Rea drafted the arguments supporting repeal; San Angelo members William H. Armstrong, Jack Ransom, and Richard Webb prepared the statement against.[23]

In his argument, Rea reviewed the AICPA's problems leading up to the consent decree, concluding with the assertion that the Texas Society was equally vulnerable. The Society's attempt to enforce Rule 3.03, Rea argued, would provoke legal action, and "if such should come about, it is highly probable that the petition for injunction would not only seek to invalidate our Rule 3.03, but also our Rules 3.01 (advertising) and 3.02 (solicitation)." The unenforceability of 3.03 meant it should be repealed, lest the failure to enforce one rule engender disrespect for all rules. Repeal of 3.03 would not undermine the profession, Rea continued, because the Texas State Board would continue to enforce its Rule 14. He also pointed out that slightly over half of the CPAs in the nation practiced professionally without 3.03, and he was sure Texas accountants could do as well.

The formal arguments supporting retention of 3.03 contended that the AICPA entered into the consent decree because, in part, it assumed that state societies and state boards would continue to enforce their rules and would thereby prohibit competitive bidding in the absence of the AICPA rule. Therefore, the Texas Society should retain 3.03, even if unenforced, to give moral support to the Texas State Board. Abandonment of 3.03 by the eight thousand members of the Society would discredit the rule and bring intolerable pressure on the State Board to repeal Rule 14 as well. Better to adopt a wait-and-see attitude, the argument ran, until the State Board, which had statutory authority to promulgate rules of conduct in the public interest, had a chance to

22. "Minutes 1972–73 Board of Directors Meeting, December 1, 1972," TSCPA.
23. Copies in "Minutes 1972–73 Executive Committee Minutes, February 17, 1973," TSCPA.

challenge the consent decree. Proponents also pointed to the Professional Service Procurement Act adopted by the Texas legislature in 1971 as having given statutory approval to the state and its agencies to contract for CPA services without competitive bidding. At the national level, it was noted that recent congressional legislation provided guidelines for the selection of architects and engineers for federal government jobs on the basis of demonstrated competence and qualifications rather than considerations of price. "The most appropriate course of action is to retain Rule 3.03 in its entirety," they said, "without the imposition of any enforcement or sanction for its violations until" accountants found out how other professions fared. The Society would be in an awkward position if it repealed 3.03 only to have the State Board or Congress force the courts to rule that it was "in the public interest" to have such rules of professional conduct.

Forty-five percent of the Society's 7,421 members voted in the referendum. The vote for repeal was 2,223; the vote against was 1,134. Needing a two-thirds majority to carry, the recommendation failed by the slim margin of 15 votes.

The membership having spoken, the Ethics Committee resumed enforcement of the rule against competitive bidding. Occasional articles also appeared in the *Texas CPA News* that reinforced the arguments supporting Rule 3.03. Writing from New York where competitive bidding was condoned, the partner of a major national firm criticized unprofessional competition that led to "pricing services below cost in order to obtain clients." Such practice often resulted in "marginal audit programs" and gave rise "no doubt to several of the lawsuits against the profession."[24] Though intended only to be an argument against competitive bidding abuses, the article clearly stated the worst that many Texas accountants feared would happen, both to the public's interest and to their own largely unspoken concern that smaller firms would fare poorly in open price competition with larger firms.

On the other hand, restrictions on the competitive behavior of professionals in fee setting, advertising, and solicitation were seen increasingly to be in conflict with a broader need to protect the public and individual practitioners from monopoly practices. In this sense, the

---

24. Richard T. Baker, "Professional Competition—Cut-Rate Audits or Quality Services?" *Texas CPA News*, Jan., 1975, pp. 12–13.

Virginia State Supreme Court ruled in 1975 in *Goldfarb* v. *Virginia* that the minimum fee schedule of a Virginia county bar association was in violation of the Sherman Anti-Trust Act. And in another case involving the legal profession, *Bates* v. *State Bar of Arizona*, the U.S. Supreme Court ruled in 1977 that a ban on advertising violated First Amendment rights of free speech. Also in 1977, following two years of legal maneuvering, the Justice Department filed suit against the Texas State Board of Public Accountancy, alleging its Rule 14 illegally restricted price competition among the state's accountants. The district court agreed and in May, 1978, enjoined the State Board from enforcing Rule 14 even during the State Board's appeal of the case to the Fifth Circuit Court of Appeals. Meanwhile, a Dallas CPA, Franklin Eugene Miller, filed a $30,000,000 damage suit against the State Board in January, 1978, because of a reprimand he had received for violating the rules against advertising. The Texas Society was also named a party in the Miller suit. On top of all this, the Federal Trade Commission launched a nationwide investigation to determine if the profession's entry requirements were too restrictive and its standards too high.

In the face of these suits and adverse court opinions, the Executive Committee suspended the rule on advertising in June, 1978, and the rules on competitive bidding and solicitation in August.[25] With relatively little discussion, all three restrictions were deleted from the code of ethics at the annual meeting in June, 1979.

The long controversy over the repeal of rules curbing promotional and competitive practices often overshadowed the enforcement of other ethical standards which, given the thrust of the Wheat report, were more important to the profession and to the public than competitive bidding, solicitation, and advertising. Chief among these were standards of independence and client and public relations embodied in Article 1 of the Texas Society code, technical standards governing the expression of opinions and the use of an accountant's name found in Article 2, and the operating policies of accountants included in Article 4. Public criticism for violations and/or deficiencies in one or more of these parts of the code were largely responsible for the crisis in the profession. The need to achieve greater uniformity between state soci-

25. As noted in official minutes of the two meetings and in *Texas CPA News*, Aug., 1978, p. 5.

ety and AICPA codes and to overhaul enforcement procedures became, in the opinion of AICPA, a top priority.

Recognizing the problem, if not the urgent need, the Texas Society continued the policy begun in 1962 of bringing its code of ethics into agreement with the AICPA code. The Society completely overhauled the numbering and much of the wording of its code to conform to the AICPA code, though it stopped short of doing as some state societies did—and as it did with regard to State Board rules—of adopting by reference the AICPA code. The Society guarded its independence from AICPA, and in 1970 when AICPA proposed a restated code of ethics, the issue attracted attention in Texas.

At the December, 1970, Board of Directors meeting, Gordon George, Leonard Brantley, and Willard Findling all directed attention to the proposed Restated Code of Ethics, most particularly the omission of Rule 3.03 prohibiting competitive bidding, and encouraged members of the board to write members of the AICPA council expressing their concern before the proposed rules were submitted for a final vote.[26] What effect letters from Texas had on other points, the consent decree of June, 1972, settled the 3.03 issue, and it is interesting to note that the restated code omitting the ban on competitive bidding was overwhelmingly approved by Texas accountants in the fall of 1972 at the same time that the fight within Texas was being made to retain Rule 3.03 in the Texas code.

## Joint Ethics Enforcement Program

Along with the Restated Code of Ethics, the AICPA proposed a number of changes in enforcement procedures which became known as the Joint Ethics Enforcement Program (JEEP). JEEP is designed to eliminate the duplication of jurisdictions and enforcement procedures between state societies and AICPA, and to provide a means for the profession to initiate actions before the state boards of public accountancy. To achieve these objectives, it was proposed that trial boards be established to act on behalf of both the AICPA and the state societies and that the workings of the ethics committees of the state societies and the AICPA Ethics Division be coordinated.

26. "Minutes 1970–71 Board of Directors Meeting, December 4–5, 1970," TSCPA.

A joint meeting in Dallas in April, 1973, of the Texas Society's Trial Board and Professional Ethics Committee thoroughly reviewed the AICPA proposal and filed a lengthy report with President Jarman Bass that was critical of the proposals.[27] With "surprising unanimity" the joint committee announced that JEEP "would not be acceptable" to members of the Society because it "was not responsive to the problem which it is intended to solve, it would involve a substantial abdication of responsibility by the Texas Society in regard to enforcement of its rules of professional ethics and standards, and at this particular time the proposal might pose a definite threat to the success of the legislative efforts of the Texas Society . . . to protect our present public accountancy act."

JEEP's stated purpose was to restore public confidence eroded away by critics who charged that the profession "might not be maintaining an acceptable level of independence and adherence to generally accepted auditing procedures and reporting standards." The Society committee said changes in enforcement proceedings would have little, if any, effect on public confidence. In its view, "the real solution" to the problem of sagging public confidence was "a more successful program of defining generally accepted accounting principles, auditing standards and a more aggressive program of continuing education concerning these matters." The committee noted that "the cases that receive and generate criticism often arise in court actions, where a judge may make a unilateral finding completely outside the thrust of professional ethics enforcement. These cases usually involve mistakes in judgment, either real or attributed in hindsight, of individuals that may never appropriately be subject to ethics enforcement."

In addition to JEEP's missing the mark of its stated purpose, the Texas committee pointed out, the AICPA proposal would "concentrate all enforcement activities of the accounting profession at the AICPA level" and it would "represent a virtual abdication of our enforcement responsibility at the local level." This transfer of responsibility "would tend to undermine the confidence of the TSCPA members . . . in the effectiveness of their state society and possibly in the ultimate fairness of the enforcement process." With regard to the legislative program of

27. Billy M. Mann and Max L. Spillar to Jarman Bass, April 9, 1973, in "Minutes 1972–73 Executive Committee Meeting, April 27, 1973," TSCPA.

the state society, the committee felt "the proposed plan of reorganization would provide support to what is now the unmerited accusation
that the accounting profession in Texas is controlled by the AICPA,"
and in view of the attacks on the Texas public accountancy act, "it
would be very unwise for our Texas members to abdicate their responsibility for enforcement of our professional standards at the local level."
In conclusion, the committee referred to the Society's practice of sharing with AICPA information concerning ethical violations. This was
the only issue that divided the members of the committee, they reported, with the majority feeling that individual enforcement case should
be conducted and concluded before there was any sharing of information with other professional groups. The minority felt information could
be shared during the processing of cases, but it was the firm view even
of the minority that ultimate responsibility for enforcement should not
be delegated by the state society.

Bass and his Executive Committee concurred in the opinion of the
joint committee, and he so notified the AICPA. Later in the year, a
more formal reply came from the Board of Directors meeting in December, 1973. It simply stated: "The TSCPA has received and considered the proposal for a joint AICPA/State Society ethics enforcement
effort. Texas has long had a history of effective ethics education and
enforcement. The TSCPA, therefore, does not choose to join in the
AICPA proposal."[28]

A year later, in December, 1974, Curtis Frazier reported that the
AICPA was moving ahead with JEEP, and if Texas should elect to join,
the state would constitute a region unto itself for enforcement purposes,
as would New York and California, two other large societies with reservations about the program.[29] Texas remained outside JEEP, however,
until June, 1980, when meeting in Houston, the Board of Directors
approved a contract bringing the Society under the jurisdiction of JEEP
Region V. There, trial boards appointed by the president of the Texas
Society and composed of Society members will hear all cases involving
TSCPA members accused of violating the Society code of ethics. The
arrangement also provided for the Society Ethics Committee to conduct
investigations involving the violation of the Texas code. James Carter,

28. "Rough Draft Minutes (December 1, 1973)," TSCPA.
29. "Minutes 1974–75 Board of Directors Meeting, December 6–7, 1974," TSCPA.

who chaired the ad hoc committee that negotiated the contract, explained, "We have dealt with all stated previous objections to the program. We have everything to gain from this joint enforcement program with the AICPA. We'll gain AICPA resources—people to assist in investigations and Trial Board action at no cost to TSCPA. We will also have available to us all sources of information from both the AICPA and the Securities and Exchange Commission."[30] By a ten-to-one margin, Society members approved amendments to the by-laws later in the year ratifying the Board of Directors' action.[31]

## Relations with the American Institute

Participation in JEEP is a sign of the strengthening relations between the Texas Society and AICPA in evidence for the last few years. At odds earlier over competitive bidding and slow to embrace AICPA's mandatory continuing education, the Texas Society also forced a restatement of an AICPA ruling virtually eliminating CPAs from holding bank directorships. In addition, the Texas Society consistently opposed mandatory concurrent membership in AICPA and state societies, and it objected to associate membership in AICPA for management advisory services staff of the larger national firms. These negative expressions from Texas no doubt led some AICPA staff to think of the profession in Texas as being isolated and provincial. On the other hand, Texas accountants frequently felt the state got less than its fair share of AICPA committee assignments, given the size of the profession in Texas.

A conscious effort to change these perceptions took shape in the mid-1970s, helped along no doubt by the warm welcome and reception the AICPA received when it held its annual meeting in San Antonio in 1975.[32] Two years later, the Texas Society formed a standing committee to improve relations with AICPA. The committee advertised AICPA services to Texas accountants, and it also provided an ample list of names of qualified Texans to serve on AICPA committees. Meanwhile, Stanley Scott's vigorous leadership as chairman of the American Institute in 1977–1978 reflected credit on the Texas Society and the practitioners of the state. As a result, by 1981 some eighty-six members

30. *CPA 80*, August, p. 16.
31. *CPA 81*, Jan.–Feb., pp. 26–30.
32. "Minutes 1975–76 Board of Directors Meeting, June 23, 1976," TSCPA.

of the Texas Society were serving on AICPA committees, leading William E. McReynolds, chairman of the Society Committee on Relations with AICPA, to observe that "the voice of the Texas CPA is now being clearly heard in AICPA meeting rooms."[33]

33. *CPA 81*, March, p. 9.

# 9

## *The Public Accountancy Act of 1979*

THE vigorous spirit in which the Texas Society approached the arena of public affairs in the 1970s may be inferred from the name "Committee for Positive Action"—the name it gave to one of several activities aimed at protecting the certificate and defending the accountancy act of 1945. On the theory that a good offense is the best defense, the Society sharpened its lobby effort, joined the State Board in legal action to prevent the unauthorized practice of public accountancy, and instituted a political action committee to help elect candidates to public office. These efforts stood the Society and the profession in good stead at the end of the decade when, in a somewhat troubled political environment, the Texas Sunset Law forced a comprehensive review of the 1945 act. As was the case in 1945, the strength of the new Public Accountancy Act of 1979 is primarily a testament to the public's need for professional accounting services, but it is also evidence of the Society's successful public affairs program.

### Professional Corporations Act of 1969

For almost a decade following the strenuous legislative activity of 1961, the Texas Society maintained a relatively low profile in Austin. Skirmishes with bookkeepers seeking recognition under the accountancy act broke out occasionally, but the Society easily repulsed these attempts to change the law. On the other hand, the Society joined other professions in gaining passage of the 1969 Professional Corporations Act permitting professionals to incorporate their practices. The initiative and major impetus for this law came from other professional groups in Texas, but President Robert Knox, upon polling Society members, found support for including public accountants in the act. At the time, professional corporations were allowed in thirty states and, it must be remembered, had been permitted in Texas before 1945. Since 1969, the number of accounting firms choosing to incorporate has reached almost five hundred.[1]

## The "Key Man" Program

Beginning with the decade of the 1970s, the legislative tempo picked up. The Society identified key members whose acquaintance with one or more members of the legislature permitted them to present the Society's case on a legislative issue in a personal and, it was hoped, more effective way. As a result of the "key man" program, Neal Y. R. Sheffield, chairman of the Committee on Legislation, reported 1971 to be "a very good year" for Society-endorsed legislation.[2] That year the Society successfully amended the accountancy act, the amendment allowing the governor to appoint "more than five" CPAs to the State Board and to increase thereby the ratio of CPAs to public accountants serving on the nine-member board. It also squashed a hastily drawn bill to reopen registration of public accountants and do away with the designation of certified public accountants. On a related matter, the Society joined forces again with other professions to support a Professional Services Procurement Act exempting professionals from competitive bidding requirements of state and local government contracts.

## Political Action Committees

During the same time the Society was becoming more actively involved in legislative matters, new state controls on lobby activities came into force in 1971 and stricter laws concerning political campaign contributions came into force in 1973. The new laws required the Society—and all other organized groups engaged in political efforts—to modify the traditional approach to these activities. In the Society's case, voluntary contributions into an informal contingency fund was for years the way the Society defrayed legal fees and miscellaneous costs associated with defense of the accountancy act and protection of the certif-

1. "Report of the Executive Committee, June 21, 1969," TSCPA.
2. "Annual Report 1970–71, Committee on Legislation Long-Range Planning," TSCPA.

icate. The contingency fund was also drawn upon for occasional contributions to political campaigns.[3] The informal nature of these activities began to change in 1971, however, when the Texas Lobby Registration Act required disclosures of lobby activities which, had they still been funded through the contingency fund, would have caused the organization to be designated a political action group under the Internal Revenue Code. Therefore, in order to comply with state law and avoid an inappropriate designation by IRS, a committee independent of the Society, the Committee for Positive Action, was formed, and $50,000 in voluntary contributions was raised to defray direct lobby expenses and other costs involved in protecting the certificate. On the other hand, the Board of Directors provided that legal services and related expenses incurred for "information and education on a continuing basis" be budgeted and paid from the Society's general funds.[4]

Two years later the 1973 Texas Campaign Contributions Act imposed such strict reporting standards for giving and receiving political campaign contributions that the Society's legal counsel advised against further activities of this nature. This brought an end to the contingency fund. James E. Jenkins, chairman of the Committee on Public Affairs, announced in June, 1974, that "the Society will no longer, as an organization, collect or disburse monies in support of political campaigns."[5] The following year, however, after a second legal opinion and a change of attorneys, the Society reversed its position. President Larry Pickens advised the Board of Directors, meeting in El Paso in 1975, that there "was an imperative need for the accounting profession to resume organized political contributions" to counter what he called "a dwindling of the CPAs' influence in Austin." The Society, Pickens argued, should again raise funds for political candidates "as it did for 10–15 years," and this activity should and could be done in compliance with existing state law.[6]

The Board of Directors responded by forming a statewide Political Action Committee (PAC) and allowing chapters to do likewise. The first meeting of the Society's CPA/PAC was held in November, 1975,

3. "Minutes 1970–71 Executive Committee Meeting, July 31, 1970," TSCPA.
4. "Minutes 1971–72 Board of Directors Meeting, December 3–4, 1971," TSCPA.
5. "Minutes 1973–74 Board of Directors Meeting, June 15, 1974," TSCPA.
6. "Minutes 60th Annual Meeting of the Board of Directors, June 18, 1975," TSCPA. See also Lawrence G. Pickens to 1974–75 Board of Directors, June 12, 1975.

at which time plans were made to raise $50,000 for the 1976 campaign year. Several of the larger chapters followed the state society's lead and established PACs of their own. In 1978, CPA/PAC contributed over $112,000 to local and statewide campaigns, roughly 75 percent of the contributions going to candidates in local contests and the remaining 25 percent being contributed to candidates for statewide office. Meanwhile, in December, 1977, the Committee for Positive Action, having disbursed all but a thousand or so dollars, contributed the remainder of its funds to the Texas Society and ceased activity.[7]

## The Fulcher Cases

Before its demise, the Committee for Positive Action reimbursed the Society for $8,000 in legal fees it incurred in court action aimed at stopping the unauthorized practice of public accountancy by bookkeepers and accounting technicians. What became an important development in case law surrounding the Public Accountancy Act of 1945 started quietly enough in 1973, when the Texas State Board of Public Accountancy, along with the Society as a party plaintiff intervenor, sought a court order enjoining William L. Fulcher of Brownsville from holding himself out to the public as an accountant in violation of the 1945 act.[8] After eight years and two favorable Texas Supreme Court decisions, the Fulcher cases have clearly established the power of the State Board to prevent this kind of encroachment.

The facts in the first Fulcher case were relatively clear-cut. Although a director of the Texas Accountants Association and the Texas Association of Public Accountants, Fulcher was neither a certified public accountant nor a licensed or registered public accountant under the Texas act. He held no permit to practice public accounting. He did, however, hold himself out to the public as an accountant and he prepared income tax returns, furnished bookkeeping services to clients, and rendered general accounting services to the public. For these reasons, the State Board took him to court.

The state district court in Brownsville found Fulcher to be in violation of the law but excused the violation and denied the State Board's

7. "Fluctuation Analysis, October 31, 1977," TSCPA.
8. "Minutes 1972–73/1973–74 Executive Committee Meeting, April 27, 1973," TSCPA.

request for an injunction on grounds that the law was unconstitutional. The act was "ambiguous, contradictory, and prohibitory, rather than regulatory," and, the court said, it failed to accomplish its purpose in a reasonable manner; that is, "unlicensed accountants are not prohibited from practicing accounting but are prohibited from holding themselves out to the public as accountants."

The constitutional issue forced and clearly drawn, the State Board and the Society appealed the trial court's decision. On September 19, 1974, the appellate court reversed the trial court and rendered a strongly worded opinion upholding the accountancy act of 1945. "The need to protect the public against fraud and deception as the consequences of ignorance or incompetence in the practice of most professions makes regulation necessary," the higher court said, adding that the intricate and technical matters with which public accountants must deal makes it necessary that the state regulate that particular profession. Furthermore, the court said, the state had legitimately determined that the use of the term "accountant" is a holding out to the public that the person using the term has a live permit to practice public accounting. "The Texas statute," the appeals court concluded, "does not prohibit an unlicensed accountant from practicing accountancy or doing accounting work. We hold that it only prohibits an unlicensed accountant who practices *public* accounting from holding himself out to the public as an *accountant*." The State Board was entitled, therefore, to the injunctive relief it sought.[9] The Texas Supreme Court affirmed the ruling of the appeals court in March, 1975, much to the relief and pleasure of the accounting profession.

The dust had barely settled from the first Fulcher case, however, when Fulcher resurfaced, using the title "accounting practitioner." In July, 1976, the State Board and the Society filed suit again. This time, the district court issued a permanent injunction against Fulcher's use of the terms "accounting practitioner," "accountant," "public accounting offices," "accounting offices," or any abbreviations or derivations thereof in connection with his business activities. When the Texas Supreme Court refused Fulcher's appeal in December, 1978, Chairman Don Lyda of the State Board announced that the opinions in the two cases had

9. Quotations are from Opinion of the Court in Case 889, Texas State Board of Public Accountancy v. W. L. Fulcher, 13th District Court of Civil Appeals.

now become widely recognized across the nation and were "leading authorities relating to the state regulatory board's power to protect the public from unlicensed individuals." [10] The victories won in the *Fulcher* cases appear to be secure, though a similar case in the state of Maryland has recently been decided otherwise, and Fulcher himself filed suit against the State Board in the federal courts in October, 1980, alleging violation of his First Amendment rights.

As the *Fulcher* cases wound their way through the state courts, the Texas Association of Public Accountants continued its persistent efforts in the legislature to reopen registration and provide for permanent two-class regulation, most notably during the legislative session of 1977. These events provoked some CPAs to call for a complete overhaul of the accountancy act, the purpose being to restore the definition of public accounting dropped from the law in 1961 and to put more teeth into enforcement provisions dealing with encroachment on the certificate. In these discussions, two other issues surfaced as needing attention if the act were redrafted. One was the authority of the State Board to mandate continuing professional education, and the other was a proper response to the enthusiasm generated by consumer and public advocacy groups to have lay members appointed to all professional regulatory boards. Responding to these suggestions, the Board of Directors in June, 1977, directed the Long-Range Planning–Public Affairs Committee, Jimmie L. Mason, chairman, to study the matter and make appropriate recommendations.

The committee reported back in November, 1977. Several matters became apparent to the committee during its deliberations, Mason wrote. The first was that the Public Accountancy Act of 1945, as amended in 1961 and recently interpreted by the courts, gave CPAs in Texas one of the strongest regulatory laws in the nation, the lack of a precise definition of public accounting providing greater, rather than less, latitude in the enforcement of the law. Moreover, reinsertion of a definition of public accounting at this point might undermine the recent favorable rulings in the *Fulcher* cases. Also, there were always dangers inherent in introducing sweeping new legislation because of the opportunity it presented groups like the TAPA to make "unfavorable amendments during the legislative process." Furthermore, the committee heard from mem-

10. As quoted in *CPA 79*, Feb., p. 5.

bers of the State Board that, given the effectiveness of the present law, it would be unwise to introduce new legislation while the board was under attack from federal agencies regarding its rule-making authority in competitive bidding, advertising, and solicitation.

For these reasons, the Mason committee argued against wholesale revision of the accountancy act at that time. On the other hand, the committee did recognize a need to prepare and have in readiness an amendment authorizing the State Board to impose mandatory continuing professional education, given the nationwide movement in that direction. With regard to lay members' serving on the State Board, the committee recommended exploratory talks with other professional groups "to develop an intelligent approach to the possibility (probability) of public members on state boards within the next few years."[11]

## Sunset Review

Change, in the form of the Public Accountancy Act of 1979, occurred more rapidly, however, than the Mason committee and the Society intended or desired, events being pushed along by forces outside the profession's control. Specifically, the Texas Sunset Act of 1977 subjected over two hundred state boards and agencies to review by the Sunset Advisory Commission and the state legislature every ten years. Those boards that failed to justify their continued existence would be allowed to expire. The luck of the draw, based in part upon alphabetical order, placed the State Board of Public Accountancy in the first group of twenty-five whose authority would be terminated September 1, 1979, unless extended by act of the legislature meeting earlier that year. There was little likelihood that the State Board would fade away and the profession be left unregulated. On the other hand, the review process included lengthy sunset commission staff investigations and recommendations conducted months in advance of the legislative session, followed in 1979 by full legislative action, all of which ran the risk that unwanted changes would be forced upon the profession. Accepting the reality of the situation, however, the Society leadership adopted a strategy

11. "Report of the Long Range Planning–Public Affairs Committee, November 21, 1977," TSCPA.

of defending the essential features of the accountancy law and preserving the status quo as much as possible.[12]

In May, 1978, however, two separate but related events occurred that made it clear some fundamental changes in the law would have to be made; the U.S. District Court in Austin ruled in the Justice Department's antitrust suit against the State Board, and the Sunset Advisory Commission revealed its staff findings and recommendations. The thrust of the sunset staff report was that the State Board should exercise greater independence in promulgating rules of professional conduct by dropping the requirement that all rules must be approved by a referendum vote of the licensees. The staff further questioned the specific rules governing competitive bidding, advertising, and solicitation as not being in the interests of consumers of professional accounting services. Also, the staff noted that Texas lagged behind most states in requiring continuing professional education and that the public's interest could be better protected by the addition of lay members to the board.[13]

The federal court's ruling in the antitrust suit touched upon some of the same points. Basically, the Justice Department's charge was that the State Board's Rule 14 against competitive bidding was a per se restraint of trade in violation of the Sherman Act and that the procedures used by the board in the promulgation of rules was an act of conspiracy on the part of the board and its licensees. In his ruling, Judge Roberts basically agreed with the government's position and ordered the cancellation of Rule 14. He then broadened the scope of the case, instructing the State Board to cease enforcement of rules against advertising and solicitation as well. The court's action made the State Board uncertain of its enforcement powers in all areas of behavioral actions, and it implied that as long as the State Board promulgated rules of professional conduct under the permissive language of the accountancy act and shared the promulgation of those rules with the licensees, it compromised its status as an arm of the state immune from federal law.[14]

12. "Minutes 1977–78 Executive Committee Meeting, February 25, 1978," TSCPA.
13. "Texas State Board of Public Accountancy: Staff Report to the Sunset Advisory Commission, April 20, 1978," copy provided by commission staff.
14. See *Texas CPA News*, July, 1978, pp. 10–11, for a review of the Sunset Commission Report and the federal court's ruling against the Texas State Board of Public Accountancy.

The State Board responded to the court's order with a complete redrafting of the rules of professional conduct, dropping altogether references to competitive bidding and liberalizing the rules on advertising and solicitation. Based upon a model set developed by the National Association of State Boards of Accountancy, the rules were submitted to a referendum vote in October, 1978, and became effective on January 10, 1979. Thus, even as the legislature convened to consider the recommendations of the Sunset Advisory Commission, the State Board had answered some of the consumer demands reflected in the commission's report.

## A New Accountancy Act

The Society drew on the political resources it had built up over the decade to see the Public Accountancy Act of 1979 through the legislature. Society President Walter Bielstein and Lloyd Weaver, chairman of the Public Affairs Coordinating Committee, joined with Don Lyda, chairman of the State Board, to coordinate the legislative activity. When the battle was over, Bielstein praised the efforts of committee members, key men, and others who worked to pass the new law, saying that "because it was able to maintain the 'status quo' the accounting profession in Texas stood stronger than ever before."[15]

The Public Accountancy Act of 1979 did represent a holding of the line in most areas. The TAPA's attempt to provide permanent two-class registration failed. The new law retained virtually intact the education, experience, and examination requirements for a licensee. It also continued in full force protections against encroachment by unlicensed bookkeepers and accounting technicians, including the restriction on unlicensed persons "holding out" as accountants. The retention of these sections of the law recognized the victories in the *Fulcher* cases and responded to the Federal Trade Commission's inquiry about entry-level requirements and professional standards being too high. Subsequent to the passage of the act, the FTC decided that these allegations, prompted in part by bookkeepers, were not the case, and the wisdom of the legislature was therefore affirmed.

The important rule-making section of the 1979 law represented a

15. As quoted in *CPA 79*, May/June, p. 4.

careful attempt to reflect the recommendations of the sunset commission and the order of the federal court. This was accomplished in part by clearly mandating the State Board's independent rule-making authority—eliminating altogether any reference to referendum approval by licensees—and then declaring that the reason for such authority was not only to guarantee integrity in the practice of public accountancy, as the old law stated, but to guarantee as well "high standards of competence" and to assure that "the conduct and competitive practice of licensees serve the purposes of the Act and the best interest of the public." With an eye toward maintaining high levels of professional competence in the future, the law permitted—but did not require—the State Board to promulgate rules requiring continuing professional education and to recognize specialities with different levels of competence in the practice of accounting.

The statute was much more explicit when it came to advertising and competitive bidding, a clear line being drawn to protect the First Amendment rights of practitioners and the consumer rights of the public on the one hand, and the obligation of the state to enforce professional standards on the other. There could be no rule against advertising, for example, unless one were needed to insure that advertising was "informative, free of deception, and consistent with professionalism." Rules on advertising could also be drawn to insure that "the conduct and dealings of licensees are free from fraud, undue influence, deception, intimidation, overreaching, harassment, and other vexatious conduct, including uninvited solicitations to perform professional accounting services."

The competitive bidding issue was handled in essentially the same manner. The State Board could make no rule against competitive bidding "except to the extent necessary to insure" that contracts or engagements with state agencies and political entitles covered by the Professional Services Procurement Act were not bid "in violation of law"; except for audit engagements with private companies with revenues in excess of $300,000; and except to insure that "no licensee engages in any competitive practice which would impair the independence or quality of services rendered or would restrict the opportunity for members of the public to seek and secure high quality professional accounting services at reasonable prices or which would unreasonably restrict competition among licensees."

In addition to the changes embodied in the rule-making section of the law, the 1979 act contained two other innovations. The first increased the size of the State Board from nine to twelve members and provided that the three new members must be "public representatives" not licensed by the board. Of the remaining nine licensed members of the board, at least seven must be CPAs. Second, in recognition of problems caused by the Texas Open Meetings Act and the Open Records Act, a new section in the law provided for reasonable protection of accountant-client confidentiality.

## Relations with the Texas State Board of Public Accountancy

While the Society welcomed the passage of the 1979 act and complimented itself on "maintaining the status quo," the law did break new ground. The extent to which substance follows form remains to be seen, but the make-up and expanded authority of the State Board under the 1979 law placed the board in a much more powerful and independent position with regard to the professional life of Texas accountants. The trend toward increased board authority began with the first regulatory act in 1945 and was appreciably extended in 1961 when the board received subpoena powers. That authority has now reached the place where the board can unilaterally promulgate rules of professional conduct, the violation of which could result in the revocation of an accountant's license and the means of pursuing his or her livelihood. The presence of lay members on the board provides another dimension to the board's outlook and perspective, and the reality of sunset review every ten years will no doubt cause the board to be more responsive to broadly defined public and consumer interests in the future than it has been in the past.

An indication that the State Board might act in a somewhat more independent fashion in the future surfaced with the promulgation of new professional conduct rules, a provisional set dated September 1, 1979, and the more permanent and current set dated December 27, 1979. Modeled again after the recommendations of the National Association of State Boards of Accountancy, the rules incorporate by reference generally accepted auditing standards and accounting principles; define standards of independence, integrity, and objectivity; describe the responsibilities of accountants to clients; and explain the rights of competitive behavior. The rules also include a lengthy list of terms and definitions, including a definition of the "practice of public accountancy" that by virtue of incorporation in the rules affords a legal definition not found in the statute itself.

The new rules met with general approval. There was considerable difference of opinion, however, over the board's definition of competitive bidding, which included the statement: "for the purposes of these rules a 'fee estimate' shall not be deemed to be a competitive bid." The problem in the minds of many Society members was that though technically nonbinding on the accountant, a fee estimate as defined in the rules was for all practical purposes a bid and should be allowed only in cases where competitive bidding was allowed, or, conversely, should not be allowed in cases where competitive bidding was prohibited, as in engagements conducted under the Texas Professional Services Procurement Act and engagements with private entities whose annual revenues exceed $300,000 annually.

The issue quickly came before the Society's Executive Committee, a majority of whom opposed the definition. Through President Carl Chilton, the committee formally requested the board to reconsider its definition of competitive bidding. State Board Chairman Lyda formally responded to the Society's request, stating that the board declined to change the rule. The board recognized a clear distinction between a nonbinding fee estimate and a competitive bid, Lyda said, adding that the "fee estimate concept was made a part of the Rules to assist the client in making an informed selection of an accountant prior to entering into a binding fee arrangement," and "to reduce the likelihood of the over-eager licensee's accepting work without adequate advance consideration." Lyda agreed that a client's "commonly perceived need for some meaningful cost information in advance of selecting an accountant is not strange, hard to understand, nor difficult of empathy. In short, the fee estimate is designed to prevent potential harm to the public, the only basis upon which a restriction of competitive practices may be justified."

Lyda also responded to the Society's implication that the State Board's rules caused Texas CPAs to "end up with a result different from what they fought to achieve" in the passage of the 1979 act. This observation "could perhaps be accurate," Lyda acknowledged. However, "such a development should not seem totally strange, unnatural, or without logic when one considers the contrasting roles of the Society and the Board. It is understandable and reasonable that the Board's objectives as to both the Act and the Rules may have been somewhat different from those of the Society," Lyda said. He noted "the society is a voluntary professional association with a primary function of promoting the well-being of its members and the profession," while the State Board "is a legislatively created agency of state government charged by statute with administering the Act and promulgating rules 'to insure that the conduct and competitive practices of licensees serve the purpose of the Act and *the best interest of the public*.' Although both the Board and the Society share a common long-term objective for a strong and healthy profession, it is not unnatural and not necessarily unhealthy that the Board and the Society have contrasting views in the short run as to certain matters. Such differences are the inevitable product of the regulator-regulatee relationship." [16]

It would be a mistake to read into Lyda's lengthy response to the Society more than was intended. However, it candidly recognized that the Texas Sunset Commission and the federal courts had forced the State Board and the Society into a different relationship than had existed before 1979. In retrospect, this may have been the most significant development in professional accountancy in Texas in the decade of the 1970s.

Regardless of the new "regulator-regulatee" relationship, the Society and the State Board worked closely together in 1981, pushing through several amendments to the new accountancy law. The most important change allows the governor, for the first time, to appoint as many as two CPAs from government or industry to the State Board. Another change permits public practitioners to participate in peer reviews without violating rules of privileged client information. Texas CPAs also applauded action removing the statutory requirement that public practitioners display a sign noting their regulation by the State Board, a requirement most thought to be obnoxious and demeaning.

16. Don Lyda, Chairman Texas State Board of Public Accountancy, to Carl Chilton, President Texas Society of Certified Public Accountants, May 2, 1980, TSCPA.

# 10

## *The Texas Society at Present*

THE accounting profession in Texas was a direct beneficiary in the 1970s of the dramatic shift in the nation's population and industrial production away from the North and East to the sunbelt regions of the South and West. In addition to its size and location, the abundance of energy resources made Texas a leader in virtually every statistical category used for measuring commercial and industrial economic growth. For example, the index of industrial production, using 1967 as the base year, rose from 113 in 1970 to 154 in 1980. The number of people employed in nonagricultural pursuits moved up from 3.6 million to 5.7 million. While real monetary gains were partly offset by inflation in the last half of the decade, measured in billions of dollars, personal income in Texas increased from $40.5 to $128; retail sales, $20.3 to $67.4; value added by manufacture, $13.1 to $46.6; value of construction contracts, $4.1 to $14.5; bank deposits, $23.0 to $76.5; mineral production, $6.4 to $23.6; and gross farm income, $4.0 to $10.6.

The state's growth rate from 1970 to 1980 in comparison with other states was equally impressive. Texas retained first place among all states in the value of mineral production, third place in gross farm income, and first place among the ten most populous states in the rate of employment. In other areas, Texas moved up from fifth to second in retail sales, eighth to seventh in value added by manufacture, third to second in construction, sixth to third in nonagricultural employment, sixth to third in personal income, and fifth to fourth in bank deposits. Finally, summarizing all the indices of growth, the population of Texas increased 27 percent during the decade, a figure twice the national average, and moved the state from fourth to third place behind California and New York.

## Presidential Leadership, 1965–1983

The industrial and commercial expansion occurring in Texas, along with sophisticated changes in the practice of accountancy itself, imposed demands on Society leadership which are reflected in the educational background and professional careers of the nineteen presidents serving since 1965. All are collge graduates, four have graduate degrees in accounting or business management, and one has a law degree. Seventeen were in public practice while in office, though one former president, Jarman Bass, went into industry later. Presidents Robert Knox, in industry, and Charles Zlatkovich, in education, were not in public practice. Illustrating the growing presence of national firms in Texas, six of the seventeen presidents in public practice were associated with national firms at the time of their service to the Society, and three others merged their local or regional firms with national firms afterwards. Thus nine of the seventeen, over one-half of the number in public practice since 1965, can be identified with national firms. This is in marked contrast to the two-to-one majority that presidents from local or regional firms held in the period before 1965. However, regardless of practice and firm affiliation, Society leaders have continued to come from and identify with cultural distinction that make Texas unique. All but three, J. Kenneth Arthur, Paul Hillier, and president-elect Lee Wilson, were born either in Texas or in the neighboring states of Arkansas and New Mexico, and only Hillier was reared outside the Southwest.

Paul Cheatham, president in 1965–1966, was born in Burnet, Texas, in 1919. He attended public schools before enrolling in the University of Texas in 1938, where he was attracted to accounting because it offered a more professional career than other programs in the College of Business Administration. At Texas, George Lafferty, Cheatham's partner in later years, taught him introductory accounting, and Fladger Tannery, a future Society president, directed his labors as student assistant. Graduating with a BBA degree in 1942, Cheatham first worked in Houston for IBM and Brown Shipbuilding Company before joining Price Waterhouse & Co. in 1943. He completed the CPA examination in 1944 and two years later opened his own firm. The practice expanded to include six partners and a thirty-five-member professional staff with offices in Houston, Dallas, and Texas City at the time of Cheatham's death in 1981. While active in many aspects of the Society's programs, Cheatham is most remembered for the emphasis he gave to the management of accounting practices.

J. Kenneth S. Arthur's roots in the accounting profession go back to Scotland, birthplace of the profession. Two uncles on the maternal side of his family were Scottish chartered accountants who migrated to Texas around the turn of the century and one, J. W. Hurst, was among the small group that met in Galveston in 1911 to organize the forerunner of the Texas Society. His mother later returned to Edinburgh to marry John F. Stuart Arthur, also a chartered accountant, and J. Kenneth S. Arthur was born in 1918 when his parents lived in London. Later, his family moved to Dallas, where his father joined Peter & Moss, which merged in 1930 with Lybrand, Ross Bros. & Montgomery (now Coopers & Lybrand).

Kenneth Arthur graduated from Terrell Prep School in Dallas and then attended Rice University, where he graduated in 1941. Graduate study at the Harvard Business School was interrupted by military service during World War II and not completed until 1947. Setting aside earlier ambitions to be a banker, Arthur joined Coopers & Lybrand. Having had only one accounting course at Rice and minimum exposure to accounting at Harvard, he prepared on his own to pass the CPA examination in 1950. Primarily involved in auditing, Arthur became partner in charge of the Dallas office and the firm's southwest group, which at the time included Fort Worth, Austin, Houston, Oklahoma City, Tulsa, and Memphis. Arthur's service to the Society included participation in virtually every major committee either before or after his tenure as president in 1966–1967. He also served from 1973 to 1979 on the Texas State Board of Public Accountancy.

Harry E. Ward served as Society president in 1967–1968. Born in 1922, Ward attended public school in Fort Worth and was enrolled in Texas Christian University when World War II broke out. He volunteered for a naval officers training program that permitted him to complete his collegiate degree in 1943, after which he served three years of active duty. While still in college, in 1942, Ward worked part time for the firm of McCammon, Morris, and Pickens and after the war returned to Fort Worth to join Patterson and Leatherwood. He successfully completed the CPA examination in 1947 at the age of twenty-five, making him at that time the youngest person to hold a certificate in Texas. Later a partner in the firm Leatherwood and Ward, the firm merged with

Coopers & Lybrand in 1974, and Ward became managing partner of the Fort Worth office.

Robert E. Knox, Jr., 1967–1968 president of the Texas Society, came from the ranks of CPAs in industry. Except for a two-year period (1947–1949) he spent as a staff accountant in the Dallas office of W. O. Ligon & Co., Knox has been a financial officer in an independent oil firm in Tyler. Moreover, his academic training gave little hint that he would one day speak for the public accounting profession in Texas.

Knox was born in Weatherford, Texas, in 1920 and graduated from Highland Park High School in Dallas. In 1942 he completed a liberal arts degree in literature and history at Rice University, having also worked during his student days as a biology lab assistant, editor of the yearbook, and assistant for the Houston Museum of Fine Arts. He took only one course in accounting during his undergraduate career. Following four years of military service in the Navy, Knox completed the Harvard MBA program in financial management in 1947. While waiting for a position in the oil business to open up, Knox gained experience in public accounting and, with considerable reading on his own, passed the CPA examinations in 1949. He first became active in Society affairs with the formation of the East Texas Chapter in 1953.

Edwin E. Merriman, who received his certificate in 1950, holds the unique distinction of being the only president of the Society to have been registered first under the 1945 accountancy act as a public accountant. The circumstances that led to this development grew in large part from the fact that when he graduated from the University of Texas in 1933 with a BBA degree in accounting, public accounting jobs were hard to find. He returned home and worked in his father's store in Throckmorton for over a year before returning to Austin and taking graduate courses in 1935–1936. In 1937 Merriman became a field representative for the Texas Employment Commission, and by the time he entered military service in 1942 he had been promoted to state director. Returning to Texas in 1946, Merriman registered under the new 1945 act as a public accountant. In 1948 he joined his cousin Parr Merriman in opening public practice in Lubbock. Although his cousin left the firm the next year, Edwin E. Merriman & Company developed a practice with eleven partners in Lubbock, Amarillo, Plainview, and Muleshoe before merging with Peat, Marwick, Mitchell & Co. in 1982.

Upon passing the CPA examination in 1950, Merriman moved

quickly into leadership roles with the Lubbock Chapter, the Society, and the AICPA. In addition, he served ten years (1958–1968) on the Texas State Board of Public Accountancy.

Miller Montag was born and reared in East Texas but has spent his professional career in San Antonio. Born in Henderson in 1919, Montag graduated from local public schools and Kilgore Junior College in 1939. Two years later, he received a BBA degree from the University of Texas. Following wartime service in the air force, Montag worked briefly in 1945 for the Reconstruction Finance Corporation and with the San Antonio accounting firm of George, Thrift & Cockrell. In 1946 he joined the Leon Lewis firm as staff accountant, passed his CPA examination in 1950, and became a partner in the firm in 1954. In 1970 the firm of Lewis & Montag merged with Deloitte Haskins & Sells, and Montag remained a partner until his retirement in 1980. Montag was active in San Antonio Chapter and state society affairs prior to his term as president in 1970–1971. He was appointed to a six-year term on the Texas State Board of Public Accountancy in 1975.

Frank T. Rea, the fiftieth president of the Texas Society, was born in Longview, Texas, in 1922. Only fifteen years old when he finished high school in 1938, he enrolled in Texas Tech where an older sister attended. After three semesters at Tech, Rea transferred to Kilgore Junior College for one term and then to the University of Texas, where he completed the BBA degree in 1943. Following his discharge from naval duty in 1946, Rea joined the Jay Phillips firm in Houston and developed a special interest in tax work. His CPA certificate was awarded in 1947, and in 1952 he successfully completed a law degree from South Texas College of Law. His tax practice brought him into contact with bank trust officers in Houston, one of whom invited him to join the trust department of the National Bank of Commerce. The invitation came on March 15, 1958, just as the busy tax season ended and the prospect of working only nine to five and no weekends enticed Rea into a two-year stint with the bank. The challenge of public practice brought him back into the Houston office of Price Waterhouse & Co., from which he retired in 1978. Rea was appointed to the Texas State Board of Public Accountancy in 1981.

Jarman Bass, president in 1972–1973, began his professional career with Arthur Andersen & Co. in Dallas in 1946. Ten years later he became a partner in the firm and upon completion of his term as president of the Society he managed the firm's Geneva, Switzerland, office for fourteen months. Bass returned to Dallas as chief financial officer of the Trammell Crow Co. in 1974. Three years later, he became president of Federal Coca-Cola Bottling Company in Dallas, a firm which operates soft drink bottling plants in Georgia and oil properties in West Texas. Bass, born and reared in Waco, was graduated from Baylor University in 1943 and awarded his Texas certificate in 1949.

Burke Haymes was born in Rector, Arkansas, in 1916, but he graduated from Houston public schools in 1933 and from Rice University in 1937. He worked in the New York office of Haskins & Sells until the war interrupted his professional career. Following military service, he passed the CPA examination in 1945 and worked two years for the Reconstruction Finance Corporation as that agency closed out its operations. Haymes then joined Arthur Young & Company when the firm opened a Houston office. In 1956 he established his own firm and developed a small but select practice that concentrates on financial statements and tax-related business. Haymes joined the Society in 1946 and participated most actively in the Houston Chapter before his election as president in 1973–1974. Following his term as president, Haymes was appointed to a full term on the Texas State Board of Public Accountancy. His service on the board concluded in 1981.

Lawrence G. Pickens, president 1974–1975, received his collegiate training after World War II and, in that sense, represents the first of the postwar generation of Society leaders. Born in Miami, Texas, in 1927, Pickens (no relation to earlier president Hatcher Pickens) graduated from Pampa High School and enlisted in the U.S. Navy. Discharged in 1946, he attended McPherson College in Kansas for two years and then transferred to the University of Texas, where he graduated in 1950. He was called back into service for two years during the Korean conflict and emerged a commissioned officer. He returned to Amarillo in 1953 and, for approximately eighteen months, worked for a local accounting firm and a like period of time for an Amarillo mortgage banking firm. Completing the certificate requirements in 1956, Pickens joined Zed Doshier in a partnership that developed into the firm of Doshier, Pickens & Francis, serving the Amarillo area. Tennessee Pickens, wife of the Society president, is also a CPA who, he likes to recall, passed the examination on her first try, a record somewhat better than his own.

Curtis Frazier has spent his professional career in Fort Worth. He was also born in that city in 1927 and graduated from Arlington Heights High School in 1943. Attending college at North Texas Agricultural College (now University of Texas at Arlington) during the war years 1943 to 1945, Frazier was frequently one of only four or five students in accounting classes. He entered the navy in 1945 and was discharged in time to enroll in the 1946 fall term at Baylor University. Graduating from Baylor in 1948, Frazier took additional accounting courses at the University of Texas at Austin for one year, returning to Fort Worth in 1949 to join the staff of J. Warren Day Company. Recalled into military service during the Korean conflict, Frazier returned to public accounting and completed his certificate requirements in 1953. In 1969, when many lcoal firms were merging with national firms, Frazier's firm of Day, Benton & Frazier moved in a different direction and joined with another local firm to form Brantley, Spillar & Frazier. With six partners and a staff of twenty-five, the firm has a practice almost equally divided between opinion, tax, and accounting services.

Stanley Voelkel, born in Breslau, Texas, in 1929, graduated from El Campo High School in 1947. He took an undergraduate accounting degree at the University of Houston in 1951 and completed the master's degree program in 1952. As a student he helped organize a student accounting club and taught an elementary course in accounting in the summer of 1951. With time out for military service in 1952–1954, Voelkel began his professional career in the tax department of Arthur Andersen & Co. After six and one-half years with the national firm, and having secured his certificate in 1958, he organized his own local firm. Voelkel Cabaniss & Co. currently has three partners, a total staff of thirty, and devotes approximately 75 percent of its practice to tax work.

The society's president 1977–1978 was Rowland D. Pattillo, born in Dallas County, Arkansas, in 1923. Pattillo's family lived in Fordyce and later Arkadelphia, where he graduated from high school in 1941. After two years as a student in Henderson State Teachers College, and following a medical waiver from the military, Pattillo enrolled in the University of Texas in 1943. Fourteen months later he left Austin with all but six hours of his academic program completed (which he later finished by correspondence) for a staff position with Peat, Marwick, Mitchell & Co. in Houston. A year and a half later, in 1946, the same year he acquired his Texas certificate, Pattillo accepted Frank Wilcox's offer to join him in Waco. Building upon Wilcox's individual practice, the firm, now Pattillo, Brown and Hill, has offices in Waco and Corsicana. With five partners and a staff in the high twenties, the firm's practice consists of about 45 percent audit, 45 percent tax, and 10 percent miscellaneous accounting services.

Walter Bielstein completed a business and accounting degree at Trinity University in San Antonio in 1947. Born in Comfort, Texas, in 1925, Bielstein graduated from Thomas Jefferson High School in San Antonio in 1942 and served three years in the army (1943–1946). His professional career, which began with Ernst & Ernst in 1947 in San Antonio, was strengthened with his CPA certificate in 1951. Three years later he joined a local partnership which, as Bielstein, Lewis & Wilson, merged in 1972 with the regional firm of Alford, Meroney & Company, which firm, in turn, merged with Arthur Young & Company in 1980. Having practiced in national, local, and regional firm settings, Bielstein was uniquely prepared to lead the Society in the year which saw the enactment of the Public Accountancy Act of 1979.

Carl Chilton of Brownsville led the Texas Society in 1979–1980. Born in Roswell, New Mexico, in 1923, his parents moved to the Rio Grande Valley in 1925, and he graduated from Port Isabel High School in 1940. Chilton attended Texas A&I in Kingsville in 1940–1942 and, after three years in the air force, he completed his undergraduate degree at the University of Texas in 1947. Upon graduation, he returned to Port Isabel as city secretary and manager of the chamber of commerce. A year later he moved to Brownsville and taught accounting at Texas Southmost College for three years. Acquiring his certificate in 1950, Chilton engaged in limited practice and opened an office in 1951. Later that same year he joined in a partnership with William Long that evolved into the firm of Long, Chilton, Payte & Hardin. With offices in Brownsville, McAllen, Harlingen, and Port Isabel, the firm has eight partners and a staff of sixty, making it the largest regional firm in the Rio Grande Valley. In addition to his practice and professional society activities, Chilton wrote *Successful Small Client Accounting Practice*, published by Prentice-Hall in 1976.

Paul Hillier was born April 22, 1930, in Pittsburgh, Pennsylvania, but moved at an early age to Cleveland, Ohio, where he graduated from public schools in 1948. Enlisting for a term in the U.S. Air Force, he was stationed at Lackland and Holloman air force bases in Texas and

New Mexico, where he acquired a desire to live in the Southwest. Hillier also took an entry-level accounting course in the air force that whetted his appetite for more formal training in the subject. Upon release from the military, Hillier enrolled in the University of Pittsburgh and graduated in 1953 with a BBA degree and a major in accounting. Accepting a position with Price Waterhouse & Co., Hillier came to the firm's Dallas office when it consisted of only seven persons. He has participated in the growth of that office to include more than two hundred persons, with new offices in Fort Worth and Oklahoma City. Hillier earned his Texas certificate in 1957 and shortly thereafter became active in Dallas Chapter and Texas Society affairs.

Charles Zlatkovich, president in 1981–1982, is the third academician to lead the Society, Laurence Fleck and Tom Leland having preceded him in the office. Born in Fort Worth, Zlatkovich attended public and parochial schools in that city, graduating from Laneri High School in 1934. He enrolled in North Texas Agricultural College (now University of Texas at Arlington) and completed his baccalaureate program at Texas Christian University in 1938 under the tutelage of J. R. Maceo, a chartered accountant, and J. Warren Day, a leading local practitioner and part-time instructor. A year later, Zlatkovich received the first MBA degree conferred by TCU. He taught accounting at TCU during the 1939–1940 academic year. Zlatkovich began his long association with the University of Texas in the fall of 1940 when he enrolled in the garduate program in accounting. World War II interrupted his graduate study, but he returned to Austin in 1946 and accepted a full-time university faculty appointment. Continuing graduate study on a part-time basis, he passed the CPA examination in 1947 and earned his doctorate in 1952. Except for a year and a half of service on the AICPA staff in New York shortly after completing his doctorate and occasional summers spent with public accounting firms, Zlatkovich has devoted his professional career to teaching. Since 1973, the year it was established, he has held the C. Aubrey Smith Professorship at the University of Texas.

Carroll W. Phillips, born in 1933 and holder of a comparatively high numbered certificate (number 4586, dated January, 1959), attended public schools more reminiscent of pioneers in the Texas profession than the current generation. Phillips spent the first five years of his public schooling in a one-room school house in Clay County, twenty miles south of Henrietta, Texas. Even when surrounding schools consolidated, only seventeen seniors were in his graduating class in 1950. Phillips, who is no relation to J. A. Phillips, an earlier president, enrolled in Texas A&M in the fall of 1950 convinced he wanted to become a medical doctor. But after one semester of "frogs and formaldehyde," he changed his major to accounting. Professors Walter Matting and T. L. Ledbetter influenced his early studies and, as was the custom at A&M, in his senior year Tom Leland took a hand in finding him a job. Leland sent Phillips to Dallas for an interview with Stuart Arthur of Lybrand, Ross Bros. & Montgomery (now Coopers & Lybrand), where Phillips was "hired on the spot." Following graduation in 1954, Phillips spent six months in Dallas before serving his two-year commisioned service in the U.S. Air Force in Germany. Returning to Coopers & Lybrand in Dallas in 1956, Phillips remained until 1971, except for brief excursions to New York and Los Angeles. He became managing partner of the Houston office in 1971.

In the last thirty years, with only rare exception, presidents of the Texas Society have come from reasonably large local or regional and national accounting firms in which other partners can take up the slack when the president is involved in the time-consuming demands of the office. This will not be the case in 1983–1984, when the president will be I. Lee Wilson. A business consultant and specialist in tax matters, Wilson has been an individual practitioner in Dallas since 1963.

Lee Wilson was born in Bridgeport, Alabama, in 1926, and spent his early years in the Appalachian region near Denton, Tennessee. In 1942 his family moved to Dallas, where he completed the last two years of high school. He entered the U.S. Navy's V-5 and V-12 officer training programs in 1944, receiving essentially two years of his collegiate education before being discharged at the end of the war. Returning to Dallas, Wilson enrolled in Southern Methodist University. After completing the BBA degree requirements, he continued his studies and, in January, 1950, became the first graduate of the school's MBA program. That same month, Wilson passed the CPA examination and accepted employment with the Internal Revenue Service. Before the year was out, however, he became an agent for the Federal Bureau of Investigation. After four years with the FBI, Wilson took an executive position with an industrial corporation, where he remained until he opened his practice in 1963.

Wilson became actively involved in Dallas Chapter affairs, serving once as chapter president and later being named Dallas CPA of the Year in 1978. He first gained attention statewide for his work with the Society's Political Action Committee.

## Rapid Growth of Society Membership

The 4,700-member society Paul Cheatham presided over in 1965–1966 increased virtually fourfold, to 18,164 members during the years ending with the Charles Zlatkovich administration in 1981–1982. In 1975, with the membership closing in on 10,000 and expanding at the rate of 1,000 per year, President Curtis Frazier suggested that the ceremony recognizing each thousandth new member be modified and thereafter performed at intervals of five thousand.[1] Instead, the Society discontinued the ritual altogether. In relation to the total number of persons eligible for membership, the Society continues to average close to 80 percent of the licensed certified public accountants, of whom there were 22,600 in August, 1981.

The Texas Society's dramatic growth, of course, partly reflected the sharply rising demand for accountants nationally. During the period 1973 to 1982, for example, membership in the AICPA increased from 95,415 to 187,188. Even so, the growth rate in Texas exceeded the national average and permitted the Society comfortably to maintain its position as the nation's third-largest state society behind New York, with 24,543 members in 1981, and California, with 21,470.

The Society's growth can be measured in other ways, especially meaningful to accountants themselves. Society expenditures, which ran about $161,000 in 1964, doubled every four or five years thereafter: $341,000 in 1969, $704,000 in 1974, and $1,634,000 in 1978. For the year ending May, 1982, Society expenses, including the CPE Foundation and Educational Foundation, but excluding the Political Action Committee, reached $3,933,898. As noted earlier, expenditures related to continuing professional education are balanced by income from the sale of courses and programs and, since 1977, have been administered by the CPE Foundation. General Society expenses consist of adminis-

1. "Minutes 1975–76 Executive Committee Meeting, December 4–5, 1975," TSCPA.

trative office expense (including the Educational Foundation); publications; annual meeting; legal fees; officers and committee expense; and other charges of a miscellaneous nature. Totaling $1,090,687 in 1982, these expenses are essentially paid from membership dues and admission fees, with much a smaller amount of income from sale of advertising in publications, annual meeting registrations, and interest on invested funds. As the administrative office expenses increased, it became necessary to raise membership dues. This sometimes painful chore was done by vote of the membership in 1963 and 1967, but in 1970 members delegated the authority to set dues to the Board of Directors, who responded with increases in 1972, 1977, 1980, and 1981.

## Changes in Society Staff

The explosive increase in membership, plus the new emphasis on continuing professional education, burdened the Society's staff as well as its volunteer officers and committee members. When William Quimby took over the executive directorship in 1964, an eight-member staff serviced the needs of four thousand members, a staff-to-membership ratio of 1 to 500 that was already high in comparison with other state societies. By 1975 the staff had exactly doubled in size, but membership exceeded nine thousand and the staff ratio was even more acute. Moreover, a "genuine crisis" developed in the continuing professional education department when, simultaneously, the director, Forrest Black, resigned and his top assistant retired; both were persons of long tenure with the Society. The failure to define procedures and give direction to the new continuing professional education director, Don Weldon, compounded the problems of a department that was understaffed and inadequately housed to do the job it was attempting to do. These problems related to continuing professional education were underscored in an auditor's report submitted to the Board of Directors in November for the year ending May 31, 1975.[2] The report went further, however, to recommend improvements in handling cash receipts and disbursements, better use of the budget to control expenditures, and upgraded computer services. In addition to the critical tone of the auditor's report, declining staff morale was matched by frustration on the part of

2. Middleton & Burns to Board of Directors, Nov. 28, 1975, TSCPA.

some leadership that the Society was becoming unresponsive and failing to meet the desires of the general membership.

The changes required to correct the problems perceived to be plaguing the Society were most forcibly addressed by the administration of President Stanley Voelkel, who, with his executive committee, set about to infuse the Society staff and leadership with a new sense of direction and purpose. Upon assuming office in June, 1976, Voelkel accepted the resignation of William Quimby and for the next six months personally directed staff and Society affairs while the search for a new executive director ran its course.[3] Lines of administrative authority and internal financial controls were sharpened, dues were increased, and an in-house computer was installed. The need to provide more office space focused attention again on the question of removing Society offices to Austin, a move which Voelkel supported but one which the Board of Directors turned down at a called meeting in Dallas in August.[4] However, Society offices did move from downtown Dallas to more commodious facilities on the edge of town convenient to Love Field and the Dallas–Fort Worth airport. Less tangible but no less important, a larger number of Society members became actively involved in committee, chapter, and continuing professional education programs.

Webster W. Sharp became the Society's fifth executive director in February, 1977. Like his predecessor, Sharp's professional background was in chamber of commerce work, coming to the Society from a position with the Clear Lake Chamber of Commerce, where he had gained accreditation for the organization and the distinction Certified Chamber Executive for himself. A native of Amarillo, Sharp was born in 1935 and graduated from Texas Tech University in 1958 with a BBA major in advertising. The skills he brought to the Society enabled him to continue the forward momentum already generated. Serving with him in other key staff positions are James A. Sanders, director of administration; Julie C. Kirksey, director of continuing professional education; Kathleen Y. Klein, director of communications; Pat Sterling, director of membership/EDP; Dorothy R. Smith, executive director, Educa-

3. Quimby's relationship with the accounting profession did not end in 1976. Five years later, in 1981, he was appointed to the Texas State Board of Public Accountancy.

4. Location of the Society office was a major concern of an Ad Hoc Committee on Facilities created in 1974. Reporting to the Executive Committee on Oct. 23, 1974, the committee stated its preference to keep Society headquarters in Dallas (TSCPA).

tional Foundation; Cheryl E. Corder, director of finance; and Pat King, meetings director. In all, the staff numbers forty-seven persons, which affords a comfortable staffing ratio of 1 to 386, comparable to the California society's 1 to 358 and the New York society's 1 to 400.

## New Directions in Communications and Public Relations

Larger and neatly balanced budgets, a more smoothly running CPE program, a well-administered Educational Foundation, and efficient staff support for committees and trustee groups provide ample evidence to insiders that the Society is keeping up with professional changes and demands in the state. Communicating the Society's activities to the general membership became vitally important as the number of CPAs increased so rapidly. The first step in the direction of changing Society publications to fit current needs occurred in July, 1974, when the Society discontinued publication of the *Texas Certified Public Accountant* and replaced it with the *Texas CPA News*. The difficulty of getting good articles, the expense of publication, and the low readership by members convinced the Editorial Advisory Board that the technical journal should give way to a "short, eye-catching, interesting" publication containing news about members, information about the Society, and short articles of member interest in the areas of tax, audit, management services, and practice management.[5] Replete with more pictures and presented in a more pleasing format, the *Texas CPA News* did more nearly serve the Society's needs until 1978, when the publication was further improved and renamed *CPA 78*. Representing almost a year's study with professional communications experts, *CPA 78* gave the Society's lead publication a more modern appearance and some new dimensions in communication with its readers. A year later, the Society adopted a new logo designed to give Texas CPAs the appearance of being "professional, knowledgeable, organized, competent, modern—as opposed to conservative—and established."[6]

Meanwhile, communicating with the public again became a high-priority matter for the Society. In 1978 the Executive Committee charged the Communications Committee to develop projects that would "in-

5. *Texas CPA News*, Aug., 1974, p. 2.
6. As described in *CPA 79*, Dec./Jan., p. 13.

crease general public awareness, acceptance and understanding of the role of certified public accountants in the modern society." Responding to the charge, the Society hosted programs for chapter public relations officials, provided manuals to help chapter publication efforts, and provided press releases of a general interest for use by the mass media.

After two years of effort, a professional poll to ascertain the public's image of CPAs revealed the Society still had work to do. In comparison with medical doctors, lawyers, teachers, and insurance agents, CPAs were found to be less visible and perceived to be less important to the general public in a number of important categories. Recognizing an urgent need to generate greater public recognition and better inform the public, the Society engaged the professional services of a public relations firm in 1981. The first evidences of the new campaign appeared later that year in the form of institutional advertisements in state magazines and newspapers.

Aside from the impact of numbers themselves, it is important to note the changing composition of Society membership, most notably the increasing percentage of members who elect not to engage in public practice, the advance of women, and the admission of black accountants. During earlier years, membership in the Society was overwhelmingly in favor of public practitioners, CPAs not in public practice being relegated to associate membership prior to 1935. Since the middle 1950s, however, the strong demand for professional accounting services in the private sector has resulted in an increase of CPAs in industry that is much more rapid than that in public practice. Among the members of the Texas Society, the CPAs in industry, government, and education outnumbered those in public practice for the first time in 1979–1980.

## Women in the Society

Women have joined the ranks of professional accountancy in much greater numbers in the last decade and one-half. As previously noted, Mary Ethel Welborn of Dallas in 1934 was the first woman CPA in Texas and also the first female member of the Texas Society. Heloise Brown Canter, in 1942, was only the fifth woman CPA in Texas and the first in Houston. Nationwide, the number of women CPAs did not reach one hundred until 1947, and it was another decade before appreciable numbers began to appear. Within the last five years, however, the number of women CPAs in Texas has jumped from 520 in 1974, approximately 3 percent of the total, to 3,095, or 13.7 percent, in 1981. Almost 30 percent of the certificates awarded in 1980 went to women. A subtle sign of the changing times occurred in 1973, when Society by-laws were amended "to recognize the feminine gender where applicable" in the use of the pronoun "he."

Accountancy is still largely a male-dominated profession, but it augurs well for the future of women that four of the five Allred Award winners since 1975 have been women and that half of the forty-four Accounting Excellence Awards given by the Educational Foundation to senior accounting students in 1980 went to women. In 1978 women won four of the five graduate fellowships awarded by the Educational Foundation. Among women Society members, Heloise Brown Canter was the first to head a committee: History and Archives in the late 1950s and Society Tours since 1964. Sara Lou Brown has led the Society Committee on Tax Courses, and Johnnie Ray Seale, an outstanding chapter president (Corpus Christi) in 1979–1980, was elected vice-president of the Society in 1980–1981. The third CPE Award, given in recognition of outstanding contributions to continuing professional education, went to Joel Ann Middlebrook in 1978–1979. Further reflecting the advancement of women accountants, Sue Wegenhoft Briscoe in 1979 became the first woman to serve on the Texas State Board of Public Accountancy. In a separate category altogether because they are not CPAs, the Society elected Dorothy Smith, long-time director of the Educational Foundation, and Pauline Thomas, for many years executive secretary of the State Board of Public Accountancy before her death in 1978, honorary members of the Society in recognition of their unique contributions to the profession.

## Breaking Down the Color Line

In terms of the numbers involved, admitting black accountants into Society membership was less dramatic than admitting women, but in terms of eliminating discrimination, the admission of three black faculty members from Texas Southern University in 1969 was a signal event. As noted, the first constitution of the Texas Society restricted membership to whites only, though there were no black CPAs in Texas in 1915 and for nearly four decades to come. The formal wording prohibiting black members was soon deleted, but informal opposition remained into the late 1960s. Meanwhile, in March, 1952, the Texas State Board issued, by reciprocity from Indiana, the first Texas certificate to a black accountant, Professor Milton Wilson of Texas Southern University. Wilson made application for membership in the Texas Society soon thereafter, but his application was pigeon-holed in deference to the argument that the Society was, in part, a private organization entitled to select its members according to social as well as professional criteria.

This view held until the civil rights movement and affirmative action programs of the 1960s brought about a change in attitude. The change reflected, in part, the growing national emphasis against minority discrimination. But it also came about as a result of pressures brought to bear on Society leadership by national accounting firms, which were recruiting black accountants for their staffs and which found the informal policy of the Society harmful to their recruiting efforts. The issue came to a head during the administration of President Edwin Merriman, at which time six blacks, four of them associated with Texas Southern University, held Texas certificates. Merriman and his membership committee removed the racial barrier and invited blacks to join. Ironically, Wilson and two of his colleagues, Calvin L. Cooke and Melford T. Thompson, left Texas for other teaching positions soon after they were admitted to the Society, but Milton Bergeron, TSU business manager, remained and took an active role in Houston Chapter affairs.[7]

Gaining membership for blacks in the Texas Society was only part of a broader effort to recruit blacks and Mexican-Americans for the profession. A survey in 1969 revealed that there were only 150 black CPAs in the entire nation.[8] The number of Mexican-American accountants was also disproportionately small. To recruit minorities nationwide, the AICPA collected over $1.2 million for scholarships and financial aid. In Texas, modest gifts totaling $1,000 from five accounting firms enabled the University of Texas to conduct a pilot program in

7. As revealed in author's conversations with Milton Bergeron, Ernest L. Wehner, Paul Cheatham, and Edwin E. Merriman.

8. Bert N. Mitchell, "The Black Minority in the CPA Profession," *Journal of Accountancy* 128 (Oct., 1969): 41–48.

1971–1972 aimed at minority recruitment.[9] More importantly, loans from the Society's Educational Foundation enabled minority students to complete collegiate degrees. These efforts yielded mixed results. Mexican-Americans moved into the profession in sizable numbers, as witnessed by the dozen individuals with Spanish surnames holding Society committee assignments in 1981. On the other hand, only 158 blacks currently hold certificates in Texas.

## Volunteer Committee System

The volunteer committee system, one of the strengths of the Texas Society, strained under the diverging interests of an expanding membership. The basic committee structure and coordination system, worked out in the mid-1960s, continued in force during the 1970s, and by 1981 more than nine hundred Society members served on eighty-five standing committees and trustee groups. These, in turn, were loosely grouped into eleven clusters, each cluster coordinated by a member of the Executive Committee. While there is obviously some overlap and duplication of committee charges, the large number provides an opportunity for the expression of new ideas and the development of new leadership, matters of great importance to the Society's future success.

The functions of many of the committees, particularly those which translate most directly into the profession's service to the public—ethics, technical standards and procedures, legislation, continuing professional education—have already been described. Committees that give direction to some other functions of a fraternal, social, and housekeeping nature also make important contributions to the Society. These include committees on annual meetings, society tours, insurance, management of accounting practice, and the development of programs attractive to CPAs in government and industry.

## Annual Meetings

The annual meeting, focal point of Society activity in earlier years when the membership numbered in the hundreds, took on a different

9. See "Progress Report: Beta Alpha Psi Project to Recruit Economically Disadvantaged Students," included in a letter Jack C. Robertson to Jim Lowrey, March 17, 1972, TSCPA.

function and purpose when membership, soaring into the thousands, became more impersonal. Attendance at annual meetings leveled off at about five hundred during the middle 1960s and then declined slightly by the end of the decade. Alarmed at the downturn at a time when total membership was increasing rapidly, the Committee on Annual Meetings in 1968 suggested that either the annual meeting be restricted to officers, directors, and committee members, or the number of technical sessions be increased to encourage attendance by younger CPAs. However, the Committee on Long-Range Objectives and Planning, while expressing a desire to see greater attendance, was not discouraged, given the larger number of professional development courses and local chapter committee activities in which members could participate. Reaffirming a recommendation it made a year earlier, the Long-Range Committee suggested a "more relaxed atmosphere" at annual meetings, with only a few high-level technical sessions aimed at the broadest possible segment of the membership and speakers from top management of major corporations, government regulatory agencies, and AICPA. Further, it was suggested the purpose of the annual meeting be redefined to include the conduct of business in accordance with by-laws, social fellowship, and the enlargement of "understanding of fields of interest outside of our own."[10]

This philosophy prevailed until the emphasis on continuing professional education emerged in the early 1970s. Instructions for the San Antonio meeting in 1973 called for technical sessions in both morning and afternoon sessions, "reversing the trend toward de-emphasizing the technical content at annual meetings."[11] Regardless of the mix between technical and general sessions, attendance showed no marked increase.

The decision to hold annual meetings outside the state proved to be almost as controversial as the content of the program.[12] The Executive Committee began meeting in such places as Cerromar Beach, Puerto Rico; Pebble Beach, California; and Guadalajara, Mexico, in the mid-1970s, and the idea caught on for out-of-state annual meetings. New

10. "Mid-Year Report, 1968–69 Committee on Long-Range Objectives and Planning," TSCPA.

11. "Minutes 1972–73 Executive Committee Meeting, November 30–December 1, 1972," TSCPA.

12. See "Minutes 1975–76 Board of Directors Meeting, December 5–6, 1975," and "Minutes 1977–79 Board of Directors Meeting, June 25, 1977," TSCPA.

Orleans, Louisiana, was the site of the first such meeting in 1977. Plans to meet in Mexico City in 1978 were changed in favor of Dallas, but the Society met in Las Vegas in 1979 and San Francisco in 1981. Critics argued that the Society should stay in Texas, but the attendance figures for Las Vegas (580) and San Francisco (481) were considerably above the 1978 meeting in Dallas (345) and the 1980 meeting in Houston (376).

## Insurance Programs

The Society's insurance program began in the early 1950s when the Sid Murray Insurance Agency of Corpus Christi was authorized to offer the members group and individual policies for major medical, legal liability, and office overhead insurance. These policies were placed with insurance carriers, most notably Mutual of New York and Continental Casualty Company, and administered for the Society by the agency. In 1961 efforts to enroll Texas Society members in the AICPA-sponsored group life insurance program ran afoul of Texas law protecting domestic companies, whereupon the Sid Murray Agency developed an individual policy to suit member needs.[13] By 1969 the total annualized premiums paid by Society members on policies administered by the agency totaled $695,822. An "interesting statistic" noted by the Insurance Committee at that time was the Society's five-year paid claim/loss ratio under the professional liability plan: only 3.4 percent as opposed to 25 percent nationwide for the carrier, Continental Casualty Company.[14]

In an effort to improve coverage and lower costs, the Society took over administration of the group insurance programs in 1976 and contracted directly with Prudential Insurance Company to provide group and individual life, personal accident, long-term disability, major medical, and in-hospital disability income insurance. Under the new arrangement, the Society established an insurance trust to collect premiums and make remittances on a quarterly basis to Prudential. Within eighteen months, by the summer of 1978, the new program had enrolled 3,319 members, who paid in total annual premiums in excess of

13. "Minutes 1960–61 Executive Committee Meeting, June 16, 1961," TSCPA.
14. "Annual Report, 1969–70 Committee on Members' Insurance," TSCPA.

$1,200,000.[15] The life insurance proved particularly successful. For the premium year 1979–1980, the trustees were able to refund approximately $100,000 to participating Society members. "This demonstrates the overall validity of tremendously favorable arrangements that can be built with joint purchasing power," Keith C. Kakacek said in announcing the dividend for the trustees.[16] In other insurance matters, the Society added group automobile and homeowner's policies in 1980 and continued to sponsor individual professional liability insurance through Alexander & Alexander, a firm into which the Sid Murray Agency merged in 1973.

## Society Tours

The speed and economy of jet travel, which makes annual meetings in Las Vegas or San Francisco no more adventuresome today than was the train trip to Galveston in 1911 by the founders of the Texas profession, also prompted the Texas Society in 1962 to consider organizing foreign travel tours as an additional membership service. Airlines eager for the business were quick to point out the considerable savings available for group tours, and when the Executive Committee ran a notice in the October issue of the news bulletin to test the market, they "expressed optimistic surprise at the high rate of interest."[17] Thus encouraged, Heloise Brown Canter was appointed to head a committee and arrange a two-week European tour for the summer of 1964.

Although the 1964 tour was successful, the next Society-sponsored tour did not occur until 1970. But thereafter, under Canter's direction, many Society tours to places around the world have taken place annually, five separate tours in 1975 being the largest number in one year. In the early 1970s, approximately 225 Society members a year participated in the tours, a number that has been reduced in the last year or two to less than half.[18]

## Management of an Accounting Practice

Addressing the nuts-and-bolts problems associated with management of an accounting practice (MAP) represents a substantial invest-

15. *Texas CPA News*, July, 1978, p. 8.
16. *CPA 81*, April, p. 8.
17. "Minutes 1962–63 Executive Committee Meeting, December 7, 1962," TSCPA.
18. Heloise Brown Canter to author.

ment of formal committee time and effort. Some seven committees currently operate under the aegis of the Society's MAP Coordinating Committee. Some of the issues now formally addressed, however, were informally discussed earlier. Mark Eaton touched upon the subject of fees and "the economics of the accounting profession" in 1957 when he advised fellow practitioners that they should provide themselves with the office amenities and staff support necessary to lend dignity to their relations with clients. A practice should also be profitable enough to allow accountants to participate actively in civic and professional affairs and provide "sufficient leisure for thought and advanced study," for, after all, Eaton said, accountancy is an intellectual occupation. Over and above these considerations, Eaton remarked, the profession must compete successfully with business and other professional groups in recruiting the best young minds into accountancy.[19]

The Society gave form and substance to the study of ways by which CPAs could "improve their own economic welfare" during the administration of President Paul Cheatham in 1965.[20] A new Committee on Management of Accounting Practice, Herbert E. Dickey, chairman, undertook to provide information on a continuing basis in the following areas: recruiting and training, professional statistics, continuation of practice, professional fees, promotions and mergers, insurance bonds and guarantees, billing and collections, practice development, and practice review. Acknowledging this to be a "massive activity," the committee nevertheless moved ahead with vigor and determination, the success of the program being attested to in 1972 when Cheatham was given the Society's Meritorious Service Award. In making the announcement, President Frank Rea remarked "some practitioners are now driving Cadillacs instead of Fords because of the efforts of Paul N. Cheatham."[21]

The device first used to carry out the committee's work was a questionnaire distributed to Society members. It was designed to give a statistical profile of public practice in Texas—specifically, the size of the office, number of partners and staff, average net and gross income, average increase in gross fees, square feet of office space per person, number of hours charged per person, percentage of fees realized, use

19. Marquis G. Eaton, "The Economics of Accounting Practice," *Journal of Accountancy* 103 (June, 1957): 31–35.

20. "Minutes 1965–66 Executive Committee Meeting, April 23, 1965," TSCPA.

21. "Minutes Annual Meeting of Members, June 19, 1972," TSCPA.

of standard billing rates, staff to be added, and other related information. The popularity of the survey in Texas attracted attention from neighboring states, and in 1972 the New Mexico, Oklahoma, Arkansas, and Louisiana state societies joined in participation. In 1977 the questionnaire was modified to make it compatible with statistics compiled by the AICPA and was also broadened to include several states outside the Southwest: Oregon, Pennsylvania, Washington, Colorado, and New Jersey. Currently, sixteen states participate in the survey.

Other MAP activities evolved from the initial surveys and questionnaires. The Society produced a popular continuing professional education course entitled "Practicing Public Accounting Profitably," and followed that in the mid-1970s with practice management workshops which also carried educational credit. In addition, practice management conferences facilitate the exchange of information under less structured conditions. Most recently, the Society has developed a survey aimed at helping practitioners to understand the client's perception of accounting services.

## Members in Government and Industry (MIGI)

Vigorous committee leadership and the sheer force of numbers has recently caused the Texas Society to address the membership needs of CPAs in government, industry, and education, who, as noted above, in 1980 for the first time outnumbered Society members in public practice. These needs have long been recognized and partly fulfilled, a number of early leaders and supporting members having come from this segment of the Society. However, as late as 1975 the Society committee for this group reported that it "doesn't have a lot of work to be done except on special occasions, e.g., funds were raised a few years ago for legislative activities and for the Educational Foundation. A good part of this year was spent in trying to better define the specific charges this committee could be doing from year to year."[22]

Momentum began to gather two years later, when Larry Gene Pointer and the CPE Committee for Members in Government and Industry surveyed members in nonpublic practice to determine their level of re-

22. "Minutes 60th Annual Meeting of the Board of Directors, June 18, 1975," TSCPA.

sponse in reporting CPE hours. A follow-up survey then elicited more information about CPE needs, and it also discovered occupational characteristics of nonpublic accountants that were helpful to the Society in a more general way. Growing out of this activity, Pointer recommended the Society establish an umbrella committee in 1978 to coordinate all efforts aimed at supporting this segment of the membership. With enthusiasm and purpose, the MIGI Coordinating Committee moved into educational and organizational activities. It sponsored an annual Decision Makers Conference, developed chapter activities for MIGI, and pushed for representation of MIGI on all Society committees and the Texas State Board of Public Accountancy.[23] By 1980 MIGI was a high-priority item for the Society, personalized by the election of one of its number, Charles Zlatkovich of the University of Texas, to be president in 1981–1982.

The philosophical and ethical issues that emerge from the circumstance that half the members are engaged in public practice and half are privately employed have also moved to the fore. A major question is whether privately employed members should be bound by the same code of ethics as public practitioners. Currently bound by only two of the Society's thirteen rules of professional conduct, members in government and industry are particularly exempted from the rules requiring adherence to generally accepted accounting principles and auditing standards as well as independence and objectivity. Given the continuing interest of congressional leaders and financial analysists in corporate reporting, a strong case is being made for those in private practice to adhere to generally accepted standards and competency. And while members in government and industry surrender claims to independence and objectivity for financial statements they have a hand in preparing, the move is also underway to include them under rules of professionalism attendant to certification and membership in the Society.[24]

## Chapter Activities

In 1967, when he was vice-president charged with coordinating chapter activities, Frank Rea reported that "the eighteen chapters of the

---

23. *Texas CPA News*, March, 1978, pp. 12–13; and *CPA 79*, November, p. 10.
24. *CPA 81*, April, pp. 10–11 and 16–19.

Texas Society are the life blood and heart beat of the organization." That observation could be repeated with perhaps more force in 1980, particularly if the reference is to the role the chapters, now numbering twenty, play in providing opportunities for intrasociety contacts of a professional and social nature and for the interface they afford between the profession and the general public. Problems occasionally arise over conflicting loyalties between one's local chapter and the larger, impersonal state society. But these are minimal when compared with the chapter system's overall strength—a healthy respect for regional differences and the encouragement of chapter initiatives in carrying out the Society's broad policies.

The most interesting development in Society-chapter relations in the last ten years, in fact, has been a move somewhat in the other direction, a move by Society members desirous of breaking away from large chapters to form smaller ones that, by necessity, relate more directly with the state society. The effort was successful in the case of members in the Bryan–College Station area, who carved the Brazos Valley Chapter out of the Houston Chapter in 1975, and members in Texarkana, who formed their chapter at the expense of the East Texas Chapter in 1979. In each of these two cases, the parting was amicable on the part of the affected chapters and the Society. A different reaction occurred, however, when accountants in the area between Dallas and Fort Worth organized a Mid-Cities Association in 1975 and petitioned for chapter status. The Mid-Cities group ran into opposition from the two established chapters as well as a Society rule that permitted only one chapter per county. Fearing a precedent would be set that might result in other local group pull-outs, Society leadership delayed approval of the Mid-Cities petition. Thus far, no generally accepted solution to the problem has been found.[25]

One of the considerations involved in the creation of new chapters, and a stumbling block in the Mid-Cities matter, is the effect loss of members and revenues from chapter dues will have on the chapter giving up members to a new chapter. Dues vary from $10 to $50 annually, and in the larger chapters—Houston, Dallas, Fort Worth, San Antonio, and Austin—the income supports a full-time office staff and a variety

25. "Minutes 1974–75/1975–76 Executive Committee Meeting, May 2, 1975," and "Minutes 1975–76/1976–77 Executive Committee Meeting, April 22, 1976," TSCPA.

of professional development programs that are in addition to the Texas Society offerings. The Houston Chapter, with over thirty-six hundred members, and the Dallas Chapter, with more than three thousand, are each larger than many state societies, and their program activities reflect that fact. At the other end of the spectrum, however, four chapters—Brazos Valley, San Angelo, Texarkana, and Victoria—each have fewer than one hundred members and are therefore considerably more dependent upon the Texas Society.

## The Texas Society in the Future

Historians, like auditors, are wary of predicting the future. In reviewing a company's financial record, however, auditors suggest its future. Similarly, history permits an educated guess as to the direction the Society is moving.

Given the promising commercial and industrial development of Texas, the demand for professional accountants will almost certainly remain strong. This demand will be met by continued high student enrollments in college and university accounting departments, but more than one president of the Society has also remarked favorably on the substantial "in-flow" of highly skilled accountants in industry who have come to Texas when corporate headquarters of national and international businesses have relocated here. The growing strength of national accounting firms, which local and regional firms sometimes refer to as an "invasion," also make available a highly trained personnel pool. National accounting firms tend to recruit locally, however, and their tendency to enter the state and expand their practice by merger with local and regional firms diminishes somewhat the national firm as a source of new manpower. This fact also reduces the fear of some that professional development in Texas will be subject to policies of national firms headquartered in New York, Cleveland, or Chicago. In truth, the Texas offices of many national firms will likely have more to say about accounting principles and auditing standards for energy-related industries, for example, than do the partners in the home office. In this sense, the invaders have been taken over by the invaded.

The national-firm presence in Texas has several implications for the Texas Society and its programs. The practice of national firms, more or less automatically, to pay Society dues for eligible staff members makes their financial contribution to the Society increasingly important. At the same time, because of their own in-house professional development programs, national-firm personnel depend relatively little upon the Society for continuing professional education courses, now the major activity of the Society as measured in financial terms. This paradoxical development is partly explained by the fact that the Society's CPE program is self-supporting from fees rather than membership dues, but it is difficult to imagine the CPE Foundation's maintaining a strong program without a correspondingly viable Society staff, which, in turn, is increasingly dependent upon the membership dues of national-firm personnel.

The future of the Society does seem to be tied to its educational programs. The Educational Foundation's student loan and fellowship programs will continue to be needed and fully utilized as long as the demand for accountants remains strong. On the other hand, mandatory continuing professional education appears to be only a matter of time for all licensed accountants, and the CPE Foundation has an obvious responsibility in that regard.

Elsewhere, the Society's jurisdiction over rules of ethical and professional conduct has been seriously limited by recent events. The courts essentially removed professional societies from enforcing rules of competitive behavior and, despite the expectations of the American Institute's Joint Ethics Enforcement Program, respect for client confidentiality made enforcement of other ethical rules difficult. A professional society's strength and major reason for existence depends upon enforcing rules of professional conduct, however, and whether it is done directly through JEEP or indirectly through support of the Texas State Board of Public Accountancy, the obligation to uphold professional standards in the future is clear.

The probability is that the Society will find working through the Texas State Board of Public Accountancy to be the most effective way to uphold standards and professional conduct. This is not a new idea. In some respects, it is as old as the original Accountancy Act of 1915, and, as the more recent controversy over the Society's rule on competitive bidding illustrates, many Society members have thought for a long time that the Texas State Board was the proper place to locate this power. In their view, suspension or revocation of an accountant's license to practice by the legal arm of the state is a vastly more powerful weapon to enforce ethical behavior than withdrawing membership in a voluntary professional society. As a result of sunset review and the Accountancy Act of 1979, the State Board operates slightly more at arm's length from the Society than was the case in earlier years. However, it is difficult to see how the Society and the State Board could have fundamentally divergent views on how best to protect the public and the profession.

The future of the Texas Society will also hinge importantly upon its success in reconciling the interests of members in public practice and those in government and industry. Considerable progress in this direction has been made recently, but much remains to be done, both from the standpoint of the Society as it tailors programs to fit the needs of members in government and industry and from those members' recognizing their obligation to keep up professionally. Failure on the part of either party will possibly lead to a two-class licensing system, confusing to the public and damaging to the profession.

In conclusion, the Texas Society of Certified Public Accountants has served the profession and the public well for almost three-quarters of a century. Activities and programs of the state office and local chapters raised high standards of competence and integrity, enhancing the stature of professional accountants in Texas and benefiting the public they serve. The Society of the future can do no less.

APPENDIX A

## Past Officers of the TSCPA

| Year | Presidents | Presidents Elect | Vice-Presidents | Secretaries | Treasurers | Executive Committees |
|------|-----------|------------------|-----------------|-------------|-----------|---------------------|
| 1915–17 | D. H. Kernaghan* | | Loyd B. Smith* | | C. E. Scales* | |
| 1917–20 | Loyd B. Smith* | | Chas. F. Bridewell* | | C. E. Scales* | |
| 1920–21 | Marion Douglas* | | Marion Douglas* Austin H. Cole* | | C. E. Scales* | |
| 1921–22 | Austin H. Cole* | | Austin H. Cole* | | C. E. Scales* | |
| 1922–23 | Austin H. Cole* | | G M. Hofford* T. J. Tapp* | | C. E. Scales* | |
| 1923–25 | George Armistead* | | Frank G. Rodgers* | | C. E. Scales* | |
| 1925–26 | Luke B. Garvin* | | A. E. Myles* | Joe E. Hutchinson, Jr.* | | |
| 1926–27 | Arthur C. Upleger* | | A. V. Seay* | John J. Gannon | | |

*Deceased

| Year | Presidents | Presidents Elect | Vice-Presidents | Secretaries | Treasurers | Executive Committees |
|---|---|---|---|---|---|---|
| 1927–28 | Bouldin S. Mothershead* | | T. F. Kennedy | | H. Brady Mayhew* | |
| 1928–29 | J. R. Nelson* | | C. W. Wittman, Jr.* | | E. R. Burnett* | |
| 1929–30 | C. W. Wittman, Jr.* | | W. M. Aikman* | | A. V. Seay* | |
| 1930–31 | W. M. Aikman* | | Forrest Mathis* | | A. V. Seay* | |
| 1931–32 | Forrest Mathis* | | W. F. Carter, Jr.* | | H. Tracy Nelson | |
| 1932–33 | J. A. Phillips* | | H. W. Goodson | | C. F. Milledge | |
| 1933–34 | Thomas W. Leland* | | J. Glen Bixler* | | C. F. Milledge | |
| 1934–35 | Thomas W. Leland* | | E. R. Burnett* | | C. F. Milledge | |
| 1935–36 | Frank G. Rodgers* | | Clifton H. Morris* | | C. F. Milledge | |
| 1936–37 | H. Tracy Nelson | | T. W. Mohle* | | C. F. Milledge | |

*Deceased

| Year | | | | |
|---|---|---|---|---|
| 1937–38 | T. W. Mohle* | Joe C. Harris* | | C. F. Milledge |
| 1938–39 | Joe C. Harris* | C. F. Milledge | Thomas W. Leland* | |
| 1939–41 | Walter C. Burer* | Fred E. Pflughaupt | Thomas W. Leland* | |
| 1941–42 | Fred F. Alford* | R. I. Mehan* | Thomas W. Leland* | |
| 1942–43 | Joseph C. Cobb* | Lyle R. Sproles* | Thomas W. Leland* | |
| 1943–44 | Lyle R. Sproles* | Ben F. Irby | Thomas W. Leland* | |
| 1944–45 | C. F. Milledge | Laurence H. Fleck | Thomas W. Leland* | Nelson D. Durst |
| 1945–46 | Laurence H. Fleck | Roy L. Pope<br>John B. Allred* | Thomas W. Leland* | Nelson D. Durst |
| 1946–47 | Roy L. Pope* | Frank L. Wilcox*<br>Waymon G. Peavy | Thomas W. Leland* | |
| 1947–48 | Clifton H. Morris* | Kenneth B. White<br>Ben M. Davis* | Thomas W. Leland* | |

*Deceased

| Year | Presidents | Presidents Elect | Vice-Presidents | Secretaries | Treasurers | Executive Committees |
|---|---|---|---|---|---|---|
| 1948–49 | Harry D. Hopson* | | Charles A. Meroney*<br>Frank C. Brock | Thomas W. Leland* | | |
| 1949–50 | Frank L. Wilcox* | | Curtis H. Cadenhead<br>Hatcher A. Pickens | Thomas W. Leland* | | |
| 1950–51 | Ben M. Davis* | | Hatcher A. Pickens<br>J. R. Jordan | Thomas W. Leland* | | |
| 1951–52 | Curtis H. Cadenhead | | Fladger F. Tannery<br>W. Charles Woodard | Thomas W. Leland* | | |
| 1952–53 | J. R. Jordan | | Osa F. Alexander*<br>Walter R. Flack* | Thomas W. Leland* | | |
| 1953–54 | Marquis G. Eaton* | | C. Aubrey Smith<br>Wm. E. Ponder | Thomas W. Leland* | | |
| 1954–55 | Hatcher A. Pickens | | Homer L. Luther*<br>Robert J. Hibbetts | O. H. Maschek | W. Boone Goode | Marquis G. Eaton*<br>J. R. Jordan<br>Thomas W. Leland* |

*Deceased

| Year | | | | | |
|---|---|---|---|---|---|
| 1955–56 Fladger F. Tannery | Wm. P. Crouch<br>Don C. Chorpening | Kenneth W. Hurst | W. Boone Goode | Thomas W. Leland*<br>Hatcher A. Pickens<br>Frank L. Wilcox* | |
| 1956–57 Walter R. Flack* | Kenneth W. Hurst<br>L. Ludwell Jones | Jordan B. Wolf | W. Boone Goode | Thomas W. Leland*<br>Fladger F. Tannery<br>Frank L. Wilcox* | |
| 1957–58 Robert J. Hibbetts | W. Boone Goode<br>Jordan B. Wolf | Sam A. Merrill* | J. Francis Middleton | Walter R. Flack*<br>Harry D. Hopson*<br>Fladger F. Tannery | |
| 1958–59 Homer L. Luther* | Jack E. Collier<br>Thomas N. Jenness,<br>Jr. | Charles T. Zlatkovich | Edward F. Chirhart* | Don C. Chorpening<br>Robert J. Hibbetts<br>L. Ludwell Jones | |
| 1959–60 W. Charles Woodard | Clark W. Breeding<br>Erwin Heinen<br>Glenn A. Welsch | Walter L. Jungmann | Walter D. Roten | Kenneth W. Hurst<br>Homer L. Luther*<br>Bouldin S.<br>Mothershead* | |
| 1960–61 L. Ludwell Jones | Paul N. Cheatham*<br>Robert E. Knox, Jr.<br>Stanley J. Scott | James F. Nigh* | Herbert E. Dickey | John F. Kramer<br>Frank L. Wilcox*<br>W. Charles Woodard | |

*Deceased

| Year | Presidents | Presidents Elect | Vice-Presidents | Secretaries | Treasurers | Executive Committees |
|---|---|---|---|---|---|---|
| 1961–62 | Stanley J. Scott | | Gordon N. George<br>John F. Lanier, Jr.<br>Sidney M. Lewis<br>Edwin E. Merriman | Walter K. Juncker | Howard L. Busby | Byron G. Bronstad<br>Jack E. Collier<br>L. Ludwell Jones |
| 1962–63 | Jordan B. Wolf | Kenneth W. Hurst | J. Kenneth S. Arthur<br>Robert A. Casey*<br>Donald R. Eaton<br>Harry E. Ward | William B. Newkirk, Jr. | Curtis L. Frazier | J. R. Jordan<br>Lawrence G. Pickens<br>Stanley J. Scott |
| 1963–64 | Kenneth W. Hurst | Gordon N. George | R. Jud Adams<br>Herbert C. Graham<br>Miller Montag<br>Adolph G. Schlossstein, Jr.* | John R. Walker | Jack O. Spring | Donald W. Dorman<br>Walter E. Vater<br>Frank L. Wilcox* |
| 1964–65 | Gordon N. George | Paul N. Cheatham* | Herbert E. Dickey<br>Donald W. Dorman<br>C. H. Hamilton, Jr.<br>Gregg C. Waddill | Zed Doshier, Jr. | Jarman Bass | Jack E. Collier<br>Miller Montag<br>W. Charles Woodard |

*Deceased

| 1965–66 | Paul N. Cheatham* | J. Kenneth S. Arthur | Robert L. Grinaker<br>Walter D. Roten<br>Walter E. Vater<br>Tom Welch | L. William Long | Leonard H. Brantley | Walter R. Flack*<br>L. Ludwell Jones<br>Harry E. Ward |
|---|---|---|---|---|---|---|
| 1966–67 | J. Kenneth S. Arthur | Harry E. Ward | Howard L. Busby<br>Lawrence G. Pickens<br>Frank T. Rea<br>Neal Y. R. Sheffield | Burke Haymes | Rowland D. Pattillo | Robert E. Knox, Jr.<br>Edwin E. Merriman<br>Jordan B. Wolf |
| 1967–68 | Harry E. Ward | Robert E. Knox, Jr. | Burke Haymes<br>Walter L. Jungmann<br>William Morphew<br>Edward P. Thompson | Daniel E. Kilgore | Kenneth C. Durbin | Jarman Bass<br>Robert A. Casey*<br>Gordon N. George |
| 1968–69 | Robert E. Knox, Jr. | Edwin E. Merriman | Carl S. Chilton, Jr.<br>H. B. Edens<br>Curtis L. Frazier<br>Jack O. Spring | James E. Jenkins | Buford J. Rhodes | Ford R. Hale<br>Kenneth W. Hurst<br>Frank T. Rea |
| 1969–70 | Edwin E. Merriman | Miller Montag | Jarman Bass<br>James C. Galbraith<br>Curtis L. Miles<br>John Patrick Thomas | G. George Varady | I. Lee Wilson | John A. Killough*<br>Lawrence G. Pickens<br>William H.<br>Shireman, Jr. |

*Deceased

| Year | Presidents | Presidents Elect | Vice-Presidents | Secretaries | Treasurers | Executive Committees |
|---|---|---|---|---|---|---|
| 1970–71 | Miller Montag | Frank T. Rea | Ford R. Hale<br>Robert S. Lipson<br>Don M. Lyda<br>Stanley H. Voelkel | Brooks Wilson | Samuel H. Tannebaum | C. L. Boggs<br>Gordon N. George<br>Tom Welch |
| 1971–72 | Frank T. Rea | Jarman Bass | Willard H. Findling<br>James E. Jenkins<br>E. James Lowrey<br>Lloyd J. Weaver | James F. Pattee | Carroll W. Phillips | William E. McReynolds<br>Edwin E. Merriman<br>Rowland D. Pattillo |
| 1972–73 | Jarman Bass | Burke Haymes | Walter A. Bielstein<br>John A. Killough*<br>Weldon J. Squyres<br>G. George Varady | Tommie E. Roddy, Jr. | William C. Hatfield | Wm. H. Armstrong<br>Lawrence G. Pickens<br>Harry E. Ward |
| 1973–74 | Burke Haymes | Lawrence G. Pickens | Rowland D. Pattillo<br>Carroll W. Phillips<br>Oscar E. Reeder<br>Charles T. Zlatkovich | Larry J. Parsons | John R. Jordan, Jr. | Glen D. Churchill<br>Edwin E. Merriman<br>Stanley H. Voelkel |

*Deceased

| Year | | | | | |
|---|---|---|---|---|---|
| 1974–75 | Lawrence G. Pickens | Curtis L. Frazier | Samuel P. Bell, Jr.<br>C. L. Boggs<br>Bruce J. Harper<br>Paul W. Hillier, Jr. | Arthur Greenspan | Robert R. Owen | Robert R. Arms<br>Frank T. Rea<br>Brooks Wilson |
| 1975–76 | Curtis L. Frazier | Stanley H. Voelkel | Patrick B. Collins<br>Doyle Z. Williams<br>I. Lee Wilson<br>James E. Windlinger | Paul J. Ellenburg | R. Allen Dodgen, Jr. | Frank S. Hardin<br>Robert E. Knox, Jr.<br>Don M. Lyda |
| 1976–77 | Stanley H. Voelkel | Rowland D. Pattillo | William E. McReynolds<br>Tommie E. Roddy, Jr.<br>Samuel H. Tannebaum<br>Brooks Wilson | William H. Armstrong | R. Allen Dodgen, Jr. | Samuel P. Bell, Jr.<br>Burke Haymes<br>Edward James Hanslik |
| 1977–78 | Rowland D. Pattillo | Walter A. Bielstein | Robert D. Clyde<br>William R. Cox<br>James R. Gilger<br>Vernal L. Huffines | Andrew G. Shebay | Bill R. Tillett | Carl S. Chilton, Jr.<br>Jimmie L. Mason<br>Lawrence G. Pickens |
| 1978–79 | Walter A. Bielstein | Carl S. Chilton, Jr. | Mason L. Backus<br>Wm. Nathan Cabaniss<br>James D. Ingram<br>Tom R. Locke | Claude R. Wilson, Jr. | Jay T. Ward | Carroll W. Phillips<br>Ronnie Rudd<br>Harry E. Ward |

*Deceased

| Year | Presidents | Presidents Elect | Vice-Presidents | Secretaries | Treasurers | Executive Committees |
|---|---|---|---|---|---|---|
| 1979–80 | Carl S. Chilton, Jr. | Paul W. Hillier, Jr. | Arthur Greenspan<br>Jimmie L. Mason<br>Charles L. Spicer<br>D. Wayne Tidwell | Raymond E. Graichen | Keith C. Kakacek | Robert D. Clyde<br>William R. Cox<br>Gene E. Glazener<br>Ronnie Rudd |
| 1980–81 | Paul W. Hillier Jr. | Charles T. Zlatkovich | Robert R. Arms<br>Dan H. Hanke<br>Ross McElreath<br>Johnnie Ray Seale | Frederick W. Nelan | James C. Hibbetts | Gene E. Glazener<br>Keith C. Kakacek<br>Robert E. Knox, Jr.<br>Claude R. Wilson, Jr. |
| 1981–82 | Charles T. Zlatkovich | Carroll W. Phillips | Walter T. Coppinger<br>Larry Gene Pointer<br>John W. Puckett<br>Ronnie Rudd | R. C. Mann | Henry R. Pearson | Nancy Boyd<br>John E. Ohlenbusch<br>Johnnie Ray Seale<br>John E. Sutton |
| 1982–83 | Carroll W. Phillips | I. Lee Wilson | Fred M. Bunker<br>Ted R. Popp<br>Karl A. Ransleben<br>J. Wayne Winfrey | Richard M. Witmer | J. Ike Guest | Walter A. Bielstein<br>John W. Burdette<br>Roderick L. Holmes<br>Pat D. McCarty |

*Deceased

# Recipients of Honors and Awards

## Meritorious Service to the Public Accounting Profession in Texas

Bestowed on a CPA and member of the TSCPA for his or her service to the Society or a chapter thereof, through direct participation in its affairs or otherwise, if circumstances justify.

1981–82—Paul W. Hillier, Jr.
1980–81—Robert E. Knox, Jr.
1979–80—Walter A. Bielstein
　　　　　Lawrence G. Pickens
1978–79—Jarman Bass
1977–78—Robert J. Hibbetts
1976–77—Harry E. Ward
1975–76—Lloyd J. Weaver
　　　　　Charles T. Zlatkovich
1974–75—Frank T. Rea
1973–74—J. Kenneth S. Arthur
1972–73—Edwin E. Merriman
1971–72—Paul N. Cheatham
1970–71—Neal Y. R. Sheffield
1969–70—Glenn A. Welsch
1968–69—Howard L. Busby

1967–68—Donald W. Dorman
1966–67—L. Ludwell Jones
1965–66—Stanley J. Scott
1964–65—Hatcher A. Pickens
1963–64—Thomas W. Leland
　　　　　(posthumously)
1961–62—Frank L. Wilcox
1960–61—Walter R. Flack
　　　　　Bouldin S. Mothershead
1959–60—Gilbert F. Orcutt, Jr.
1958–59—Lionel E. Gilly
1957–58—Louie B. Green
1956–57—Jack E. Collier
1954–55—J. R. Jordan
1953–54—Kenneth W. Hurst
1952–53—Homer L. Luther

## Distinguished Public Service

Granted to a CPA and member of the TSCPA and a local chapter who is actively engaged in various community, charitable, and civic activities on a local and, preferably, a statewide or national basis in such manner that such activities reflect favorably on the Texas Society and the profession as a whole.

1981–82—Robert J. Cruikshank
1980–81—Miller Montag
1979–80—J. Kenneth S. Arthur
1978–79—Don M. Lyda
1977–78—A. G. Schlossstein
1976–77—Angus Cockrell
1975–76—Robert S. Rosow
1974–75—Clark W. Breeding
1973–74—Kenneth W. Hurst

1972–73—Erwin Heinen
1971–72—C. L. Boggs
1970–71—Walter A. Bielstein
1969–70—John M. Grimland, Jr.
1968–69—Wylie O. Webb
1966–67—W. Dewey Presley
1965–66—Lloyd J. Weaver
1958–59—J. A. Phillips
1957–58—Charles H. Cavness

## Outstanding Chapter President

Made to chapter presidents, based on size of chapter, in recognition of chapter accomplishments taking into consideration the overall goals and objectives of the Texas Society as well as chapter initiative and leadership.

1981–82—Kenneth C. England, El Paso
Mark H. Lawley, Texarkana
A. R. Richardson, Houston

1980–81—Robert F. Anderson, Dallas
Johnny Lacy, Panhandle
Larry L. Lyles, Rio Grande Valley
Carlton D. Stolle, Brazos Valley

1979–80—Cecil E. Smith, Fort Worth
J. W. (Larry) Anderson, Lubbock
Johney L. Williams, Central Texas

1978–79—Larry G. Beaumont, Southeast Texas
Johnnie Ray Seale, Corpus Christi
B. J. Montgomery, San Antonio

1977–78—Jerry M. Baker, San Angelo
John W. Puckett, Panhandle
Ronnie Rudd, Houston

1976–77—Larry Gene Pointer, Brazos Valley
John R. Jordan, Jr., Dallas
Bruce G. Bixler, El Paso

1975–76—Roderick L. Holmes, Central Texas
J. Reed Warner, Lubbock
John A. Poteet, Jr., San Antonio

1974–75—Raymond E. Ellis, Fort Worth
Edgar L. Moody, Central Texas
Jim A. Smith, Austin
Gerald L. Brady, Beaumont

1973–74—Doyle Z. Williams, Lubbock
Frank C. Wilson, Fort Worth

1972–73—Harvey E. DeFord, Austin
Bruce J. Harper, Houston

1971–72—Charles E. Reed, Beaumont
Oscar E. Reeder, Fort Worth

1970–71—M. Dan Howard, Lubbock
Tommie E. Roddy, Jr., Fort Worth

1969–70—Bobby J. Melson, Abilene
Charles W. Pope, San Antonio

1968–69—Dennis A. Riddle, Rio Grande Valley
Willard H. Finding, San Antonio

1967–68—C. L. Boggs, Lubbock
Stanley H. Voelkel, Houston

1966–67—Allen R. Greenstein, Central Texas
Jarman Bass, Dallas

1965–66—Ben F. Robinson, Lubbock
Edward P. Thompson, Dallas

## Outstanding Committee Chairman

Granted to a member of the Texas Society of CPAs in recognition of his or her outstanding performance as a committee chairman during the current year.

1981–82—Lamar W. Gardner, Jr.
Professional Ethics
1980–81—Karl A. Ransleben
Communications
Coordinating
1979–80—Morris D. Johnson
Professional Ethics
Larry Gene Pointer
Members in Industry and
Government (MIGI)
Coordinating
1978–79—Jimmie L. Mason
Public Affairs

1977–78—Ross McElreath
Management of an
Accounting Practice
1976–77—Arthur Greenspan
Public Affairs
Dan M. Guy
CPE Council
1975–76—Raymond E. Graichen
Committee on State and
Local Taxation

## CPE Award

Recognizes an individual for his or her outstanding contribution to continuing professional education in the accounting field.

1981–82—Tom R. Locke
Michael J. Deppe
1980–81—Tommie Roddy
1979–80—James F. Dunn, Jr.

1978–79—Joel Ann Middlebrook
1973–74—David E. Lajoie
1966–67—Harry S. Long

## Young CPA of the Year

Bestowed on a CPA and member of the TSCPA and a local chapter. The individual, thirty-five years or under, has made significant contributions to the accounting profession and the community and is a member of at least one other professional organization.

2001-2002  Brao O.
1981-82—Rudy Q. Ramirez
1980-81—James C. Hibbetts
1978-79—Keith C. Kakacek

1977-78—Bill R. Tillett
1976-77—Ronnie Rudd
1975-76—Dan H. Hanke

## Honorary Fellow

Bestowed on a CPA and member of the Texas Society of CPAs who has distinguished himself or herself within the accounting profession as well as his or her community.

1981-82—Edwin E. Merriman
1980-81—J. Kenneth S. Arthur
1979-80—Gordon N. George
1978-79—C. A. (Jake) Freeze
1978-79—Leon O. Lewis
1978-79—Stanley J. Scott
1977-78—Erwin Heinen
1976-77—Lloyd J. Weaver
1975-76—Kenneth W. Hurst
1975-76—Robert J. Hibbetts
1974-75—Fladger F. Tannery
1974-75—H. Tracy Nelson
1974-75—T. W. Mohle
1974-75—J. R. Jordan
1974-75—Laurence H. Fleck
1972-73—A. Lawrence Markham
1970-71—W. Charles Woodard
1970-71—Homer L. Luther
1970-71—L. Ludwell Jones
1970-71—Harry D. Hopson
1970-71—Walter R. Flack
1970-71—Don C. Chorpening

1965-66—Frank L. Wilcox
1965-66—Hatcher A. Pickens
1965-66—Bouldin S. Mothershead
1965-66—C. F. Milledge
1965-66—Ben M. Davis
1965-66—Curtis H. Cadenhead
1957-58—C. Oliver Wellington
1957-58—J. A. Phillips
1957-58—Thomas W. Leland
1957-58—Charles B. Couchman
1952-53—A. C. Upleger
1952-53—J. R. Nelson
1952-53—Albert G. Moss
1952-53—Charles M. Grider
1940-41—Frederick H. Hurdman
1940-41—George Cochrane
1938-39—Clarence Longnecker
1938-39—J. E. Hutchinson
1938-39—Charles F. Bridewell
1938-39—E. J. Archinard
1938-39—William M. Aikman

## Honorary Member

Presented to a person who is not eligible for regular TSCPA membership but who has distinguished himself or herself at least within the accounting profession on a statewide basis. The award is generally reserved for those who have benefited accountancy for a significant period and who will, by position, employment, or activity, continue to be identified with accountancy, its literature, or its profession.

| | |
|---|---|
| 1980–81—William H. Gregory (posthumously) | 1971–72—William H. Quimby |
| | 1967–68—John Arch White |
| 1976–77—Dorothy R. Smith | 1967–68—J. A. Gooch |
| 1974–75—Pauline Thomas | 1938–39—John L. Carey |

## TSCPA 50-Year Continuous Fellows

Bestowed on an individual who has distinguished himself or herself as a member of the Texas Society of CPAs for 50 years.

| | |
|---|---|
| 1979–80—R. Glenn Davies | 1977–78—Ben M. Davis |
| 1979–80—Wm. F. McCroskey | 1977–78—George N. Kerby |
| 1978–79—Fred E. Pflughaupt | 1977–78—C. F. Milledge |
| 1978–79—Hatcher A. Pickens | 1974–75—Bouldin S. Mothershead |
| 1977–78—H. T. Nelson | 1974–75—J. A. Phillips |
| 1977–78—O. H. Maschek | 1974–75—Frank L. Wilcox |

## Kenneth W. Hurst Fellows

Recognizes long-time contributors and supporters of the Educational Foundation of the Texas Society of CPAs, Inc.

| | |
|---|---|
| 1981–82—Madie Ivy | 1977–78—Stanley H. Voelkel |
| 1980–81—Carl S. Chilton, Jr. | 1977–78—Byron G. Bronstad |
| 1979–80—C. Tom Frazier | 1977–78—Wayne K. Goettsche |
| 1978–79—Ford R. Hale | |

## John Burnis Allred Merit Award

Granted to an individual who "has evidenced unusual knowledge and ability in accountancy by the record he/she made on the Uniform Certified Public Accounting Examination in the current year and has demonstrated high moral and ethical standards of character."

1981–82—Thomas M. Dethlefs
1980–81—John Todd McCall, Jr.
1979–80—James Gifford Russell
1978–79—Heidi Ann Langsjoen
　　　　　Callaway
1977–78—Anne Louise Londeree
1977—Donald W. Callaghan
1976—Mary Elizabeth Rader
1975—Randi L. Harry
1974—Patrick William Lenahan
1973—William Roger Strait
1972—George Harvey Matters
1971—Richard Thomas Guinan
1970—Andy Clyde Payne
1969—Chester F. White
1968—Richard Ellis Bean
1967—Mark J. Brookner
1966—David C. Holland
1965—John R. Jordan, Jr.
1964—Joe Nelson Prothro
1963—Albert Johnny Rexnicek

1962—William Giles Nolen
1961—Walter L. Colwell
1960—Wayne Kenneth Goettsche
1959—Weldon Roy Aston
1958—Robert Stephen Rowland
1957—John Dennis Trent
1956—Dan Rogers Farmer
1955—Kenneth K. Byrd
1954—James T. Fort
1953—John Rex Walker
1952—Robert Calvin Bennett
1951—Alexander E. Wiskup
1950—Wayne Horn
1949—Elmore Cammack
1948—Jerome H. Parker
1947—John Ralph Holmes
1946—Robert H. Gregory
1945—Robert S. Turner
1944—John B. Cookenboo
1943—Stanley W. Smith

APPENDIX C

## Past Officers and Trustees of the Educational Foundation, TSCPA

| Year | Presidents | Vice-Presidents | Secretaries/Treasurers | Other Trustees | Executive Director |
|------|------------|-----------------|------------------------|----------------|--------------------|
| 1957–58 | Bouldin S. Mothershead* | Curtis H. Cadenhead | Harry D. Hopson* | Walter R. Flack*<br>Frank L. Wilcox*<br>Fladger F. Tannery | Lod C. Allison* |
| 1958–59 | Curtis H. Cadenhead | Walter R. Flack* | Harry D. Hopson* | Frank L. Wilcox*<br>Fladger F. Tannery<br>Bouldin S. Mothershead* | Lod C. Allison* |
| 1959–60 | Walter R. Flack* | Frank L. Wilcox* | Kenneth W. Hurst | Edwin E. Merriman<br>Harry D. Hopson*<br>Curtis H. Cadenhead | Lod C. Allison* |
| 1960–61 | Kenneth W. Hurst | Edwin E. Merriman | Robert J. Hibbetts | Walter R. Flack*<br>Harry D. Hopson*<br>L. Ludwell Jones<br>W. Charles Woodard | — |

*Deceased

| Year | | | | | |
| --- | --- | --- | --- | --- | --- |
| 1965–66 | Stanley J. Scott | Donald W. Dorman | Jordan B. Wolf | Paul N. Cheatham*<br>Bert Rush<br>Don C. Chorpening<br>Kenneth W. Hurst | William H. Quimby |
| 1966–67 | Donald W. Dorman | Walter D. Roten* | Leonard H. Brantley | J. Kenneth S. Arthur<br>Edwin E. Merriman<br>Bert Rush<br>Don C. Chorpening<br>Walter E. Vater<br>Kenneth W. Hurst | Dorothy R. Smith |
| 1967–68 | Leonard H. Brantley | Walter E. Vater | L. Ludwell Jones | Don C. Chorpening<br>Walter D. Roten*<br>Harry E. Ward<br>Donald W. Dorman<br>Kenneth W. Hurst<br>L. William Long | Dorothy R. Smith |
| 1968–69 | Leonard H. Brantley | Walter E. Roten* | L. William Long | Donald W. Dorman<br>Robert E. Knox, Jr.<br>Walter E. Vater<br>Kenneth W. Hurst<br>L. Ludwell Jones<br>J. W. Giese | Dorothy R. Smith |

*Deceased

| Year | Presidents | Vice-Presidents | Secretaries/Treasurers | Other Trustees | Executive Director |
|------|-----------|-----------------|------------------------|----------------|--------------------|
| 1969–70 | Walter D. Roten* | J. W. Giese | L. William Long | Kenneth W. Hurst<br>Miller Montag<br>Leonard H. Brantley<br>Joseph M. Conder<br>H. B. Edens<br>Ford R. Hale | Dorothy R. Smith |
| 1970–71 | J. W. Giese | Joseph M. Conder | Carl S. Chilton, Jr. | Leonard H. Brantley<br>Frank T. Rea<br>Walter D. Roten*<br>H. B. Edens<br>Robert J. Hibbetts<br>Kenneth W. Hurst | Dorothy R. Smith |
| 1971–72 | J. W. Giese | Carl S. Chilton, Jr. | Tommie E. Roddy, Jr. | Jarman Bass<br>Walter D. Roten*<br>H. B. Edens<br>Robert J. Hibbetts<br>Kenneth W. Hurst<br>Walter H. Hanshaw | Dorothy R. Smith |

*Deceased

| 1972–73 | Carl S. Chilton, Jr. | Walter S. Hanshaw<br>Ford R. Hale | Ford R. Hale<br>Thomas J. Hayes, Jr. | H. B. Edens<br>A. Burke Haymes<br>Madie Ivy<br>Kenneth W. Hurst<br>J. W. Giese<br>Stanley H. Voelkel | Dorothy R. Smith |
|---|---|---|---|---|---|
| 1973–74 | Carl S. Chilton, Jr. | Ford R. Hale | Madie Ivy | Kenneth W. Hurst<br>Lawrence G. Pickens<br>Thomas J. Hayes, Jr.<br>J. W. Giese<br>Stanley H. Voelkel<br>Tommie E. Roddy, Jr. | Dorothy R. Smith |
| 1974–75 | Ford R. Hale | Tommie E. Roddy, Jr. | Madie Ivy | Curtis L. Frazier<br>Robert S. Lipson<br>Doyle Z. Williams<br>Stanley H. Voelkel<br>Carl S. Chilton, Jr.<br>Kenneth W. Hurst | Dorothy R. Smith |

*Deceased

| Year | | | | | |
|---|---|---|---|---|---|
| 1978–79 | Miller Montag | Anne D. Snodgrass | Morris D. Johnson | Carl S. Chilton, Jr.<br>Richard B. Counts<br>J. W. Giese<br>Dan M. Guy<br>Robert A. White<br>John Patrick Thomas | Dorothy R. Smith |
| 1979–80 | Miller Montag | Anne D. Snodgrass | Morris D. Johnson | C. H. Hamilton, Jr.<br>Paul W. Hillier, Jr.<br>Robert G. Kralovetz<br>John Patrick Thomas<br>J. W. Giese<br>Emerson O. Henke | Dorothy R. Smith |
| 1980–81 | Morris D. Johnson | C. H. Hamilton, Jr. | Pat Thomas | Robert G. Kralovetz<br>Anne D. Snodgrass<br>Charles T. Zlatkovich<br>J. W. Giese<br>Emerson O. Henke<br>Miller Montag | Dorothy R. Smith |

*Deceased

| Year | Presidents | Vice-Presidents | Secretaries/Treasurers | Other Trustees | Executive Director |
|------|-----------|-----------------|------------------------|----------------|--------------------|
| 1981–82 | Morris D. Johnson | C. H. Hamilton, Jr. | Pat Thomas | Carroll W. Phillips<br>J. W. Giese<br>Emerson O. Henke<br>Miller Montag<br>Betty Bell<br>Gene E. Glazener | Dorothy R. Smith |
| 1982–83 | Pat Thomas | C. H. Hamilton Jr. | Betty Bell | J. W. Giese<br>Emerson O. Henke<br>Keith C. Kakacek<br>Gene E. Glazener<br>Morris D. Johnson | Dorothy R. Smith |

*Deceased

# A Note About Sources

THE archives of the Texas Society of Certified Public Accountants, located in the Society's Dallas office, were opened to the author without restriction. Committee reports, membership rosters, minutes of committee and Society meetings, and other official records found there vary considerably in terms of their historical significance and usability. Full and complete records have been kept only since the middle 1940s. The archives hold a small but important collection of letters and papers relating to the early history of the Society which were taken from the personal papers of William P. Peter after his death. A manuscript by Forrest Mathis entitled "History of the Texas Society of Certified Public Accountants to June 27, 1945" was of value.

The files and records of the Texas State Board of Public Accountancy, housed in its Austin office, also contain valuable information on the development of the profession in Texas. The records are more complete for the period after 1945 when the board hired permanent staff employees, but there exists a complete set of minutes of all board meetings back to 1915.

Tape-recorded interviews with each living former president of the Texas Society provided first-hand knowledge and valuable personal insights into the Society's history. Over forty interviews were conducted in connection with the first history written in 1962. Unfortunately, those tapes were discarded during an office cleaning in the 1960s. The research for the revised history included interviews with each president since 1962, along with Don Lyda and Lloyd Weaver, former chairmen of the Texas State Board of Public Accountancy.

The *Texas Accountant* (1928–1954), the *Texas Certified Public Accountant* (1954–1974), *Texas CPA News* (1974–1978), and *CPA* (Current Date), are the official publications of the Texas Society.

Outside the official records and publications of the Society, the *Journal of Accountancy* (New York, 1905–), official organ of the American Institute of Certified Public Accountants, and the *Certified Public Accountant* (Washington, 1922–), counterpart publication of the American Society of Certified Public Accountants until the two organizations merged in 1936, were the best sources reflecting trends and movements within the national profession. *Accounting Review* (Urbana, 1926–) is also helpful.

The following select bibliography will acquaint the reader with the national and international history of public accountancy: Nicholas A. H. Stacey,

*English Accountancy, 1800–1954* (London: Gee and Company, 1954); *A History of the Chartered Accountants of Scotland* (Edinburgh: privately published by the Institute of Chartered Accountants of Scotland, 1954); Ananias C. Littleton, *Accounting Evolution to 1900* (New York: American Institute Publishing Company, 1933); and, by the same author, *Studies in the History of Accounting* (London: Sweet & Maxwell, 1956); Richard Brown, *A History of Accounting and Accountants* (Edinburg: T. C. and E. C. Jack, 1905); Norman E. Webster, comp., *The American Association of Public Accountants: Its First Twenty Years* (New York: AIA, 1954); *The American Institute of Accountants Fiftieth Anniversary Celebration* (New York: AIA, 1938); James Don Edwards, *History of Public Accounting in the United States* (East Lansing: Michigan State University, 1960); John L. Cary, *The Rise of the Accounting Profession: From Technician to Professional, 1896–1936* (New York: AICPA, 1969), and *To Responsibility and Authority, 1937–1969* (New York, AICPA, 1970); John W. and Marlene H. Buckley, *The Accounting Profession* (Los Angeles: Melville Publishing Company, 1974); Paul D. Montagna, *Certified Public Accounting: A Sociological View of A Profession in Change* (Houston: Scholars Book Company, 1974); and Stanley Charles Abraham, *The Public Accounting Profession: Problems and Prospects* (Lexington, Mass.: D. C. Heath, 1978).

# Index

Accountancy Act of 1915, 182

*Accountant* (journal), 4

accountants: chartered, in Scotland and England, 4; institutes of, 4; certification of, by state, 7–8; early concerns of, 10; status of, with clients, 58; relations of, with bankers and lawyers, 63–64, 87–91; and controversy with lawyers, 64–71; certified and noncertified, relations between, 82; on State Board, 83–84; as tax consultants, 90; and public relations, 92–94; incorporation of, 143–144

accounting: British influence on, 4; origins of, in America, 5–7; Texas beginnings of, 10–12; division in, 25–26; advertising of, 33–35; early educators in, 35; regulation of, 36–38; ethics in, 54–59; public, defined, 73; schools of, 132; management of practice in, 176–178

Accounting Excellence Award, 131, 171

Accounting Principles Board, 123

Adams, Nathan, 29

advertising: of professional accounting, 33–35; institutional, 34–35, 92–93; relaxation of rules governing, 133–134; restrictions on, 136–137. *See also* publicity

Aikman, Griffin, and Mothershead, 42, 44

Aikman, William M.: at first TSSPA meeting, 14; in San Antonio, 18; waiver certification of, 20; membership certificate of, 29n; on publicity, 34;

practice of, with B. S. Mothershead, 42; as TSCPA president, 44; and accountant-lawyer controversy, 64; and accountant-lawyer tensions, 68–69; as representative of TSCPA, 69; on Legislative Committee, 71; and F. G. Rodgers, 75; on tax work in accounting, 90

Alamo Auditing Company, 77

Albertson, B. F., 14

Alexander & Alexander, 176

Alford, Fred F., 54, 56, 72, 77–78

Alford, Meroney & Company, 163

Allday, Thomas Elbert, 27

Allison, Lod C., 85, 104

Allred Award, 171

Alpha Kappa Psi, 42

American Accounting Association, 61–62

American Association of Public Accountants, 4–7

American Institute of Accountants, 9; encroachment of, on state boards, 25–26; opposition of, to regulation, 37–38; Loyd Smith and, 39; G. Armistead and, 40; A. C. Upleger and, 41; merger of, with ASCPA, 51–53; argument of, against competitive bidding, 55–56; on lawyer-accountant cases, 69; T. W. Leland and, 75; Texas meeting of, 75–76

American Institute of Certified Public Accountants (AICPA): A. C. Upleger and, 42; meeting of, with Wartime Accounting Conference, 50; J. A. Phillips

Mexican-Americans, in accounting, 172–173

Middlebrook, Joel Ann, 171

Milledge, Cyril Frederick, 29n, 49, 78–79

Miller, A. E., 17, 23

Miller, Charles Edgar, 28n

Miller, Franklin Eugene, 137

Miller, Henry J., 56, 71

minorities, in accounting, 171–173

Mohle, Theodore W.: membership certificate of, 29n; membership recruitment activities of, 47; at cooperation conference, 52; as TSCPA president, 76; and W. C. Burer, 77; and H. D. Hopson, 113

Montag, Miller, 125, 160

Moody, Dan, 45

Moore, Ervin C., 99

Moore, Revely A., 29n

Morgan, Charles G., Jr., 16, 21, 27

Morris, Clifton H.: on Texas State Board of Public Accountancy, 20; certification of, 20; at first TSCPA meeting, 22; on outside auditors, 58–59; on Legislative Committee, 71; as TSCPA president, 112–113

Morris, Milton, 14

Morrison, William D., 52

Moses, Elkin, 30

Moss, Albert G.: as TSSPA associate member, 16, 17; firm of, 18; certification of, 21; as fellow member, 23; and annual meeting, 29

Moss, John, 123–124

Mothershead, Bouldin Shivers: in TSCPA, 27; on code of ethics, 32; as TSCPA president, 42–43; and revision of 1961 accountancy law, 86; and Educational Foundation, 99; on Professional Development Council, 100; on competitive bidding rule, 133

Mothershead, Hamilton, Day & Mayo, 42

Mutual of New York, 175

Myles, A. E., 21, 27, 36–37

National Association of Accountants, 42, 104

National Association of Accountants and Bookkeepers, 13

National Association of Certified Public Accountants, 26, 31

National Association of Public Accountants (NAPA), 82

National Association of State Boards of Accountancy, 153–154

National Conference of Lawyers and Accountants, 69

National Conference of Lawyers and Certified Public Accountants, 89

National Society of Public Accountants (NSPA), 80, 81, 87

Nelson, H. Tracy, 29n, 43, 54, 76

Nelson, Jesse Ray: waiver certification of, 20; at first TSCPA meeting, 22; as accounting educator, 35; on regulation, 37; practice of, with A. H. Cole, 40; as TSCPA president, 43; on accountant-banker relations, 63–64

Nelson Audit Company, 43

Nelson and Nelson, 43

Newlove, George H., 29

Newman, E. D., 27

New York Institute of Accountants, 6

New York School of Accounts, 7

New York Society of Certified Public Accountants, 52

North Texas State University, 132

offices, location of, 105–106

Oglesby, John S., 29n

Open Records Act, 153

Pace, Homer, 34

Pace Institute, 34

Patillo, Brown and Hill, 163

Patillo, Rowland D., 113, 162–163

Patterson and Leatherwood, 158

Paulk, C. V., 24

Peat, Marwick, Mitchell & Co., 17–18, 24, 159, 162

Peter, W. P., & Company, 18, 41

Peter, William Preston: and early TSCPA, 13, 14, 15, 17; to Texas State Board of Public Accountancy, 20; certification of, 21; as fellow member,